Jason Webster went to Spain to learn to play the flamenco guitar. He currently lives outside Valencia with his Spanish wife. The author of the critically acclaimed *Duen_____ _____ _____ _____* while researching this book, tha_ _____ _____ _____ been a gunrunner in the Spanish Ci___ ____.

For more information see www._____

Critical _____

'Moving and succinct . . . generous and humane . . . With this book, Webster definitively joins the long line of Anglophone writers who have interpreted Spain to the world: Richard Ford, Nathaniel Hawthorne, Ernest Hemingway, Gerald Brenan, Hugh Thomas, and Ian Gibson. It is distinguished company but he deserves his place in the pantheon'
Sunday Telegraph

'An absorbing book that conveys the raw Spanish experience – its heat, dust, light and shade – with rare and startling actuality. Admirers of his first two books will have their high regard confirmed by this one. Newcomers should start here. They will not be disappointed'
Literary Review

'The term "romantic traveller", once used indiscriminately by Spaniards to describe any foreigner with a passionate interest in Spain, seems particularly applicable to Jason Webster . . . you are likely to be seduced by his powers as a storyteller. Such familiar incidents as the assassination of the poet Lorca are retold with such panache that you are made to feel that you are reading about them for the first time'
Independent

'Perhaps only a foreigner, and a foreigner who lives in Spain, could give a truly accurate picture of how the memory of the Civil War still dominates so many people's lives in the country. In all its glare and gloom, this is what Jason Webster's vivid and perceptive journey through the tortured memory of modern Spain provides'
Professor Paul Preston

'Written with considerable power and beauty'
Sunday Times

'There are many . . . dirty deeds recorded but, partly because of Webster's essentially happy character, his heartfelt prose and his deep love for modern Spain and its vibrant people, this positive and optimistic book leaves an impression of hope after the horror'
Daily Mail

Also by Jason Webster

Duende: A Journey in Search of Flamenco
Andalus: Unlocking the Secrets of Moorish Spain

and published by Black Swan

¡GUERRA!

Living in the Shadows of the Spanish Civil War

JASON WEBSTER

BLACK SWAN

TRANSWORLD PUBLISHERS
61-63 Uxbridge Road, London W5 5SA
a division of The Random House Group Ltd
www.booksattransworld.co.uk

¡GUERRA!
A BLACK SWAN BOOK: 9780552772815

First published in Great Britain
in 2006 by Doubleday
a division of Transworld Publishers
Black Swan edition published 2007

This book is a work of non-fiction based on the experiences and recollections of the
author. In some [limited] cases names of people, places, dates, sequences or the detail
of events have been changed solely to protect the privacy of others. The author has
stated to the publishers that, except in such minor respects not affecting the
substantial accuracy of the work, the contents of this book are true.

A CIP catalogue record for this book
is available from the British Library

Addresses for Random House Group Ltd companies outside the UK
can be found at: www.randomhouse.co.uk
The Random House Group Ltd Reg. No. 954009

Typeset in 11.5/14pt Bulmer by
Falcon Oast Graphic Art Ltd

11

The Random House Group Limited supports The Forest Stewardship
Council® (FSC®), the leading international forest-certification organisation.
Our books carrying the FSC label are printed on FSC®-certified paper.
FSC is the only forest-certification scheme supported by the leading
environmental organisations, including Greenpeace. Our
paper procurement policy can be found at
www.randomhouse.co.uk/environment

Printed and bound in Great Britain by Clays Ltd, St Ives plc

For Mum and Dad

The Spanish Civil War . . . came from the scarcity of water and excess of fire in the Spanish temperament. When the ardent sun of Spain dries up the land . . . the parched earth splits open. The well-meaning foreigner, set ablaze himself by Spanish passions, says, 'This earth here on the right . . .' or else 'This earth here on the left is responsible.'

But there is but one earth.

Salvador de Madariaga

Contents

Note

The Civil War is still a sensitive subject in Spain. Some of the people mentioned in this book have asked for their names to be changed so that their privacy may be respected.

Acknowledgements

The following people have been of enormous help during the research and writing of this book and it gives me great pleasure to be able to thank them here: Francisco Sánchez Montoya, Dr Miguel Botella, Manolo Martínez, Paco González, Ángel Olmedo, Diego Peral, Antonio Moya, Sargento Primero Rosado, Abdelkrim Bentato, David Smith, Rafael Paniagua Sánchez, Jim Carmody, Anthony Ham, Toby Follett, Cordula Reinhart, Paul Sapin, José 'El Taponero', Emilio Silva, Peter Carroll, Mary Dowley, Marlene Sidaway, Christopher Ross, Paul Preston, Gerald Blaney, Clive Maltby, Michael Alpert, Vicente Botella and Mike Ivey.

La Asociación para la Recuperación de la Memoria Histórica, el Instituto Cervantes de Tetuán, el Cuartel de Regulares No. 3 de Ceuta, and the International Brigade Memorial Trust were all generous in their assistance. Sadly, the Fundación Francisco Franco failed to cooperate or respond in any way, despite my approaches.

Thanks also to Natasha, for her invaluable contribution; to Sarah, for another exceptional effort; and to Salud – *sin tí, ya sabes, nada de esto hubiese sido posible.*

THE STAGES OF THE SPANISH CIVIL WAR

FRANCE

FERROL
OVIEDO
BILBAO
HENDAYE
PERPIGNAN
GUERNICA
2
VIGO
BURGOS
1
SARAGOSSA
SALAMANCA
BELCHITE
3
BARCELONA
MADRID
MALLORCA
2
TOLEDO
TERUEL
CASTELLÓN
VALENCIA
BADAJOZ
CASTUERA
ALBACETE
IBIZA
2
ALICANTE
1
SEVILLE
GRANADA
1
CARTAGENA
MALAGA
TANGIER
CEUTA
TETOUAN
MELILLA
1
CANARY
ISLANDS
CASABLANCA
SPANISH
MOROCCO

P O R T U G A L

1. Nationalist controlled territory July 1936

2. Nationalist gains by October 1937

3. Nationalist gains by July 1938

0 MILES 200

JULY, 1936 - JULY, 1938

1

The Pit

*B*egoña stood at the entrance to the house, leaning on her staff as her little mongrel, Rosco, panted nervously at her feet. A straw hat was tied under her chin with a dark-blue scarf, partly shading a worn, landscaped face, and eyes that shone like cinnamon stones from within layers of protecting skin.

'One of the goats has fallen down a hole.'

Normally her husband brought the herd up here to graze, but today she had taken his place. 'Hugo's in the city,' she said by way of explanation. 'Doctor's appointment.'

I grabbed some rope and a knife and stepped out for her to show me the way. The code up here in the mountains was never to ask for help, simply to explain a problem, and people would naturally respond. In their turn they would receive a minimum of thanks – assisting one another was how the community in this sparsely populated landscape survived. Favours were repaid with favours.

'Where is it?'

I followed in her footsteps as we passed through fields of dry grass and sprouting blue peach-leaved bellflowers. Spring was almost over but the pale almond blossom on the slopes below us still glistened in the sunlight. Small and compact, Begoña skipped over the stones and rocks that pushed out of the thin dry soil, her cloth bag with her water-bottle and food to last the day swinging across her lower back above a wide rump. She and Hugo had both been born up here, in farmhouses across the valley that were now abandoned like the rest of them. I sometimes wondered how long ago that had been: still active, she had an outdoor face that could belong to anyone over fifty.

Begoña had always been more open and keen to chat than Hugo. You had the sense that her husband was happier with his goats, singing in solitude as the herd scattered a trail of droppings and kicked up stones wherever they trotted. Begoña, on the few occasions when she had come up to the farm, had always stopped by to say hello, accepting my offers of red wine from dusty tumblers and telling me stories of life in the valley from when she was a little girl. There used to be more rain here, before the weather started changing. Snow up to your knees every winter. Now you were lucky to get any at all. Used to be a big grape-growing area, but the farmers had switched some years back to olives and almonds, which could cope better with the drier conditions.

Her animals would mill around her, munching their way through everything in my budding garden, Rosco growling them back into place if they strayed too near the fig trees, while she talked on regardless, lapping up the opportunity for conversation as though quenching a great thirst.

'You need some tomatoes here. They like this soil. My uncle used to grow them up over the other side of the mountain, next to his tobacco plantations. Before everyone left and moved to the towns, that is . . .'

I loved the remoteness of this area – the mountains of

Castellón: it was one of the reasons why Salud and I had looked for a house here in the first place. I'd been living in Spain for some twelve years now, mostly in the city, but the landscape surrounding us here tapped into an enduring vision I had of my adopted homeland: the silence, the spectacular mountain views, the scent of pine forests; often we caught sight of eagles soaring in the sky overhead, brightly coloured butterflies would flutter around our feet, while Spanish ibex, their horns like lyres, would sometimes come to drink at sunset in our little spring on the other side of the hill. Yet for Begoña the silence was a source of sadness. These had all been bustling farms once; now Salud and I were the only ones living so far up the valley, slowly renovating a small group of ancient stone cottages – a *mas* – that hadn't been lived in for decades.

The area was rich in history: the Maestrat had once been the battle ground of El Cid, later a domain of the Templars and Hospitallers, presented to the knights as a gift by King James I the Conqueror after winning it from the Moors. Cathar refugees had settled here after being persecuted and all but exterminated in southern France by the early fourteenth century. It was said there were still heretical motifs on the churches from those times, mysterious symbols as little understood as the palaeolithic wall paintings depicting strange fertility dances that decorated some of the caves nearby. This had been the heartland of the ancient Iberians, the 'swarthy-skinned and curly-haired men' described by Tacitus, a warrior people who worshipped doves and a sea goddess, and who cremated their dead before burying their ashes in urns.

We walked on over the fields, scampering down the banks of terraces where the old dry-stone walls had crumbled away through lack of care. Even now, there were no telephone wires or electricity pylons to be seen: no signals or reminders of modern, mechanized man.

'Before my mother was born,' was all Begoña would say when I asked if she knew when all these terraces had been built. Their imprint was visible on almost all the faces of the surrounding hills and mountains, but many were thickly overgrown. I'd resisted asking when her mother had been born. It wouldn't have shed much light on the matter anyway. How *long* before her mother was born? They could have been there for hundreds of years.

The goats bleated and groaned as we covered territory they had already crossed that day. They had eaten the best of the grass already and were now being presented with their own left-overs. Still, they munched on, managing somehow to eat and walk at the same time. Every so often the dog gave a threatening growl.

After a half-hour stroll we passed a ruined old house that stood further down the slope, and turned sharply off the path to descend through gorse and pines sheltering in the shadows of the tallest peak in the valley. The sheer cliff face was a mosaic of orange and pink rock, curling round like the inside of a barrel.

'Rosco!' The dog was ordered to keep the animals at bay as we pushed downwards.

'I don't usually bring them here,' Begoña explained. 'But there's been so little rain this year.' She pushed the branches and bushes out of her way with her wooden staff as she followed a path on the hillside I could barely make out.

Halfway down the slope, in the shade of a cluster of holm oaks, was a hole: an irregularly shaped fault in the ground with a fifteen-foot drop to the bottom. Gorse bushes smothered the rim, so that it was almost impossible to see it until we were nearly falling into it ourselves. At the sound of our voices, the fallen goat started bleating.

'Come round this side,' Begoña said. 'There are a few foot-holds.'

She pushed the bushes back as I edged to the side and looked down. The small brown goat was standing on an outcrop of rock near the bottom, bellowing now it could see us, pleading for help. Judging by the way it was standing, it seemed to have broken something.

I climbed down, trying not to fall or push any loose rock down on to the already frightened animal. It didn't look too difficult. Once I reached the goat, it should be just a matter of tying the rope around its body and hauling it back up.

The creature gave a start as I skipped down the last few feet to reach it, but it seemed to understand that I was there to help, staring up into my face and bleating plaintively as I stroked its head. Begoña threw the rope down to me, keeping hold of one end while I wrapped the other underneath its belly several times and through its legs, following her instructions as to how best to support the animal's weight. I fumbled with the rope until it felt reasonably secure, finishing off with a reef knot. It was the only knot I could remember, but it seemed to do the trick.

Getting out of the hole proved more difficult than getting in, as the flaky limestone rock easily gave way under my weight, but after a couple of attempts, holding on to clumps of wiry grass growing out of the sides, I was back with Begoña at the top.

'*Bien*,' she said. Wrapping the loose end of the rope around her waist, she started to heave the animal up, her strong arms tensing with the strain. Down in the hole the bleats turned to screams as the goat took off from the ground and immediately crashed into the side. It kicked out at the rock with its knees, unable, it seemed, to straighten its legs and fend off with its hooves. It was already damaged enough, I thought. If we weren't careful we were going to hurt it even more in trying to save it. Crouching down on the ground, I tried to lift the rope as far as possible from the side of the hole, hoping to spare the animal too many bruises during its ascent. I would have taken the rope myself but Begoña barely paused for breath as she hauled the beast up, her powerful squat body twisting like a spring as, inch by inch, the goat rose towards us.

With a couple more tugs the animal was within my grasp. Grabbing it by the upper part of its front legs I lifted it the final two feet, pushing it in Begoña's direction for her to take a look. One leg was clearly broken: the goat was hopping around bleating frantically, obviously in some pain. We'd probably have to carry it all the way home. The leg would take time to heal – a few weeks at least.

I bent down to brush the dirt from my legs and glanced into the hole again. It was a long way down. No wonder the poor thing was in such a state.

As I was caught by the sense of falling into this empty void, the bleating behind me stopped. I looked over to where Begoña was attending to the animal, wondering how she had managed to silence it so suddenly. She was wiping her hands on her hips. The goat lay limp on the ground like a rag doll, its eyes half closed, tongue poking out between the teeth of its open mouth.

'You've killed it?' I asked, trying to check a note of incredulity in my voice.

'We lost one last year as well,' she said. 'Can't take your eye off them for a second.'

She bent down and with a short swinging motion lifted the dead beast up on to her shoulders, holding it on either side by its legs. Back up the hill Rosco gave a bark, sensing that his mistress was about to return.

I watched for a moment as she pushed her way back up the slope, flicking the bushes aside with her staff to get through as she had done before. On her back the goat's head flopped like a heavy shopping bag: lifeless, motionless meat. There was no blood; she must have broken its neck while my back was turned. Swift and efficient. I felt dizzy.

Eventually I started up the hill after her, fighting feelings of sentimentality about the fate of the animal. Goats were just goats, I reminded myself. If someone offered me goat stew that evening for dinner I would happily eat it. This was just one goat more. And Begoña, who'd been a goatherd all her life, knew how best to deal with them. They weren't pets: they were her livelihood. A goat with a broken leg was a liability.

Yes, I thought, but even still.

As this conflict churned inside me, I only half registered that we were not going back up the way we had come. Rather than cutting across the almond orchards, we had walked further down the valley, and round to an area at the side of the mountain I had never been to before. The area was thick with dark-green Austrian pines, their trunks bent out of the sloping ground like the necks of flamingos. Dragonflies fluttered from stone to stone under squat dusty oaks, the shine from whose thick stunted leaves was already baked dry in the heat.

The sweat quickly evaporated from my forehead in the mountain air, and I felt the back of my throat begin to itch. I wondered why Begoña had decided to go back this way. She pushed on, a tanned paw-like hand held out in front of her with a bent finger pointing ahead.

We came out from under the shade of the trees on to an open stretch of land facing east. In the distance a few fields were still being cared for, with rows of almond trees bursting through ploughed pink soil. But mostly this area had been abandoned.

'You might want to see this,' Begoña said simply. I looked around – beneath the wild grass there were odd dents in the earth, unnatural creases snaking for a hundred yards or more in the direction of the sun. Away to the left I could make out a dark pit, partially obscured by gorse bushes.

'This is where the bodies are buried,' she said.

For a moment I thought she meant a place where they dumped the bodies of goats like the one slung over her

7

shoulders. But something in her expression made me wonder. 'What bodies?'

The massacre had taken place here in the mountains in the early summer of 1938. In the USA and Britain audiences were flocking to see Errol Flynn at the cinema in *The Adventures of Robin Hood*, Germany had just absorbed Austria in the Anschluss, the first *Superman* comics had recently been published, and oil had been discovered for the first time in Saudi Arabia. But Spain at that point was caught up in a vicious and bloody civil war that would cost at least half a million lives, force a similar number into exile, and see the eventual victory and establishment of one of the twentieth century's most enduring dictators, General Francisco Franco, an austere and ruthless Catholic soldier from the northwest of Spain. A second world war, as many already sensed, was just around the corner, but in the meantime a bloody dress rehearsal was under way on Spanish soil as the Soviet Union, Germany and Italy carried out a proxy war in preparation for the real thing.

By the late spring of 1938 the Spanish Civil War was almost two years old and entering its final phase. General Franco and his supporters, who called themselves the Nationalists, were slowly beating their opponents – the Republicans, defenders of the democratic state Franco was trying to overthrow. The Nationalists were backed by Hitler and Mussolini's weaponry and soldiers, while the Republicans were relying ever more heavily on their only serious international backer, Stalin. The Republicans were in disarray at this late stage in the war: Franco had reached the Mediterranean and had cut their remaining territory in two. He was now moving his army down the coast towards Valencia.

As I now learned, it was at this point that the front line had reached where I was standing that morning, surrounded by goats on a dry mountainside, a jittery dog scuttling about my feet and a dead animal hanging over the shoulders of my elderly neighbour.

I knew only a little about the war. It was not a subject you talked about much in Spain, where people usually wanted to forget and get on with their lives, even now, almost seventy years since it had begun. Friends had often dismissed the subject as unimportant. It was politics, nothing more, just a scrap between some people on the Left and some others on the Right. And anyway, it was all history, finished. Caught up as I had been by other aspects of the country – the colour and passion of Spain, things that usually drew people here – I had side-stepped this part of Spanish history. I had been too busy enjoying everything that fitted in with my romantic dreams of what Spain was all about: the sensuality of flamenco, the exoticism of the country's Moorish past

Nonetheless, I was fascinated by what Begoña began to tell me.

'This is where the Republicans had their last defences,' she said. 'These lines here' – she nodded towards the zigzag markings – 'were the trenches.'

It wasn't easy to make them out, with the flat midday light almost obliterating the contours in the landscape. But as she pointed, they began to stand out more clearly: man-made shapes that appeared somehow out of place in their natural surroundings. Mostly filled in now, the trenches were about two metres wide, each stretch some eight or ten metres long before a dogleg bend to another stretch, creating a jagged effect.

Begoña told me how Republican fighters had made a stand out here in the countryside as Franco's men marched southwards. It was difficult mountainous territory, and while the Nationalists' capture of the nearby village had been straightforward, the Republicans hoped to slow the advance by leading the enemy out into the hills. They hadn't lasted more than a few days.

'Franco's planes came from over there' – she pointed towards the northeast – 'and shot them up.'

The shape of the defences, it seemed, was supposed to offer some protection against a linear attack from the air. But the planes returned again and again, manoeuvring so that their machine-guns could fire the length of each stretch of the trenches.

'Some managed to escape but most of them were killed.'

There was nothing but wild flowers and birds today; only a lifetime ago, this place had been a killing field. I looked around at our peaceful, pastoral surroundings and struggled to imagine what must have happened that day.

'And it took place right here?' I said, as though demanding confirmation from her. Begoña took a swig from her water-bottle and nodded. The dead goat's head swung limp and senseless on her back, its half-open eyes now mere balls of drying jelly.

I glanced up in the direction from which the Nationalist fighters had approached. In the distance the Penyagolosa, the highest mountain in this part of Spain, once sacred to the Celtic sun-god Lugus, pushed upwards into a cloudless sky. Further up the valley I could make out the whitewashed walls of my own farmhouse glinting in the sun.

'The bodies,' I said to Begoña. 'Are they . . . ?'

'They're still here,' she said matter-of-factly.

I looked again at the trenches and the scarred earth where we were standing. I felt uneasy about walking on people's graves, thinking about the men who were lying here, about the kind of people they'd been, about their wives and lovers, their children.

'How many Republicans were here?' I asked.

About seventy of them were buried there, she told me.

'I was eight at the time,' she continued. 'I came with my

mother and brother to sow wheat that morning. We saw the Francoists dig a pit, a *fosa*, and then throw the bodies in from a lorry on top of each other.'

For the first time I caught the emotion in her voice, a tightening in her throat.

'My mother didn't stop weeping all day.'

Only her voice betrayed the depth of her emotion, her face screwed tight as it had been for decades against the sun and the elements. And perhaps, also, against the memories of what she had witnessed here as a little girl. The experience she had had, the event that had occurred here, filled the space around us like lead.

My mind was filling with questions: why had they dumped the bodies here rather than giving them proper burial? What had happened to their families? Why hadn't anyone moved them since? Franco had been dead for almost thirty years. The country was a democracy once more. Couldn't a memorial be erected at least? It was disturbing to think that here in this lost, sun-drenched valley, with its fields of wild flowers, the smell of blossom filling the air, bursts of birdsong set against a blanket buzz of honeybees, something so terrible could have happened.

The questions and thoughts filled my mind, but it was almost impossible to speak.

'I'm the only one left who saw what happened,' she said at last. Rosco was curled around her feet, looking up at me with mournful eyes. 'I'm the only one left.'

Grief and sorrow now seemed to flow like an electric current from her skin. If I put a hand on her arm, in some inadequate gesture of sympathy, I was sure I would feel a shock. There was one thing, however, that I had to ask. Why had she brought me here?

'I don't know,' she said, turning away. 'I don't know.'

*

I watched her walk away with the herd down the dirt track, the dead goat still on her shoulders, the dog scampering about making sure the rest of the animals moved forwards. From behind, the blue scarf holding down her straw hat looked like a dark gash across the top of her head. The weather seemed to be changing, and from the west a hot suffocating wind was beginning to blow, bringing with it the dust and sand of the plains. It passed over the cliff face and down into the hollow of the valley, circling and tightening before whipping round and surging up into my face in concentrated, melting bursts. My eyes stayed fixed on the old woman's compact form, her skirts flapping around her ankles as she gradually disappeared into the distance. So much strength and energy seemed to be held within her, it was strange to think that one day, like the men dumped in the field she had shown me, it would be extinguished. It was as though she had given a small part of herself to me by taking me to that place.

I walked back up the slope towards home, but the house, the farm, was different. The change was subtle, but immediate, and the cracks in my vision of what I thought I had were already starting to show. Violence and blood had stained my perfect world.

2

Prelude

*T*wo murders in Madrid acted as a catalyst for the Spanish Civil War: the assassinations within hours of each other of a policeman by political activists, and of a political activist by policemen.

On the night of 12 July 1936, a young police officer, Lieutenant José Castillo, left his new bride to walk to work from their home on Augusto Figueroa Street, in the old working-class district in the centre of the capital. Castillo was part of a special force of shock troops known as the Assault Guards, a body set up five years previously to defend Spain's nascent and fragile republic. An active left-winger, Castillo had been involved in the killing of a leading member of Spain's fascist party, the Falange, during a riot in April earlier that year. They were violent times: political murders were taking place almost every day, hundreds of thousands of Spaniards were on strike, churches were being burned down. There were whisperings of a military coup against the newly elected government – a left-wing coalition – now in charge in Madrid. Falangists had sworn revenge against Castillo for the death of their colleague, the Marquis of Heredia, and had sent the policeman's wife, Consuelo, a note the day before her wedding advising her not to marry a man 'soon to be a corpse'.

It was normally only a ten-minute walk to work, but that night Castillo didn't make it. On Fuencarral Street four gunmen were waiting for him; they shot him down and disappeared. A passing journalist tried to help the wounded man, but arrived only to hear his last words: 'Take me to my wife.' He was dead by the time they got him to a nearby medical centre.

News of the killing quickly reached the police station. Castillo was the second officer in the local force to be killed that year – Captain Carlos Faraudo had been gunned down in the centre of Madrid as he was taking a walk with his wife. Angry and determined to exact revenge, the officers drew up a list of suspects and then, as night fell, began leaving the police station in small groups to make arrests. Suspicion fell on right-wingers, particularly the fascists of the Falange party and their associates. It was late by the time the last group of policemen headed out into the streets, taking a police lorry, number seventeen, out into the wealthy Salamanca district of Madrid. They were led by Captain Fernando Condés of the Civil Guard, Castillo's best friend. Not all in the vehicle were police officers, however: two were members of the communist-socialist youth movement; another was a young Galician socialist called Luis Cuenca.

Police lorry number seventeen headed first to the home of a leading politician named José María Gil Robles. A heavy-jowled, trilby-wearing man, Gil Robles was a prominent figure on the Right, leader of the Catholic CEDA coalition party, who had tried but failed to win power and establish an authoritarian Catholic regime through the ballot box earlier that year. Fortunately for him, that night he wasn't at home, having left to spend the weekend in Biarritz with his family. The policemen would have to look elsewhere.

One of the men in the lorry mentioned that another leading

right-winger lived close by. José Calvo Sotelo, an economist, had been a finance minister before the establishment of the Republic, and was a brilliant orator who was quickly eclipsing Gil Robles as the leading light on the opposition benches. With his clean good looks and more radical policies, he was gaining many followers, moving ever closer to the Falange against the backdrop of a country rapidly falling apart.

By now it was around three o'clock in the morning on 13 July. Calvo Sotelo was at his home on Velázquez Street that night, having spent weeks moving from place to place for fear of assassination. The policemen drove to his house, roused him and ordered him to get dressed and accompany them to the police station. As a member of parliament, Calvo Sotelo was granted freedom from arrest. Still, he decided to go along with them, promising his family he would call them as soon as he arrived at the station. 'Unless,' he added as he was being led through the door, 'these gentlemen are going to blow my brains out.'

With the politician inside, the police lorry set off at top speed through the streets of Madrid, Calvo Sotelo wedged in the front between a couple of policemen. After several minutes, Luis Cuenca, sitting in the back, fired two bullets into his head. The body stayed upright until they reached the East Cemetery, where they left it with the night guard.

'As they were in uniform, I didn't object,' the guard later told an inquest.

The body wasn't identified until the following morning.

Condés later said he had only meant to arrest Calvo Sotelo, and that Cuenca had shot him without his orders.

A day later, on 14 July, two funerals were held. At one the coffin of Lieutenant Castillo was draped in a red flag, socialists, Republicans and communists raising clenched fists in revolutionary salute. Several hours later Calvo Sotelo's body was buried at the same cemetery, his coffin marked with a cross, mourners stretching their right arms out in the fascist salute.

The murders had split the country in two. Three days later the Spanish Civil War began.

The murders of Castillo and Calvo Sotelo were the spark that set the Civil War in motion, but came after a long period in which Spain had become increasingly polarized and fractured, hatred and violence taking root as the country was torn apart by extremist forces. By the time the policeman and the politician were killed, there was no way of avoiding war, so intense was the loathing between conservatives and progressives, right-wingers and the Left, and so fragile was the state meant to hold them together.

Spain in 1936 was a republic, officially the country's second after an unsuccessful and short-lived experiment with republicanism in 1873. The second fall of the monarchy had come in 1931, when King Alfonso XIII abdicated after elections for town halls across the country showed a collapse in his popularity. Preferring self-imposed exile to a possible civil war, he departed for France, and in a bloodless transition to a republican regime, power fell into the hands of liberals and left-wingers who had been pushing for years for modernization and an end to the monarchy. The new prime minister was the Andalusian barrister Niceto Alcalá Zamora, who formed a government made up of socialists and Republicans. The industrial revolutions that had taken place elsewhere in Europe were still in their infancy in Spain in the 1930s – new industries were concentrated principally in the northern areas of Catalonia and the Basque Country – and the main foreign export earner was still agriculture. Illiteracy rates were as high as 50 per cent, while millions lived in semi-slavery on vast feudal estates in the south – *latifundios* – where hunger was the norm and work scarce. Life there was primitive. Landowners were often absent, preferring the life of the city, while a surplus of labourers paid a daily rate meant farm managers had complete control over the lives of the workers, employing them or sending them away each morning as they saw fit. Much of the soil was poor and the climate was dry, and many landlords left swathes of their farms uncultivated, preferring the land to stay as an arid wasteland under their own control than be farmed by hungry peasants. And so the aristocrats and gentry and their moneyed offspring – *señoritos* – would spend their time in luxury in the capital and other big cities, while country folk starved – some even having to eat grass to survive – stuck in a pit of poverty and ignorance. What had been the point of abolishing black slavery, the socialist politician Indalecio Prieto asked, if white slavery still existed in Spain?

The country, then with a population of around twenty-four million people, was sharply divided in two, and there was immense pressure on the new Republic to produce much-needed reform, with hopes that after centuries of stagnation Spain would finally catch up with its neighbours. But while liberals and left-wingers dreamed of a better future, there was also fierce resistance to any change, principally from three powerful groups with a strong interest in maintaining things as they were: the old ruling class, the Church and the army.

The early thirties was a bad time to be building a new state. The world economy was still suffering from the crash of 1929, while political extremism was on the rise from the Soviet Union to Italy and Germany. But external pressures on the young Republic were almost nothing to the problems at home. The liberal intellectuals leading the new Spain made great moves to create the country they had always dreamed of, setting up almost ten thousand new schools in their first year, freeing the press and passing reformist agrarian laws. They also tried to modernize the country's top-heavy army, where there were some seventeen thousand officers for a force of around a hundred and fifty thousand soldiers: a ratio of one to nine. Attempts to improve this, and obliging officers to swear allegiance to the new Republic, won the liberals many enemies in the armed forces.

But while conservatives dug in their heels over any change, the Republic's own supporters complained things weren't moving fast enough. And one of the biggest groups on the Left, the anarchists, whose support for the liberal government would ebb and flow over the coming years, was against the idea of a state altogether. More and more, the men in the centre felt attacked from all sides.

What made matters worse was the impression the liberal rulers gave of being unable to maintain law and order. Less than a month after the Republic came into being, six churches were burned down in Madrid after disturbances between supporters of the Republic and monarchists. The police did nothing to stop the attacks, the then war minister Manuel Azaña exclaiming that he would prefer all the churches of Spain to burn than that harm should come to a single Republican.

Likewise, conservatives, who were slowly organizing themselves into political parties and formations, felt increasingly alarmed at the growth in regionalism in the country. The idea of 'Spain' had always been a problematic concept, the country being more a collection of nations than a single entity. What were now called regions had almost all been, at some time in the distant past, independent kingdoms, principalities or counties, tiny fiefdoms which had been born at the time of the Reconquest and which had grown as Christian territory expanded southwards at the expense of the Moors during the Middle Ages. Through a succession of wars, treaties and marriages these had eventually been united under a single crown some five hundred years earlier. Now that the king had gone, however, Catalonia in particular started to test its strength, drafting a 'statute of autonomy' in 1932 which gave the region its own government – the Generalitat – with powers over local administration, civil law and health. For the army, ever the defender of the *patria*, the fatherland, nothing was more sacred than the unity of the country. The Catalan move was seen as a dangerous threat and prompted the first attempt to bring the young Republic down, a rebellion that became known as the Sanjurjada.

General Sanjurjo was a hero of Spain's wars against the Riff tribesmen in northern Morocco. On 10 August 1932 he took part in a *pronunciamiento* – a coup typical of the nineteenth century, whereby a military officer would make a proclamation against the government, either rousing enough support to take over the country or getting shot down in glory. Although momentarily successful in Seville, where he launched a mani-festo, Sanjurjo's co-conspirators failed in their uprisings in Madrid and other major cities across the country after their plot was betrayed by a prostitute. Sanjurjo was arrested while trying to flee to Portugal and was imprisoned.

The time was not yet right to bring down the Republic, but conservatives were shortly to gain the upper hand. Frustrated by the slow pace of reform, anarchists were encouraging peasants to occupy villages and plots of land spontaneously and start farm-ing them for themselves. One of the most famous cases occurred in January 1933 in the Andalusian village of Casas Viejas. Unlike earlier disturbances, which had involved church burning, this time the authorities used extreme measures to restore control. Police reinforcements stormed the village and violently imposed order. As they were carrying out house-to-house searches, one of the villagers, known as Seisdedos, locked himself in with a handful of other anarchists and refused to come out. In the gun battle that followed, two policemen were shot. Eventually the police burned the house down, killing all inside, although Seisdedos's daughter, Libertaria, had managed to escape. Later the police shot dead fourteen anarchists who had surrendered earlier in the operation. The massacre caused an outcry and the socialists decided to withdraw their support for the liberal government. In the following elections in November 1933, conservative parties were duly elected to power.

There followed two years of rule by right-wing coalitions. Agrarian reform was not just halted but reversed, many peasants ending up worse off than they had been before. The period became, for the Left, the *bienio negro*, the 'black biennium', with its lowest point in October 1934. The Left became alarmed at the entry into government at this time of the Catholic authoritarian CEDA coalition. The group was led by José María Gil Robles, an admirer of Hitler and Mussolini who had been present at one of the Nuremberg rallies. He allowed himself to be addressed as *Jefe*, or 'Chief', in imitation of *Führer* or *Duce*, and was keen to introduce Nazi propaganda techniques to Spain.

Convinced that Gil Robles's party's inclusion in the cabinet marked the first step in the creation of a fascist state, left-wing groups organized a general strike and staged a series of revolts across the country, all doomed to failure. Only in the northern mining region of Asturias did the rebellion hold out, thanks to a rare alliance between socialists, anarchists and communists. There, local troops weren't able to quell the movement, and so the government in Madrid called in the toughest forces that Spain then had – the Army of Africa, based in the Spanish territories in northern Morocco. Led by General Francisco Franco, colonial troops and soldiers from the Spanish Foreign Legion suppressed the left-wing miners using merciless and blood-thirsty methods they had developed in the Riff mountains. In an operation which lasted a fortnight, two thousand people were killed and a number of towns and villages destroyed. General Franco became a pin-up for the Right and a hate figure for the

Left. Few then realized it, but a precedent had been set for the coming Civil War.

The repression and defeats of two years of right-wing governments served to reunite left-wing parties, so that by the time elections came round once again in February 1936 they were able to stand on a united ticket – the Popular Front, a name thought up by the communists. This time the anarchists decided to vote, if only to secure the release of their imprisoned comrades. On the Right, the CEDA leader Gil Robles presented himself as the last hope against the threat of Marxist revolution, leading a coalition of parties known as the National Front. Both sides were already referring to themselves in the language of confrontation. The Popular Front, again promising sweeping social reforms, won the vote by a whisker.

Gil Robles's plan had been to gain power through the ballot box, much as Hitler had concentrated his efforts after the failure of the Munich Putsch. After the CEDA's electoral defeat in Spain, this strategy lay in ruins. Fifteen thousand members of the youth movement of Gil Robles's party switched en masse to the radical Falange party, the Spanish fascists.

The Falange had been set up in 1933 by the young aristocrat José Antonio Primo de Rivera. It was a radical, extremist group that called for social reform and authoritarian nationalistic rule, while engaging in a violent conflict with left-wing groups. Inspired by Italian fascism, it had been named after an ancient Macedonian battle formation. Until the elections of February 1936, when the Popular Front came to power, the Falange had been a small fringe organization, but now, with a new influx of members, it became a more important player on the stage. After acts of increasing violence, including murders and bombings, in March its offices were closed down and its dapper young leader was imprisoned. José-Antonio would never know freedom again, although he was later destined to become a mythical figure in Spanish politics.

For the extreme Left, the victory of the Popular Front at the elections in itself was not enough, and it urged that the pace of social reforms be increased. The leader of the radical wing of the socialist party, a semi-literate former stucco worker called Francisco Largo Caballero, was travelling around the country making increasingly inflammatory remarks about revolution, and was flatteringly dubbed 'the Spanish Lenin' by the Soviet press. Meanwhile, on a single day in March that year, over sixty thousand peasants in the western region of Extremadura spontaneously took over almost three thousand farms. Having feared for their property, landowners were now beginning to fear for their lives. Both sides seemed to be hell-bent on confrontation, with frequent gun battles in the streets between left-wingers and Falangists and other far-right groups. And the violence continued. On 16 June 1936 the CEDA leader Gil Robles claimed in parliament that in the four months since the Popular Front had won the general election 160 churches had been destroyed, 269 people assassinated, 10 newspaper offices sacked, 113 general strikes called and 146 bombs set off. Anarchy ruled; the government had lost control.

At the centre, the liberal intellectuals in the Popular Front, once again in charge, proved incapable of holding these forces of mutual destruction in check. Warnings came that right-wing army officers were planning another coup, but almost no counter measures were taken, ministers refusing to arm the people whose votes had given them power, but whose radicalism they feared. As a precaution they removed from Madrid those generals most suspected of plotting against the government and sent them to the outer regions. Franco, famous for his repression of the left-wing rebellion in Asturias eighteen months earlier, was packed off to the Canaries, General Manuel Goded went to the Balearic Islands, while General Emilio Mola was sent to Pamplona in the north. Sanjurjo, now out of prison, was in exile in Portugal.

Mola's forced move to Pamplona was a godsend for the plotters. This tall, bespectacled general now became the mastermind of the coming coup from the centre of a highly Catholic, conservative part of the country, and was nicknamed el Director. Secret plans were drawn up for the army to rise simultaneously across Spain and Spanish Morocco, thus delivering a knockout blow against the government and preventing what was seen as an otherwise inevitable Bolshevik revolution. The key was to be the use of extreme violence. 'We must sow terror,' Mola insisted to his co-conspirators. 'We must give the sense of domination by eliminating all those who do not think like us, without scruples or hesitation.'[1]

On 7 July the annual San Fermín bull-running fiesta took place in Pamplona. Mola used the holiday to organize a clandestine meeting with the other plotters. They had to move fast or the government would eventually smoke them out. But there were problems: the local conservatives of Pamplona, the Requetés, were demanding more concessions for their pet causes; others were urging caution. Franco sent a telegram from the Canary Islands saying the time still wasn't right. Mola was furious. Franco was an important figure, a well-respected soldier, and would be a key factor in the success of the coup. Mola decided to carry on regardless.

Two things would work in his favour. In Madrid, Prime Minister Casares Quiroga studiously ignored the barrage of warnings about the coming disaster, like a Cassandra figure in reverse. And then, on 13 July, José Calvo Sotelo was shot dead in a police lorry.

At once all the doubts and calls for caution were silenced. Policemen had murdered a leading politician on the Right. No further justification was needed for a coup. Franco telegrammed again from the Canaries. This time, he was on board.

The rebellion was set for 18 July at five o'clock in the afternoon, just after siesta time. The starting point was to be the home of the Army of Africa – the Spanish Protectorate in Morocco.

3

Anything Goes

*T*he hall was dark, the only light coming from the red and orange spotlights shining on the surface of the ring in the centre. I followed Luis down concrete steps into the clashing noise of hundreds of raised voices, unnerved still by the growling Rottweiler at the door, its strange forehead-marking giving a fleeting, disturbing impression in the gloom that it had three eyes. Two boys of no more than eight years old were playing with bright-yellow space-fantasy machine-guns that flickered scarlet sparks and gave off a high-pitched scream every time they pulled the trigger. As the warehouse was built half underground, the late-night summer air seemed stickier and clammier than outside, where the occasional gust of sea breeze might bring momentary relief. Down in the hall the only movement came from the hot breath of the crowd. Most of the people there appeared to be young muscular men dressed in T-shirts and shorts, with stout necks and cropped hair – the kind you saw hanging around outside the entrances of gyms with their arms slung over one another as they looked the girls passing in the street up and down. Slouched on white plastic chairs aligned in rows, there were a few women dotted in among them – girlfriends and wives, perhaps – some with young children cuddled on their laps. One of them was smiling, her broad white teeth seeming to shine in the dark, shoulder-length hair fixed in an artificial wave as though she had just come out of the hairdresser's.

Luis led me to our seats – a slow and lengthy process, as he stopped to greet friends and acquaintances along the way. Many of them, I noticed, were wearing baseball caps with an embroidered silhouette of a bull on the front. It was the same bull you often saw dotted around the Spanish countryside – huge black billboards originally put up as adverts for Osbourne sherry, but which had since become something of a national symbol. Years back, when the authorities had talked about taking them down, there had been a public outcry and protection orders had been placed on them. Now you some-times saw the same image on car stickers, or as an emblem on items of clothing, as here.

'I'm going to a fight,' Luis had said a couple of nights before when I'd bumped into him in the street. 'Why don't you come along?'

As well as the farm, Salud and I kept a small flat in the coastal city of Valencia, where I had come to spend a few days after Salud had unexpectedly been called away on a flamenco tour abroad. One of the girls in the troupe couldn't make it and so she had been called in as a last-minute replacement. It looked as if she was going to be away most of the summer. I'd arrived look-ing for a dose of the city stimulation that was lacking in the mountains, and was slowly getting used to being on my own again for the first time in years. In other circumstances I might have turned down Luis's invitation, but caught up in the light-ness of being temporarily single, and thirsty for excitement, I agreed to go along.

Luis was an old acquaintance from fencing school in Valencia. Small and wiry, his face always wore an apologetic expression, and his hair was rapidly greying as he fought an ill-tempered custody battle over his children with his ex-wife. Caught up with other things, I'd stopped attending the fencing classes, but in the village atmosphere of our part of the city we'd see each other out and about and sometimes get together for a drink. It was the usual way in this Mediterranean environment, where socializing always happens outside, often spontaneously, sometimes with people with whom you have only the most casual of connections. Luis had been the first one to recommend looking for a place in the Maestrat, where his family had had a summer house when he was a child.

'Come along. Just a few beers and a laugh.' I thought he meant a wrestling match, or perhaps boxing, which I knew was another interest of his. It would be fun, I thought. I remembered the comical wrestling performances I'd seen on television as a child: huge men in leotards bouncing off the ropes and pretending to hurt one other, each bout a kind of primitive struggle between good and evil, light and dark.

After more talk and handshakes we finally made it to our seats. We were seven rows up from the ring. At a glance I reckoned some three, perhaps four hundred people were there. Next to me was a man in his early twenties wearing a white vest, his brown flesh carved into hard bulges around his shoulders and arms. He turned and leaned to shake hands with Luis, pushing into me roughly with his bulk. Spots bulged on the back of his neck where he'd shaved.

'Just a friend,' Luis said in reference to me. The man sat back in his chair, giving me a quick hard look. I held out my hand to him but he pretended not to notice.

'They're just a bit nervous,' Luis whispered in my ear. 'They've had a few problems with these events. Red-tape stuff.

It's all good fun, though. People just want to control things and they got the wrong impression.'

I had no idea what he was talking about, but alarm bells were already beginning to ring inside me. I'd always liked Luis, though. He was the kind of man who made friends with anyone immediately. There was something unthreatening about him and, with his dimpled smile and high-speed chat, you could easily spend an entertaining evening with him.

I looked again at the musclemen taking up most of the seats around us. At the side of the ring there seemed to be an area set aside for VIPs; more children were playing there, running in and out of the adults and scrambling over them as if they were living climbing frames. I'd always loved this side of Spain – the way children were included in everything, even late-night events and parties. A great contrast to the 'seen but not heard' mentality that had still prevailed in the England of my childhood.

'Luis,' I said, turning towards my friend, 'what type of a fight is this?'

At that moment a roar went up and the lights, which had been focused on the centre of the ring, started dancing around the hall like fire-flies. Everyone rose to their feet, cheering and clapping. After several minutes of whistling and shouting, I caught sight of a half-naked man moving through the crowd towards the centre. He was young and wore tight shorts and padded fingerless gloves. His body was powerful and well built, but not in the sculptured way of so many dumb-bell pushers. The muscles under his skin were smooth and taut. No overdeveloped pectorals, no washboard stomach, no skinny ankles. Everything about him spoke of strength. The man raised his two fists above his head as the audience cheered him on, but the atmosphere lacked something of the theatricality I had expected. There wasn't even the overdone seriousness and intensity of boxers when they are led to the ring draped in hooded capes. He smiled and waved, but as though he really didn't care about the audience. You got the impression he had simply come to fight, and win. Pleasing the crowd came a very low second. As he climbed into the ring I couldn't help but notice how different he was from other fighters preparing for a bout. He didn't jump up and down to warm up, or jerk his head from one side to the other to loosen the muscles – all signs of nerves. Standing straight and tall in one corner, he remained still and calm, sometimes looking at the crowd around him, occasionally pushing his right fist into the palm of his left hand as though testing the knuckle padding on his gloves. His skin shone under the lights. He was ready for combat.

'He's a local boy,' Luis shouted in my ear. 'Our champion.'

The cheers continued for a few moments as his opponent seemed to slip unnoticed towards the ring, but once the crowd saw the dark shape of the new man swaggering towards the centre the shouts quickly turned to whistles and screams.

'*Hijo de puta*,' came a cry from behind us. Son of a bitch!

The opponent was darker skinned than the local fighter – a mulatto, perhaps. He looked Brazilian. The alarm bells began to ring slightly louder. I struggled to remember what someone had told me once about a Brazilian style of martial arts.

The whistling continued as the darker man climbed into the ring. He tried to give off an air of confidence, flicking his legs out in a kind of strut while raising a fist up in salute to the baying crowd, but his head was just a fraction too high, his eyes seeming to look inwards, towards himself, rather than out to the audience. The local boy stood in the corner, motionless.

A man dressed in black who appeared to be the referee came to the centre of the ring. He went up to the fighters and directed a few words to them individually in their corners, spending considerably more time with the white man, then clapped his hands. A bell was struck at the side and the combat began.

There was an upsurge in noise from the public, but then the screaming, whistling and shouting quickly dropped to a low murmur. The two men approached each other, circling like crabs, their shoulders raised, hands ready to clasp one another. Then with a low, dull clap they came together in a huddle, grasping at each other's breastbones, trying alternatively to stamp on each other's toes.

'¡*Venga!*' Come on! came the cry from a woman sitting at the side of the ring. Her little boy had jumped off her lap and was perched on top of a stool, his chin resting on the edge of the canvas that fenced the ring, his bright blond hair almost as white as his T-shirt.

For a few seconds the fighters barely seemed to move, caught in a tight struggle of strength, then with a flip they fell to the ground and began writhing over each other like snakes, twisting and sliding between grips and holds. The audience roared again: the local champion had his opponent by the neck and was turning upwards and sideways, as though trying to snap the man's backbone. The mulatto was clearly in pain and banged his fist against his opponent's arm. But the local boy was in a bad position, not able to control his opponent with his weight, and with a slicing motion the mulatto swung his leg round and kicked the Valencian on the side of the head. It was enough: for a second the white man's grip loosened and his opponent jacknifed up into the air free from his grasp. The Valencian immediately rushed towards him, but the local boy was hurt: the kick had cut the side of his head above the ear and blood was beginning to drip down on to his shoulders. He seemed not to care, though: with a torrent of fists he attacked the mulatto, who covered his face with his gloves. Then came another kick to the side, like a Thai boxer, and the two were on the floor again. The audience rose as one to its feet.

'*Dale, dale,*' came the cry. Go on, give it to him.

This time the mulatto had his opponent in a tight neck hold, his forearm pressed against the Valencian's throat, slowly choking him, while his right hand rained punches on to the top of his head. His teeth were clenched, spittle foaming from his mouth. The Valencian was turning red, his fingers clawing at the arm that was pressing the life out of him. Reaching for the mulatto's fingers he gave a jerk, and suddenly the hold was loosened. He slipped out and head butted the other man as they both sat on their knees on the canvas.

'*Dale*,' shouted the little boy at the side of the ring. Behind him his mother was jumping up and down hysterically.

Blood was now seeping all over the ring, the mulatto's nose smashed by the force of the Valencian's forehead. He stood up in a red haze but was submitted at once to a new barrage of blows. The Valencian held him at arm's length with his left hand while his right fist bludgeoned down again and again on to his face. His glove became wet with blood, while red spatters covered his neck and chest. The mulatto began to weaken, unable to defend himself against the heavy blows distorting his face. The referee was nowhere to be seen. In any other kind of fight he would have intervened much sooner, given the amount of blood both men were now losing. But I now realized what type of fight this was: the kind where anything goes, and these two were giving each other hell.

The muscleman at my side was on his feet, barging violently from side to side as he raised and dropped his clenched fists in excitement at the events unfolding in the ring. His arms were tensed, a powerful scent of anti-perspirant radiating from every pore. In his mind he was clearly in there himself, pummelling the mulatto with all his rage. For a second I looked around in the half-light at the other spectators. Countless bulging eyes feasting on the bloody spectacle were fixed on the centre of the hall. On my other side, Luis was punching down into the darkness at an imaginary foe.

But my own attention could not drift away from the fight for long. Within seconds I was drawn back to the two men in the ring, as if in a nightmare. The mulatto had fought back now and was pushing the Valencian against the ropes, fingers pressed hard into his shoulders as he tried to drag him down to the floor again. A stream of red poured down from each nostril and he spat to clear his mouth of the blood. His opponent was too strong for him, though: as they fell to the canvas the mulatto found himself twisting in mid-air and with a slap landed face up. The Valencian was straddling his chest in an instant, pinning him down with his weight. The mulatto couldn't move. And then the punches started once again: left, right, left, left, right. His face became a mass of pulp, arms flapping uselessly at his sides as his opponent decided to finish him off.

'*Mátale, mátale,*' came the cry. Kill him! The little blond boy at the side of the ring was slapping the canvas again in excitement. '*Mátale.*'

Not a single person was seated now, the entire audience chanting and screaming, shouting and whistling. Spaniards, whom I had always thought of as the most sympathetic and compassionate of people, were howling like mad dogs.

The mulatto appeared to be almost motionless, but still the punches hammered down. How did one of these fights end, I wondered. I couldn't believe – didn't want to believe – that it could be a struggle to the death. But the mulatto was going to fall unconscious, or worse, if it didn't stop soon.

Finally, with a weak downward motion he gave a tap on the floor as a signal of submission. The Valencian was on his feet in a flash, jumping around the ring in jubilation, the cut above his ear now congealed into a black mass. The mulatto lay still, his stomach and chest rising and falling sharply as he gasped for breath, blood dripping on to the canvas beneath him.

The audience was out of control. People were jumping on to

their chairs, waving and screaming. The man at my side was shuddering with excitement, bubbles of white saliva spilling from the corners of his mouth as he bellowed hoarsely like an ox. I was gripped by a sudden urge to get out, half suffocated by the mass of bodies now surging in an orgiastic crush, half disgusted at what we had seen, at what my own eyes had followed and watched from start to finish. But there was no way of leaving: the press of bodies was too strong.

In the ring the winner was being towelled down and handed a prize of some sort. There was little attention for the mulatto – just a helper nursing him back to his corner, trying to push a bottle of water into his broken mouth. The man needed a doctor, but there seemed to be no medical attention available. As he crouched on his stool, the Valencian came up and put his arms round his opponent's shoulders in a victorious gesture. The mulatto acknowledged him then let his head drop, supporting his forehead with his hands. He had done his job – victory for the local boy had never been in doubt.

I found myself trembling as the crowd slowly began to disperse and we were at last able to make it to the door and out of this hellhole. From a corner of the hall I could hear shouting: *Arriba España*, 'Up with Spain!' Perhaps, I thought, in the minds of the crowd, the fight had turned into some kind of nationalistic battle – the local boy against the foreigner. Their cries were an echo from the past. There seemed to be a fervour and aggression in the room I was unused to in Spain; although perhaps it was more in tune with the bloodier country it had once been. The screaming of the little blond boy for the mulatto to be killed had chilled me: it seemed so out of step with a people I knew for their love of children and their cherishing of human life.

The boy scrambled past me as we climbed the steps up back towards the exit. '*Mátale, mátale,*' he was shouting, like a chant. His elder brother ran after him, giggling.

'*Eso es, hijo*,' one of the crowd shouted in encouragement. That's it, lad. Like the others I'd noticed at the start, he too was wearing a baseball cap with an embroidered black silhouette of a bull.

We came out into the open at last. The dog with the strange marking was still there, checking everyone that walked past with brutish condescension, like a bouncer. I breathed in deeply, as though trying to cleanse myself of what I'd just witnessed. The fight had been short, just the one bout, but the crowd had seen blood, that was all that mattered. It felt like a warm-up spectacle for a night on the town, a clandestine fix to quicken the nerves before staying up till dawn dancing and drinking. I wanted to leave straight away, but out of politeness decided at least to say goodbye to Luis before heading off. I'd seen enough here. There was no point hanging on too long.

Luis was held up inside talking to his friends, though, and as I waited for him to appear from the hall I caught sight of some posters on the outside walls. I pushed past the crowd and walked up to have a closer look, grateful to have something to distract me momentarily.

IMMIGRANTS OUT! screamed one. SPANIARDS FIRST, said the other. The writing was laid over images of sub-Saharan Africans and Moroccans huddled in little wooden and rubber boats, the kinds that thousands travelled in every year as they tried to reach Spain and cross into Europe. Many died in the attempt. Near the top of the posters I noticed the same Osbourne bull everyone seemed to be wearing that night. The text was an angry rambling attack on everything from Brussels to 'blacks', with a scattering of hackneyed phrases like 'stealing our jobs' thrown in. It also mentioned contests like the one I'd just witnessed, and attempts by the authorities to ban them. But the authors were defiant. It was time for ACTION. They weren't going to take anything LYING DOWN. Then at the bottom came the signature: the director of some political party I'd never heard of, in conjunction with the Spanish Falange.

The Falange. The Spanish fascist party, the party that had supported Franco during the Civil War. I was surprised to see it still existed. And so openly, like this. Were they behind what I had just witnessed? It felt bizarre that what I had assumed to be a ghost of Spain's violent past should still be in existence and connected to this bloody spectacle. What's more, it was taking place right here in Valencia, a city I felt so at home in. The cries of *Arriba España* I'd heard inside the hall began to make sense: it had once been the rallying cry of the Falange and the Nationalists. Yet instead of resting safely on the pages of a history book, it was being shouted here right in front of me: it was happening now. Silently I cursed Luis for having brought me here. It had been such a casual invitation. Did he think this was normal? Was Nationalism, Francoism, still active in Spain today? I'd thought until then that only old men and nostalgia junkies still hankered for the days of the dictatorship.

Luis came over and placed his hand on my shoulder. He was smiling broadly, as though we'd just come out of a cinema or a comedy show.

'So,' he said, 'what did you think?'

I struggled to find something to say. I had just witnessed one of the most brutal acts I had ever seen, with hundreds of people screaming and shouting in blood-crazed lust. Children had been there, running around, baying out with the rest of them. I was used to bullfighting in Spain, but here we were watching human beings rip each other apart. I couldn't comprehend what had happened. Spain, despite its faults, was for me a country where people felt the pain of others and never failed to be moved by suffering. But this, what had happened here, went against all my assumptions, all the ideas I'd built up about the country after a dozen years living there. And to make it worse, the event was being sponsored, perhaps even organized, by fascists, like some dirty secret left over from the dictatorship and the Civil War. For a moment the image of the mass grave I'd seen back near the farm flashed in my mind. What had been happening here in Valencia during that time? Had men been killed and dumped as mercilessly in the city as they had been in the country? Had the place been split in two, divided between Left and Right? There was a side of Spain that I had not wanted to acknowledge, and yet here it was, on my doorstep. I'd thought it was part of history. Now, it seemed, I had walked into a world where distinctions between past and present were less clearly discernible.

'It was a bit *heavy*, right?' Luis answered for me. 'The mulatto will be all right. I've seen this kind of thing before. It looks worse than it actually is. He'll be fine in a couple of days. Just a few bruises, that's all. But it was a good fight. The local boy did us proud.'

I felt part of me was already moving away, had already gone home and was back at the farm, reeling from the violence and cocksure pantomime we'd just seen. I needed to get as far from here as possible.

'Do you want to come for a drink with the others?' Luis asked. 'There's a disco near here.'

'No, thanks,' I finally managed to say. 'I've got to get back.'

'Sure. I'll see you around, then.'

I walked away from the crowd of heaving, sweating, inflated muscle buzzing under the lights of the entrance and headed into the night, alone. Hoping, above all, that I would never again see Luis or the side of my beloved Spain he had opened my eyes to that night.

4

The Flying Dragon

On the morning of 11 July 1936, a silver twin-engine biplane took off from Croydon airport in south London, bound for Casablanca. In the cockpit was Captain William Bebb, formerly of the RAF. The passengers, officially off on a hunting expedition in the High Atlas mountains, were a former army officer Major Hugh Pollard, Pollard's daughter Diana, her friend Dorothy Watson and a Spaniard, Luis Bolín, of the *ABC* newspaper. The weather was bad on that summer morning in Britain, but the plane, a de Havilland Dragon Rapide, managed to take off nonetheless and within a few hours had landed in Bordeaux to refuel before continuing its lengthy journey. The Dragon Rapide was one of the best civilian planes around at the time for such a trip. With seating for nine people, a range of over 550 miles and a cruising speed of 130 mph, it would require only three or four stops en route and would be able to reach Morocco in about two days. Captain Bebb was an experienced pilot.

What most people at Croydon didn't know, however, was that the story about hunting in the High Atlas was actually a cover for a far riskier venture. Pollard, a Catholic who had previously fought in Morocco, was a British intelligence agent,[2] and the plane in fact was not ultimately bound for Casablanca, but for a rendezvous in the Canaries with a figure who would be crucial in the plot to bring down the democratic government in Madrid. Bebb and Pollard were to bring him to join his fellow plotters in northern Morocco, one of the launch pads of the coup. It was to be the beginning of a long journey that would eventually see him become dictator of all Spain.

Franco had spent the spring and early summer of 1936 in the Canaries in a kind of semi-exile, following the victory of the left-wing Popular Front in the February elections. It was a step down for the former chief of staff, a man widely suspected of plotting against the new government. Franco had taken it in his stride, however, adjusting to the slower pace of life on the edge of the tropics by attending private English lessons and taking up golf. With little to do but revise the coastal defences, he could but look on from afar as tensions increased in the capital, while perhaps reminiscing on a glorious military career to date. In other circumstances he might well have been entering the twilight of his soldiering days. In fact, the most important part of his life was just about to begin.

Franco was born in 1892 in the small naval town of El Ferrol in the northwestern Spanish region of Galicia. It is often said that to understand Franco you need to understand the Galician character, marked by an evasiveness and caution known as *retranca*. Galicians are famed for being hard to nail down – a trait often remarked on by those who knew Franco. It was a quality that was to serve him well as he rose from middle-class military cadet to head of state. Franco's mother was a devout Catholic and a very conservative woman, while his father, a pay-master in the navy, was a passionate man who liked drinking, gambling and chasing women, and who often beat his children –

Franco was the second of five: three sons and two daughters. When Franco was fourteen, his father left the family home and set up with his mistress in Madrid. Franco, however, was always closer to his mother, both emotionally and in temperament. He was later to write that the Spanish Republic had been set up by men who cheated on their wives.[3] His hatred towards it, you sense, was fuelled by an association in his own mind between the liberal government and the father who had abandoned his family when he was a boy.

As a child, Franco had wanted to join the navy, but government restrictions on entry meant he ended up training at the artillery academy in Toledo. Never brilliant, but meticulous and with a strong nerve, he rose quickly through the officer ranks, his big break coming in 1920 when, as a major, he was offered the post of second in command of the newly formed Spanish Foreign Legion. Based on its French namesake, the force was an elite unit in the Spanish Army, being made up largely of criminals and fugitives, and was headed by Colonel José Millán Astray, a man close to King Alfonso XIII and with certain dubious ideas about soldiering that were supposedly based on the samurai code. The main function of the Legión, as it was called, was to help police Spain's territories in northern Morocco.

In 1898 Spain, once the greatest empire in the world, had finally lost the last of its colonial possessions – Cuba, Puerto Rico and the Philippines – to the United States in a war that became known as the Disaster. It was a wake-up call that, after centuries of decline and decadence, the country was no longer a player on the international stage. So when the opportunity arose in 1906 to take over northern Morocco, the government in Madrid took little convincing. France was busy extending its north-African territories westwards from Algeria into Morocco, but the Germans were unhappy about this. So in a compromise deal reached with Britain and the USA at the Conference of Algeciras, Spain was invited to set up her own 'Protectorate', stretching east–west from Larache to the Algerian border along Morocco's Mediterranean coast, while the French took the bulk of the country to the south. The city of Tangier, meanwhile, would be controlled by an international committee.

Spain's Moroccan possessions, however, became something of a poisoned chalice. The terrain in the area was largely mountainous, and the people were Berber tribesmen with a long tradition of scant respect for the authorities – whoever they were. Over the years the area was brought under control only at great expense, at the cost of many Spanish and Moroccan lives, and sometimes, humiliatingly, only with the military cooperation of the French from the south. Nonetheless, the Spanish occupation of northern Morocco tapped deeply into the national psyche with its echoes of the ancient struggles to clear the Iberian peninsula of the Moors. Although the Reconquest had ended in 1492 with the capture of Granada, the conflict still resonated deeply both culturally and psychologically. Fourteen ninety-two was not only the year the Reconquest concluded, it was also the date of Columbus's famous journey and of the publication of the first Spanish grammar – the first such work in any modern Western language. It was the year in which 'Spain' as a concept was truly born. 'Moor-slaying' was part of the glue that held the fragmented nation together.

The period of the Reconquest was also the age of chivalry in Spain. Young men like Franco seeking adventure were naturally drawn to the new Protectorate, with the opportunities it gave for glory, exoticism, a life away from the humdrum and the chance to live out childhood fantasies about knights in armour beating up *Moros*. Franco was to draw on this romantic imagery when he referred to his later campaign against the Republic as a 'crusade', shamelessly using the language of Spain's medieval past.

Franco's years in Morocco made him as a soldier, as he readily admitted. It was there that he famously led his troops from the front against Moroccan rebels in the attack on the coastal rebel-held town of Alhucemas, only one of several actions which earned him the respect of his men and saw him rise even faster through the ranks. He was seriously wounded once – a bullet in the abdomen which, some said, made him impotent – but his career was set on an upward trajectory. Mentored by his superior, Millán Astray, who seems to have hero-worshipped his brave young second-in-command, Franco was also brutalized by his Moroccan experiences. Committing atrocities against the men, women and children of rebel villages was the norm, while punishments within the Legión itself were extremely harsh. Franco even shot dead one of his own men after he refused to eat his ration of beans. All this was done with a coldness and apparent lack of regard for human suffering which would remain with him for life. Even when close to death in 1975, he insisted on the execution of two ETA members and three Maoist activists, despite calls from world leaders and even the Pope for the sentences to be commuted.

Thanks to his Moroccan successes, in 1926, at the age of thirty-three, Franco was promoted to general. He was the youngest man of that rank in Europe at the time – an honour which Napoleon had enjoyed in his day. At the same time, Franco's brother Ramón was in the public eye after successfully flying across the South Atlantic to Buenos Aires – the first ever such journey. The two brothers were national heroes, although Ramón, far more of a playboy than his serious and austere sibling, dominated the headlines. People associated the name 'Franco' in those days more with the airman than with the soldier. Ironically, one would end up an authoritarian dictator, the other an anarchist revolutionary, although the two were eventually reconciled once the Civil War broke out in 1936.

Promotion took Franco away from Morocco and brought him back to the Spanish mainland. A favourite of the king and well liked in government, he was made head of the new military academy at Saragossa, a position he relished. Yet the abdication of Alfonso XIII and the establishment of the Spanish Republic in 1931, headed by a centre-left government, saw the first serious setback in his career. Manuel Azaña, the minister of war, closed the Saragossa academy and removed Franco from his post as part of his project to reform the top-heavy and inefficient armed forces. Franco was to hold a grudge against Azaña for this for life – the two would later become adversaries when Azaña became president of the Spanish Republic and Franco's opposite number during the Civil War.

In 1933, however, the left-wing government was voted out of office and a series of right and centre-right governments held power until February 1936. Franco was back in favour. Militarily, the most important event of these years, both for Franco and for Spain, was the crushing of the left-wing revolution in the northern region of Asturias. Franco was put in charge of the operation and took the innovative step of bringing in troops from Spanish Morocco to combat the Asturian miners. The troops, known as Regulares, were made up mostly of Moroccan Muslims who had joined the Spanish Army in their policing of the Protectorate. Brutalized, like the Spanish legionaries, by the harsh conditions in Morocco, they were highly effective and thoroughly ruthless against the Spanish revolutionaries, who were killed in their thousands. People were shocked that *Moros* should be used against Christian-born civilians, but their effectiveness had been proven. More importantly, a precedent had been set which would be followed on a much greater scale once the Civil War itself began – Franco, nicknamed the 'hyena of Asturias', once again sending Moorish troops to fight against his fellow countrymen.

Franco did well under the right-wing governments of the Republic. He was promoted to chief of staff, while his success in Asturias hardened his belief in a role for the military in politics, preferably with himself in charge. The event, however, further polarized the left and right wings of Spanish society, both of which were trying to push the shaky new Republic to its limits. One half was calling for violent revolution to undo social injustices, the other half demanding violent authoritarian measures to maintain the status quo. Mutual hatred was growing by the day, and the country was very quickly falling apart, yet the role, if any, for Franco in the coming conflagration was still uncertain.

Then, with the fall of the right-wing governments and the victory of the Popular Front in February 1936, Franco once again found himself in the cold. This time his enemy, Azaña, was prime minister. The close-won election had, if anything, heightened political tensions, and on the night the results came in Franco, still as chief of staff, had come close to backing calls for a coup d'état. Many on the Right were convinced that revolution was around the corner if the centre-left got back in.

Once in power, Azaña had lost little time in sidelining Franco again, on this occasion giving him the post of military governor of the Canary Islands. It got him out of the way, while making contact between him and other potential conspirators that much more difficult.

Franco, however, for all the suspicions surrounding him, did not spend his time in Tenerife plotting the downfall of Azaña's government, although he did manage to communicate with those who were. He had learned from the mistakes of other coup attempts over the decades that had failed. His Galician caution made him hesitant about making such a move, while his evasiveness meant no one was ever sure quite what he was thinking.

Franco may have been biding his time, but others quickly got down to the business of plotting the overthrow of the government. And they desperately wanted Franco, as one of the most able soldiers of his generation, to join them. General Mola, based in Pamplona, was setting out plans for a take-over of power by the military.

As the plans for the coup progressed, Franco refused to say definitely whether he was with Mola and the others or not, while always making enough positive noises for them to think he was on the brink of throwing in his lot with them. Mola, however, was absolutely relying on him and was already working out how to get Franco from the Canaries to Spanish Morocco, where, as a highly respected founder member of the Legión, he would secure the Protectorate for the uprising and command the army there. Through various contacts and financial backing from wealthy Spaniards abroad, a plane was arranged to fly from England to the Canaries to pick Franco up. This plane was the Dragon Rapide, chartered by Hugh Pollard on the instructions of Luis Bolín, the *ABC* correspondent in London. It was decided that an English plane would be faster and an English pilot more reliable than their Spanish counterparts.

Pollard decided to take his daughter and her friend along to give more credence to their cover story about the plane being used for nothing more sinister than a hunting jaunt in Morocco. But as they made their way down through France to Portugal and then on to Morocco, Franco, in the Canaries, was having more and more doubts about joining the uprising. On 12 July, the day the Dragon Rapide reached Casablanca, he sent a coded message to Mola reading '*geografía poco extensa*' – the circumstances for a coup, in Franco's mind at least, were still not right.

But over the next few hours, events were to take place in Madrid that would change his mind.

The news of Calvo Sotelo's murder by police officers shocked the whole country, not least of all Franco. The event seemed to confirm to the Popular Front's enemies that the government was unable to control the cycle of violence into which the country had fallen. It was one thing for the authorities to stand by while anarchists burned down churches; quite another for the very forces of law and order to murder a member of parliament in cold blood. It was the trigger Franco needed. 'We can wait no longer,' he said on hearing the news. 'This is the signal.' All doubts were cast aside and he immediately sent another telegram informing Mola he was on board. It was a momentous decision which would have huge repercussions both for him personally and millions of Spaniards over the course of the next forty years.

But first he had to get from the Canaries to Morocco. On 14 July the Dragon Rapide left Casablanca to begin the secret part of its mission. Leaving Luis Bolín behind, Bebb and Pollard flew southwest, not to Tenerife, but to the island of Gran Canaria, where they landed that afternoon. Franco was being watched and to land on Tenerife would have aroused suspicions. Bebb stayed behind with the plane while Pollard and the two girls caught the ferry to Tenerife, where they were to make contact with Franco via a clinic on the island with the code phrase 'Galicia saluda a Francia'. This done, Franco had to deal with the difficult question of how to get to Gran Canaria. In order to travel there he would need special permission from the ministry in Madrid. A trip to examine the coastal defences was out of the question as he had done precisely this only a couple of weeks beforehand; a repeat request would only have raised eyebrows and all efforts had to be made to avoid attracting attention. The government had wind of a potential coup, although as yet it was doing precious little to prevent it. On 16 July, however, the perfect excuse presented itself. That morning, the military commander of Gran Canaria, General Balmes, shot himself while out at target practice. It was a bizarre death, as Balmes was regarded as an excellent marksman, but meant that Franco was able to travel to Gran Canaria on the pretext of having to attend the general's funeral the next day. The coup was due to begin on the eighteenth. There was no time to lose.

No one has yet clarified the mystery surrounding Balmes's timely demise. Was it really an accident? Did the general commit suicide because he knew what was coming and, as a loyal Republican, felt he could do nothing about it? Or did Franco have him bumped off? The fact is that this was just one of a series of 'fortunate deaths' which eased Franco's rise to power throughout the course of the Civil War. The man seemed to have some sort of evil lucky star supporting him along the way, mercilessly removing people at just the right moment. None of the subsequent convenient deaths (Generals Sanjurjo, Goded and Mola, or the founder of the Falangist party José-Antonio Primo de Rivera, among others) were demonstrably of his doing, despite suspicions to the contrary. So perhaps Balmes's accident should be seen in the same light, despite the temptation to suspect foul play.

Whatever the reasons for Balmes's death, Franco was granted permission to attend the funeral and that night, leaving instructions for his supporters about the uprising in Tenerife, he caught the midnight mail-boat over to Puerto de la Luz, Gran Canaria, along with his wife Carmen and their daughter. Pollard was also on the same boat. After spending the next morning presiding over the funeral ceremony, Franco spent the rest of the day in Las Palmas preparing for the coup and drawing up his manifesto. In it he made no mention of the other conspirators, claiming that he was rebelling in order to save the *patria*, the fatherland, from anarchy. Nothing in the document could pin him down to being either a monarchist or a Republican, while the ambiguous and rather out-of-place French Revolution rallying cry with which he signed off was changed in order from 'Liberty, Equality, Fraternity' to place 'fraternity' first. There was to be little room for 'liberty' in the future Spain that Franco had in mind.

Everything was set for 18 July, but on the afternoon of the seventeenth rebel officers in the Spanish Moroccan town of Melilla anticipated the uprising by several hours when the plot was in danger of being discovered. Franco was woken with the news in the middle of the night, and by five o'clock in the morning on the eighteenth he had declared martial law on the island of Gran Canaria. Falangists and right-wing officers quickly joined him and Las Palmas was eventually secured for the rebellion. The rest of the island remained in government hands for some time, but Franco was itching to get to Morocco, where the main action would be. Securing his wife and daughter a passage on a German ship to France, he sailed around the island to where Captain Bebb was waiting for him with the Dragon Rapide at Gando airstrip. Lifted ashore on the shoulders of his men, he took off for Morocco, flying first to Agadir before heading north to Casablanca. Carrying a forged diplomatic passport in one pocket and, it is said, a letter addressed to the prime minister in the other explaining that he was travelling to Madrid to help defend the Republic, Franco changed into civilian clothes during the flight and threw his military identification papers out of the window, anxious in these delicate first hours of the uprising lest he be found out. Disorganized as the rebellion was, not all the garrisons across Spain had come out on the same day, some waiting to see how things developed before committing themselves. In the end the declarations were staggered over the next few days.

At Agadir they had difficulty finding fuel to continue their journey, while at Casablanca, as they were coming in for a night landing, the landing lights suddenly went out. Were the French authorities on to them? Had the coup failed and the Spanish authorities requested Franco's arrest, or, worse, were they trying to kill him? Bebb managed to land the plane anyway, and discovered that the blackout had been caused by a simple blown fuse.

Franco and Bolín, who had joined him by this point, slept for a few hours in a Casablanca hotel that night. Here Franco famously shaved off his moustache to disguise himself further. A fellow conspirator, General Queipo de Llano, who despised Franco despite being on the same side, later quipped that this was the only sacrifice the future Generalísimo ever made for the rebellion.

The following morning the Dragon Rapide set off again, this time for Tetuán, the capital of the Spanish Protectorate in the north. As soon as they crossed into Spanish airspace Franco put his military uniform back on. Arriving at Tetuán's Samia Ramel airport, they circled around for a few moments, uncertain as to whether they were about to be greeted by friends or enemies. Finally Franco caught sight of one of his old comrades, whom he knew was with the rebellion, and he called out to Bebb that it was safe to land.[4] He had good reason to be cautious. Until a few hours previously, his own cousin, Major Ricardo de la Puente Bahamonde, had been trying to secure the airport for the Republic. Outnumbered by the rebels, he had had to surrender, but not before sabotaging the planes at the airfield. He was to pay for it with his life, Franco facilitating the execution of a man who, as a child, had been like a brother to him.

Back on the ground, Franco immediately took charge of the uprising. But the Dragon Rapide's mission was not over yet. Realizing he was short of military supplies, Franco instructed

Bolín to leave immediately to secure more aircraft and bombs from abroad. Bolín set off with Bebb in the Dragon Rapide for Rome, where he would seek an audience with Mussolini.

Meanwhile, in Tetuán, once he'd ensured the support of the local Muslim leaders and visited the barracks of the Legión, where the commander, Colonel Yagüe, gave him a hero's welcome, Franco began to inform himself about how the rebellion was progressing across the rest of Spain. There had been some important successes: General Mola and his supporters had secured Pamplona and much of the north of the country, apart from a strip running along the coast including the Basque Country. Saragossa and Teruel were also captured. Meanwhile, in the south General Queipo de Llano had given the rebels a foothold in Andalusia by taking Seville. The coup had suffered some major setbacks, though, having failed or at that moment being crushed in the major cities of Barcelona, Valencia, Bilbao and Málaga. In Madrid, the rebels had delayed in making their move and were soon to be massacred at their barracks by armed worker militias – fighting forces linked to left-wing parties and trade unions.

As information about how the rebellion was faring came in to Franco, now based at Tetuán, his understanding of the importance of the Spanish Army in Morocco for its future success grew by the minute. The coup had essentially failed to deliver a knockout blow – a civil conflict of some sort was becoming virtually inevitable. Yet the rebel-held territory on the mainland was split in two – with Mola in the north and Queipo with his pocket in the south. The conspirators controlled none of the big industrial areas in Catalonia or the Basque Country, while Spain's biggest foreign export earner at the time – the rich fruit- and vegetable-growing area around Valencia – was in government hands. The titular head of the rebellion, General Sanjurjo, had been killed when the plane carrying him from Portugal back to Spain crashed on take-off, while the man leading the uprising in Barcelona, General Goded, one of the more able rebel generals, was about to be shot. In the circumstances, the only real asset in the rebels' hands was Spanish Morocco, home to the best fighters in the armed forces. And with Franco in charge, they were being led by a man with watertight self-belief. 'Stand firm,' he telegraphed Mola in those difficult early days, 'victory certain.' This latecomer to the uprising was about to take over the whole operation.

The main question, though, was how to get his soldiers across the Strait of Gibraltar to mainland Spain. The navy was largely in government hands, as on most ships the lower decks had mutinied against their largely pro-rebellion superiors once they'd heard about the uprising. These warships were now cruising around the Mediterranean watching for any sign of movement from Morocco. The only solution would be to fly the troops over to Seville. But there were virtually no planes available in the Protectorate. Franco would have to look for help from outside.

Like attracts like, and both Mussolini and Hitler came to Franco's rescue. Mussolini initially played it cool when Bolín handed over Franco's first request for aid, but warmed to his cause once it appeared that Britain and France would not respond belligerently if he helped the Spanish rebels. Eventually he despatched a dozen Savoia-Marchetti bombers to help Franco, though only nine arrived after three ran out of fuel and crashed or were forced to land. Meanwhile, Hitler agreed to help Franco as well by sending Junkers Ju52 bombers. Approached by Franco's representatives after he had seen a performance of *Siegfried* conducted by Wilhelm Fürtwängler at Bayreuth, he whipped himself up into an anti-communist frenzy during a two-hour rant, eventually agreeing to their request. Still under the influence of Wagner, he decided that the plan was to be called Operation Magic Fire and that Franco was to have twenty bombers rather than the mere ten he'd asked for. The international dimension to the Spanish Civil War, which would convert it into the ideological battleground of the great Left–Right conflict of the 1930s, had been set.

Hitler later said that Franco should erect a monument to the Junkers planes that subsequently carried his soldiers over from Morocco to Seville, as the saviours of the Nationalist Uprising, as the coup became known. Certainly his intervention gave a failing rebellion the shot in the arm it needed to avoid being snuffed out completely, and the initial supply of bombers was followed by a fairly steady stream of supplies, ammunition and men from both Germany and Italy. Boats were eventually used to carry some of Franco's men over the Strait, with cover provided against the Republican navy by the new planes, but the airlift of equipment and soldiers was the first operation of its kind on such a large scale in military history – by October some 14,000 men and 44 artillery pieces had been transported over a total of 868 flights.

On 7 August, Franco – the Caudillo, or 'chief' as people were calling him – eventually landed in Seville and took charge of his army's campaign to conquer the Spanish mainland. From his HQ in Tetuán he had turned the Nationalists' fortunes round almost single-handedly. Where once the odds had been heavily against them, they were now looking more even and their one major asset, the forces of the Legión and the Moroccan Regulares, was now effective. Three weeks had passed since Franco had left the Canaries in the Dragon Rapide and embarked on his journey to absolute power. The first part was over. Spain's suffering was only just beginning.

5

Ceuta

*T*he fight had disturbed me deeply, but it had also sparked something off inside, like a fly buzzing angrily at a grimy window. First the mass grave near my house, then discovering an underworld of far-right thugs in Valencia which included someone I had considered a friend. I was used to Spain being a country where people turned away from the past, drawing a veil over anything that was too unpleasant or painful to remember, or which failed to fit in with whatever world-view held sway at the time. Often there was a sense that people skated over the surface of life without asking themselves what they were really doing. Yet I was beginning to confront the country's darker history, which I myself had brushed over: a cruelty and violence I could no longer ignore. I wanted to understand what those men buried in the valley below my house had been fighting for. What were the passionately held beliefs that had set one countryman against another? And I wanted to know how a party bearing the same name as their killers could still be active almost seventy years later. Once upon a time

Spain had been ripped apart by such as these. Could they do it again?

My growing fascination with the conflict was fuelled by the discovery that my great-grandfather, Jack Warnock, had been a gun-runner during the Civil War. I was already familiar with the stories concerning his Antarctic explorations during the 1930s (there was a group of islets named after him off Kemp Land); but on a brief trip back to England, Jack's only remaining son, my Great-Uncle Iain, had told me about his father's Spanish adventures.

Once he'd returned from the southern seas, Great-Grandpa Warnock, it turned out, had worked for the Stanhope Steamship Company, run by the ship-owner J. A. Billmeir. Billmeir had made his fortune by trading with the Spanish Republican government during the Civil War, at a time when few other people would. Dodging the Nationalist blockades and land-mines, his crews often smuggled weapons in the holds of their vessels, thereby breaking the rules of Non-Intervention – an agreement by European powers not to send arms or military assistance to either side in the Spanish conflict. It was a farce, as Germany and Italy did little to hide their support for Franco, and Mussolini had thousands of men on Spanish soil. But the British went along with the pretence on the grounds of appeasement and in an attempt to prevent another pan-European war. Billmeir's ships, along with a handful of other shipping companies, were one of the main lifelines for the Republic.

My great-grandfather had been running in and out of Spanish ports in the Mediterranean – Barcelona, Valencia, Cartagena – during the late spring and summer of 1937, almost a year after the conflict had started. Uncle Iain remembered his father telling of how he had almost been killed during a Nationalist air raid on Barcelona. The force from one of the blasts had thrown him to the ground, breaking the blue china plate he was holding in his hands at the time.

The traditionally Tory-supporting family back in Lancashire had tended to keep quiet about Jack's smuggling of machine-guns past the international blockade to the under-armed 'Reds' of Spain. Jack survived Franco's bombs only to die in an accident at the outbreak of the Second World War. Great-Uncle Iain, lung cancer gripping his chest, took any more details he might have known with him when he died shortly after my visit, and my own subsequent research had failed to bring up anything more. But the story gave me a personal link to the subject.

Some weeks after the fascist-sponsored wrestling match, an opportunity came up by chance for me to visit a part of the country I had always wanted to explore. Ceuta was an anomaly – a piece of Spain on the very tip of Africa, a large rock jutting out into the sea connected to the mainland by a tiny isthmus, very much like Gibraltar across the Strait on the northern horizon. A border outpost butting on to Morocco to the south, it was a fascinating little city, geographically cut off from the country to which it belonged, and culturally divided from its immediate neighbour. Here Christians, Muslims and Jews lived in relative peace, in a mirror image of what Spain might have been had its Jewish and Morisco populations not been expelled in the fifteenth and seventeenth centuries.

Ceuta and the area around it had been one of the main start-ing points for the coup which had led to the Spanish Civil War back in 1936. An invitation to a wedding in nearby Tetuán in northern Morocco gave me a chance to explore. A friend from university had fallen for a local girl – Muna – and was holding the Muslim ceremony for their nuptials in her home town. History books talked about Franco's secret journey to this part of Morocco at the start of the conflict in order to take control of the Army of Africa. I would pass through Ceuta on my way down to the celebrations and get a flavour of the place. The city was the home of the Spanish Foreign Legion – the Legión – hardened fighting men who, the Spanish asserted, always made their French counterparts look like pussycats. They had played a key role in Franco's campaign.

The modern barracks of the Legión were, unsurprisingly, closed to the public, but they had a museum in the centre of town. The place was dark and grotty; the main curator was an affable old Sikh with proud grey whiskers and a pot belly, who talked at length about his former life as a merchant seaman. Rows of guns and bombs sat next to photos of Franco and General Millán Astray, the co-founders of this elite force. Brightly coloured flags drooped sorrowfully from the walls while stiff dusty mannequins were used to display the evolution of the Legión's uniform, a strangely macho affair where the men's chests were exposed almost to the navel in true Latin style. Apart from the Sikh, who kindly informed me that he'd written to the colonel three times now complaining about the damp, there was just the man on the desk, who seemed keen to strike up a conversation.

'This was the bullet that killed Kennedy,' he told me.

I looked carefully at the pointed piece of metal he was holding up, imagining it hurtling through the air one November morning in Dallas. Strange that it should have ended up here in this forgotten corner of Spain. Strange, too, that the man holding it up to me should be the spitting image of Abraham Lincoln, that other assassinated American president. Apart from the military uniform and the tattoos, he might well have been the man himself, complete with fur-lined chin.

'What, you mean *the* bullet?'

The soldier laughed contemptuously.

'No. The same type of bullet. Six point five millimetre.'

A macabre image flashed through my mind of it crashing into JFK's skull.

'Did they use those in the Spanish Civil War?'

A munitions expert, Abe was more than happy to talk at length on the huge number of different bullets used during the war. Republican soldiers, he told me, often used to throw away their rifles once they'd finished the cartridges, as it was generally impossible to find the right-sized replacement bullets. With guns coming in from so many disparate sources – some of them brought in illegally by my great-grandfather – a company of men might be using over twenty different calibres at any one time. Grenades were so unreliable that the men refused to use them, preferring instead to stick a piece of dynamite in a tin can and throw it at the enemy.

It was a wonder many Republicans had guns at all. The government in Madrid had been very reluctant to hand out weapons to the unions and other left-wing groups at the start of the coup. When they finally capitulated and distributed rifles from the Ministry of Defence, the militiamen found that only five thousand out of a total of sixty-five thousand had bolts and so could be fired.

'At least Franco's forces had proper guns,' Abe beamed through blackened teeth. I wondered if the state of this once historic fighting force was as bad as their museum. If so, there was little hope for them.

Fascinating though this all was, the place was a disappointment, and I had given up on finding anything more interesting when Abe pulled me outside to the entrance patio of the museum and pointed out over the sea and the curve of the bay south towards Morocco. In the distance I could make out the border checkpoint dividing Europe from Africa, the First World from the Third World. Beyond, the hillsides were dry scrubland, a few houses and villas dotted along the grey tarmacked road passing down the coast. The sea was surprisingly rough here, I noticed. I wondered if anyone ever tried swimming over the border.

'Can you see?' Abe said energetically. I looked in the direction he was indicating, not sure what I was supposed to be looking at. 'There, the building just to the left of the white apartment blocks in the distance.'

I saw a smudge on a hill, over in Moroccan territory. It was hard to make out, but it appeared to be an old building.

'That was our first headquarters,' Abe said. 'Our old home. Where Franco and Millán Astray first set up the Legión.'

I shook his hand: I knew immediately where I had to go.

An hour later I was crossing the border and heading in a tin-can taxi down the ancient Barbary Coast. Deep potholes made for wayward driving, the tarmac blending seamlessly with the sand and grit at the sides. Alongside the five-star hotels there for summer holiday-makers up from Casablanca and Rabat, elderly men in overalls and woollen hats stood at the entrance of a mechanic's oily workshop, scratching their heads over deconstructed cars in pieces on the forecourt. Bars fronting on to the sea served mint teas and iced sherbets, without a sign of a cool beer anywhere in sight. Policemen in light-blue and grey uniforms and bubble-shaped helmets with bug-eyed goggles stood by their magnificent motorbikes and directed the careering traffic, whistles blowing furiously above the sound of the crashing waves on the beach below.

The taxi-driver knew exactly where I wanted to go, and after four or five miles stopped by the side of the road and pointed to a dirt track leading up a slope away from the coast.

'That's where it is,' he said.

I quickly paid and set off up the hill at speed, not hearing what the taxi-driver shouted to me as he drove off, his words lost in the sound of the sea and the traffic.

Franco had come to this place as soon as he landed in Tetuan at the start of the coup. Colonel Yagüe, a member of the Falange, had been waiting for him, the troops primed for the coming assault against the government, with the secret rallying cry *CAFE*, an acronym for *Camaradas ¡Arriba la Falange Española!* – Comrades, Up with the Spanish Falange! Not all the soldiers were in the know, however. At a banquet just days before the coup, the Spanish High Commissioner in Morocco, a former artillery captain, was confused to hear other officers calling for 'coffee' as the fish course was being served. Later he was captured by the rebels when the coup broke out and shot for his loyalty to the government.

I clambered up the hill away from the road and the hooting of the taxi to where I thought the former Legión headquarters must be. As I reached the crest it came into view – a vast crumbling edifice, the shell of a once proud neo-Classical structure, now covered in weeds. I stood in awe. It was hard to believe that this had once been a military barracks. It reminded me of grand old Spanish tobacco factories, like the building in Seville – today a university – where Mérimée had situated the cigar-rolling women of *Carmen*. Either that or a palace for some long-forgotten duke. In front of me, a flat square of land that would once have been a parade ground stretched up to the main building – a rectangular construction covering an area of almost two acres. I walked across, stepping over flattened rusty cans among the knee-high dry grass, smudges of fox-brown in a sea of yellow and grey. The place had enormous presence and energy. Some ruins are simply dead – of architectural or historical interest, but little more. These barracks, the Dar Riffien headquarters of the Spanish Foreign Legion, were alive. Perhaps because they had been abandoned for so little time, or perhaps because they hadn't been touched since. The ghosts that lived here had been left in peace, I felt, undisturbed and free to haunt their old home.

Large fig trees were growing inside the main building. The roof had fallen in and the remaining walls must have acted as a windbreak against the breezes blowing in from the sea. Great glassless windows eight feet high ran along the outside, delicate masonry curling around their empty frames. Inside, it was difficult to see anything for the mass of foliage that had taken over, trees and flowers claiming the place for themselves as though it were a vast conservatory. Dark-purple morning glories smothered the lower walls, gradually creeping their way into what once had been offices, a canteen, kitchens. Nature had quickly taken over the buildings, but something of the spirit of the place remained.

It was hard to believe that the Civil War had been launched from a place of such beauty and grandeur. This was a palace more suited to ballroom dancing than to drills and firing practice. Yet as I scrambled around, amazed at the scale of the building, so splendid and yet so decrepit, I began to understand the emotions that a structure like this could invoke, and how it might fuel the energy and drive needed to wage the kind of war that had ripped through Spain. Here I could imagine how you could easily fall into fervent dreams of superiority, order and resistance to change. Like the cloisters of a monastery, or the courtyard of an ancient university, such a building was flattering by association: 'I belong here: this place is magnificent and therefore so am I.' The soldiers of the Legión stationed here, with their traditions of strict discipline and hierarchy, would have needed little convincing to fight the church-burning anarchists and revolution-waging Marxists who were trying to take over Spain. It was their natural duty, and inclination, to defend the old ways.

What puzzled me, though, was why this once great building

had been left to fall apart like this. I could appreciate that it no longer stood on Spanish territory – the tiny peninsula of Ceuta was visible from this vantage point back northwards up the coast: the place from which Abe had earlier shown me this very spot from outside the Legión museum. But surely the Moroccans could have made use of such a complex, perhaps for their own army. Then again, associations with the former colonial rulers might have left a nasty taste in the mouth. The Spanish had not been the most beneficent of masters in northern Morocco, spending much of the time fighting bloody and brutal campaigns against the locals. Incorporating Moroccans into their own forces – the Regulares – and then using them against their own kind in the Civil War had been one of the methods the Spanish used to channel the rebelliousness and aggression of the native tribes. Even so, to let the buildings fall to ruin like this?

As I was wondering, I spotted some Arabic lettering on the walls of a separate building set away from the main palace where I was standing. I could make out the words GOD, THE KING AND THE FATHERLAND – the motto, I remembered from somewhere, of the Moroccan Army. Then, among the ruins and the invading plant life, I caught sight of a line of clothes hung out to dry and some cooking utensils on the ground. Clean and rust-free, they must have been used recently.

As these images registered, two things happened almost simultaneously: a strong sense that I was in trouble came over me, a split second before I felt a hand grab me roughly by the shoulder. I spun round in surprise – two young Moroccan soldiers armed with rifles were staring at me with a combination of curiosity and menace.

'Come with us,' one of them said. 'You're under arrest.'

Speechless, I turned and walked away between the two of them. One of them held me firmly by the elbow. It was unnecessary: the suddenness of their appearance and the implicit threat of their weaponry left me no choice but to go with them. As they led me away, I began to realize just how blind I'd been to think the place deserted. Signs of life were everywhere – not just the clothes, but I could now hear faint Arabic music from a radio in a room somewhere. There were fresh animal droppings on the ground, chickens roaming among the dry weeds, bits of rubbish thrown about that were only days or weeks old. As I was escorted down the dusty track, everything around me seemed to talk of the present.

We headed to some green outbuildings on the edge of the complex. I had failed to notice them before, half hidden behind a cluster of strawberry trees. They were modern, undecorated cubes built out of breeze block, the red Moroccan flag with its green five-pointed star hanging limply in the still, hot air from a pole thrust into the flat roof. I sensed my nerves kicking in as we headed towards the front door, a black rectangular hole in the dusty facade. A coldness came over me, spreading across my chest and shoulders. I'd been a complete idiot. God knew how this was going to end.

The soldiers marched me down chipped blue-painted steps to a square blank room lit by a single bulb hanging from the ceiling. A small table stood in the middle, with white, scratched, dirty wooden legs. The soldiers closed the door. I expected to hear the clunk of a key locking me in, but instead, through the small hole at the top of the door where once a window might have been, I could see one of the soldiers standing on guard while the other climbed back up the stairs. I looked for a place to sit but there was nowhere to rest. Leaning in a corner I tried in vain to calm myself and remain positive, justifying what I'd done and trying to rehearse what I'd say. I had obviously broken the law by trespassing on military property, but only in-advertently; and from what I'd seen here this was not an important base. They couldn't have been doing much more than standing guard at this old site. No matter – they'd caught me, and it was going to take some explaining. Curious about the Civil War? Wanted to see the old HQ of the Legión? They would think I was mad.

After a long hour's wait I crouched down in the corner to rest my legs. The air was still and hot, while the floor looked just that bit too disgusting to sit on. But I found it hard to keep still, my cold, moistened fingertips circling around one another frantically as I waited. As the minutes passed my mind seemed to move into a kind of empty trance, my only thought being to try to remember the French word for 'sightseer'. A kind of paralysis seemed to be coming over me. The soldiers who had once occupied these barracks, the Spanish legionaries, had been hardened killers, famed for their brutality. They particularly enjoyed cutting off the heads of anyone who got in their way.

Eventually I heard someone coming down the stairs and I stood up, my head reeling from the heat. A young officer came in, his sandy uniform as ruffled and unkempt as those of the soldiers who had arrested me. He looked me up and down with a rough disinterested stare, while I tried to gauge what kind of a man he might be. One of the soldiers brought him a chair. He demanded my passport and started meticulously taking down my details on a bundle of forms and papers he'd brought with him. He leaned his small head in as he wrote, concentrating on every letter, checking and rechecking several times that he'd got it right. The fact that it simply said 'passport agency' for place of issue gave him great concern.

'*C'est où, ça?*' he barked. They were the first words he'd directly addressed to me. I had no idea where the passport agency was, but he needed a city to place on his form, so I gave him one.

'*Londres*,' I replied. Sounded reasonable enough. His head bent down again as he scribbled away.

Then came a barrage of questions, very fast and all in French. Unfortunately, 'being arrested' hadn't featured in the role-playing situations I remembered from French lessons at school. I silently cursed my teachers as I tried to understand what was being asked of me. A simple grammatical mistake might end me up in more trouble.

Who was I? I repeated my name.

Nationality? He had my passport in his hands.

Where was I staying? I gave the name of my hotel in Ceuta.

What was I doing here? This was the difficult one. I could only tell him the truth, but depending on what kind of a person he was – and I could already see he was not the most imaginative of people – it might only make things worse.

I told him the truth. I lived in Spain, I was a writer researching the Civil War, I had wanted to see the Legión's old headquarters . . . and so I plodded on, hoping I wasn't digging my own grave.

He held his palms together in front of him as though in prayer while I spoke. Anxious as I was, I forced myself to speak as slowly and clearly as possible, not wanting to make the slightest mistake that might give him the excuse he wanted to jump down my throat. But I was well aware of the danger of incriminating myself through zeal of innocence.

'You're lying!' he shouted, interrupting me mid-flow. Something in me jumped, my heart freezing, then pounding violently in my chest. But as fear cast a net over my mind, I sensed his move was forced. It seemed mad, helpless as I was, but I couldn't help feeling that his outburst had been planned from the beginning, as though it was some primitive interrogation technique he'd been taught on a course.

'Who are you?' he demanded again. I forced down a desire to

be facetious and repeated my name. The man might have been an idiot, but he was an idiot with power, and the soldiers outside were carrying rifles. My only concern was to get out of there.

'Where are you staying?' Ceuta, I said.

'Where are you heading next?' This was a new one. 'Tetuan,' I answered. The old capital of the Spanish Protectorate was only a few miles further south. The first of the wedding guests would be arriving by now, I thought. God, did I wish I was with them. A quick trip back to Ceuta to pick up my things and I could be there in a couple of hours.

At this point the officer stood up, picked up the chair and walked out, carrying my passport with him. He muttered something to the soldiers on the door, one of them staying put while the other accompanied him back up the stairs. That's it, I thought. I should have insisted I was only staying in Ceuta, not planning on travelling down to Tetuan as well. As a tourist staying in Spain on a day trip I might have had some more protection. Now that I had admitted I was going to be travelling inside Morocco as well, they could do with me what they liked.

The interrogation had made me light-headed, my nerves and the effort of answering the officer's questions leaving my mouth clammy and dry. What was he doing? Perhaps he needed to get clearance to have me locked up for the night? Or taken to another army base? I tried to keep a check on my thoughts, with only partial success. I would find out in good time. Meanwhile, I could do nothing.

The officer returned sooner than I'd expected.

'Where are you going in Tetuan?' he asked directly. I had nothing to lose so I mentioned Daniel and his wedding to Muna.

'Muna Bouaiss?' he asked. I had no idea of Muna's surname, but decided to take a punt on it. The expression of surprise on his face when I'd mentioned her seemed promising.

'Yes, that's her,' I said, not sure if I was digging an even deeper hole for myself.

In a flash he was gone again, this time running up the stairs. The other two soldiers remained behind, peering in through the open door and smiling. Why hadn't they shut me in this time? I wondered. What did those sudden grins mean? I smiled back, confused.

When my interrogator returned, he walked in, passed round the table to approach me and with his hands outstretched patted me on the shoulders in a kind of half-embrace. His face was all light and joy.

'Please pardon our mistake,' he said. 'We did not know you were a friend of the colonel's.'

'Ah, of course.' I was desperately trying to think on my feet. The colonel? 'That's quite all right,' I said with a laugh. 'How were you to know?' I had no idea who this mysterious benefactor was, but I was quickly becoming very fond of him.

'We have all heard of his niece's wedding to the Englishman,' the officer explained. He led me out of the door and up the stairs again. My knees were still shaking, my heart slowly trying to recover its poise. I wasn't sure what was going on, but from the rapid change in manner and tone it looked as though I was being released. Was Muna's uncle in the military, then? (Later I would find out that indeed he was.) I quickly looked back: the soldiers were smiling and laughing sheepishly behind us. Suddenly they were the ones to be frightened.

'The colonel, as you know, used to be the military governor of this region,' my former interrogator told me. 'Until only four months ago, in fact. We have to be careful. This is army property. It is our duty to stop people.'

'Yes, that's fine,' I said. As quickly as I'd been arrested, I was now a free man.

'Would you like some tea?'

*

Twenty minutes later I was driving back up the coast to the border with Ceuta in a pale-blue taxi hailed down on the road for me by one of the soldiers who had originally taken me in. The churning waters of the Mediterranean lapped at the oily beaches beneath us, while boys with skinny brown legs cycled barefoot in and out of the traffic. The sweet peppermint tea had helped quench my burning thirst somewhat and calmed me a little, but my head still reeled from what had happened, and how close I'd felt to disappearing into the Moroccan jail system altogether. Daniel and Muna would doubtless laugh when I told them the story, and I longed to meet the mysterious colonel whose name alone had secured my release, but at that moment I wanted nothing more than to get back to the relative safety of Ceuta and Spain.

At the border there was the same chaos I'd witnessed when I'd crossed into Morocco earlier in the day. Bread-sellers huddled around the makeshift taxi rank perched on a dusty outcrop overlooking the sea, while spherical women from the Riff mountains in bright-red and white shawls and straw hats with dark-blue bobbles struggled with canvas bags full of goods to sell. No one here, at least, wanted Ceuta handed over to Moroccan control, as the politicians in Rabat were demanding. There was too much money to be made from the situation as it stood.

Hustlers selling exit documents jigged energetically among the heaving cars lined up trying to get into Spain. The Ceutans had expensive new vehicles, with the usual bumps and scratches you expected from Spanish driving; the Moroccans' cars were ancient and dusty, the majority apparently held together with bits of string. Choking on the exhaust fumes, I handed my passport to the Moroccan authorities for the superfluous stamping procedure, adrenaline pumping nervously through my veins.

But after a haughty delay it was handed back to me and I was free to cross the border. I wandered down long wire tunnels to where the Spanish police were waiting, keen to get back to the European side and the safety of my adopted country for a while before heading back into Morocco for the wedding.

A typical member of the Civil Guard was on duty, all lime-green uniform and paunch. This paramilitary police force had originally been set up in the nineteenth century to combat bandits in rural areas. Franco had later used it as one of the pillars of his regime, and its members had developed a reputation as authoritarian thugs. But now in democratic Spain they were milder – polite, bored-looking, but usually all right. A couple of Muslim girls dressed in Moroccan-style clothes were ahead of me. The guard scanned their Spanish passports, flicking through the pages as though trying to see if they were forged. Not finding anything amiss, he handed them back with a grunt.

'We're Spanish, you know,' one of the girls said. 'Just like you.' And they walked on. I had the impression they had to face this kind of thing every day.

'Spanish,' the guard said as I approached, with a tone of disbelief and resigned despair. 'What do they mean, Spanish?'

As a rule I tried never to speak to customs people or policemen at borders. They were a mild annoyance – obstacles to get past as quickly as possible, without drawing their attention to you. But after my recent experience at the Moroccan barracks, I felt the urge to talk to this surly Spaniard and found myself blurting out my story in a desperate bid for sympathy.

'Can you believe it? I've just been arrested,' I said. 'Over there in Dar Riffien.' As I indicated behind me with my thumb I could barely hear the voice of warning screaming at the back of my head, *What are you doing? You don't tell border guards you've just been arrested!*

The policeman had been about to hand me my passport, but

pulled it back and started checking again. Meanwhile my voice had a life of its own and was continuing with the story.

'At the old barracks of the Legión,' I said. Somehow I thought the man would applaud me for trying to visit such a site. And as a Spaniard he would immediately give me the sympathy I craved for having been so mistreated by those nasty *Moros* on the other side of the border.

'Where are you staying?' he snapped. I told him the name of my hotel.

'How long are you going to be in Ceuta? What's your business here?'

Still holding my passport, he had stood up from his stool and was towering over me from inside his control booth. I drew a deep breath, realization of what I'd done seeping slowly into my brain.

'Why were you arrested?'

It seemed I was back with the Moroccans. Having blundered into being arrested that morning, I was on the brink of repeating the same mistake.

I told him what I'd said to the Moroccan officer. But my voice was trembling from the mental kicking I was giving myself for being so stupid. I looked beyond the checkpoint towards the city in the distance. There was a row of taxis waiting only a few steps away, ready to take me into town. I imagined sitting in one, being whisked away from all this, back into the warm, welcoming safety of Spain.

The guard looked at me with an expression of disgust.

'I can't stop you crossing this border,' he said. 'But would to God I could. We get enough arseholes like you coming here.'

I stared at him in disbelief. Although officious, Spanish policemen in my experience always had good manners. I had never been spoken to like this before, as he dropped the respectful *usted* form for the familiar – and in this case rude – *tú*.

'I don't want to see you here again.'

He handed me back my passport. It took me a second to react and take it out of his hand before he could drop it on the floor.

'Now fuck off!'

I walked over the border and into Spain in shock, the noise of the waves beating at the crumbling coastline crying in my ears.

6

Mountain Tears

*T*he last days in the life of Federico García Lorca read like a chronicle of a death foretold. The story grips you powerfully as you find yourself praying till the final page that the hero might somehow be saved. At every turn you beg him to change his mind or take some decision that will steer him away from his inevitable fate. But he never does; the conclusion is always the same: his body lifeless on a Granada hillside, his killers laughing their way to victory. Hundreds of thousands were murdered behind the lines under Franco's terror regime. Lorca was merely one of many, but he was one of the most famous, and his murder has become a lasting symbol of the horror of Spain's Civil War.

On 14 July 1936, the day that Lieutenant José Castillo and José Calvo Sotelo were being buried in the Eastern Cemetery in Madrid, Federico García Lorca was having lunch with a friend on the outskirts of the capital. He was at the peak of his career – celebrated nationally and internationally as an important Spanish poet and playwright, he had recently finished writing one of his great works, *The House of Bernarda Alba*, and was planning a trip to Mexico, where he would present the play to his favourite actress, Margarita Xirgu. He had already bought his ticket for the journey and had been on the point of leaving Madrid during the tense days in the capital before the outbreak of the war. But the events around him were causing him deep distress and he was unclear about what to do: stay where he was, leave the country, or head down to the family home in Granada where he usually spent the summer. The eighteenth of July was his saint's day and family tradition was to celebrate it with his father – also called Federico. As the violence increased, friends became worried for Lorca's safety. Although not a member of any political party, he was alive to the injustices that marked Spain at that time and advocated social reform. 'I shall always support those who have nothing and who are even denied the tranquillity of nothing,' he once said. This sympathy for the rural poor had been the impetus behind his Barraca theatre project, which had put on plays and brought literature to the feudal backwaters of the Spanish countryside during the early years of the Republic. As an artist, an intellectual and a rumoured homosexual, for the reactionary Nationalist rebels he belonged – despite numbering several Falangists among his friends – to the 'other Spain', the one they planned to annihilate.

Lorca himself was aware he might become a target. But the moments before the outbreak of a war can be confusing, optimistic doubts struggling with premonitions of disaster: will it be a quick bloodless power struggle or a drawn-out bloody conflict? The poet in him, with half an eye to the future, seemed to know what was coming. 'Rafael,' he told his friend at that last lunch in the countryside outside Madrid, 'these fields are going to be filled with the dead.' In that he was right. But regarding his own fate and what he should do, he was less prescient. On several occasions in his work he seemed to have predicted his own death. But now, fearful, and perhaps in several minds as to the right course of action, he opted for the safety of his family home in Granada. It was his first mistake.

It is possible that on the very train that carried Lorca to Granada in those last days before the war there sat the man who would bring about his downfall: Ramón Ruiz Alonso was also leaving the capital for his home town at about that time. It was midsummer and many people across the country were heading out from the major cities for the coast or the countryside. But Ruiz Alonso was not going on holiday. A member of the far-right Catholic CEDA party, he had lost his seat in parliament to the Popular Front in February that year and had become involved in the plot to stage a military coup. The murder of Calvo Sotelo had galvanized the conspirators into naming a date for the uprising and now at last General Franco had thrown in his lot with the rebels. All was set – timetables, targets, lists of people destined for the firing squads.

'It is necessary to create an atmosphere of terror,' General Mola, the organizer of the coup, had made clear to his followers in the run-up to the uprising. 'We have to create the impression of mastery. Anyone who is overtly or secretly a supporter of the Popular Front must be shot.'[5]

In the weeks to come, Ruiz Alonso would make sure he followed Mola's instructions to the letter.

Lorca's arrival in Granada did not go unnoticed. The local papers carried the news, *El Defensor* even placing the story at the centre of its front page. And during the few remaining days of peace the poet was often seen out and about, ever garrulous and sociable. Granada was a town he loved, yet which exasperated him. Granadan society was dominated by a largely conservative, frowning Catholic elite that seemed at odds with the essential magic of the place: the last stronghold of the Moors, home to the Alhambra and infused with the romance of

Spain's oriental past. Lorca's family had often felt out of step with Granadan society, being well-read and musical – they were well-to-do country folk more suited to a spontaneity and creativity which was lacking in many of those around them. There were notable exceptions – the composer Manuel de Falla, who lived on the Alhambra hill, was a friend of Lorca – but many had been annoyed at Lorca's attack on Granadan conservatism in a piece in a Madrid newspaper only a few months before. As far as the poet was concerned, Ferdinand and Isabella's conquest of Granada in 1492 and the end of the Moorish kingdom there had been the greatest disaster to befall the city, a place he now saw as being in the hands of the 'worst bourgeoisie in Spain'. This kind of thing didn't go down well among the Granadan grandees.

There was a party at the Lorca family's house as usual on St Frederick's Day, 18 July, Federico and his father celebrating their saint's day together, but the mood was changed from other years. News had just come in of a military uprising in Spanish Morocco; there were rumours that Seville had fallen too and that General Franco was on the side of the rebels. The situation was unclear and panic set in, despite claims from the city authorities that matters were under control. No one imagined how bad things would get.

On 20 July the plotters in Granada made their move. Conspirators inside the military garrison joined with the Falangists, and within hours of taking to the streets during the heat of the siesta, the city was theirs; the police quickly joined the uprising once they knew what was happening. Only the Albaicín, the old Moorish quarter on the hill opposite the Alhambra and a largely working-class district, put up any resistance. It held out for three days with hardly any weaponry, but was eventually crushed. The city's military and civil governors were both relatively new to their posts and were easily overwhelmed. Granada fell quickly to the rebels. But there was a problem: the city was isolated – the countryside around remained loyal to the government. The conspirators would have to wait for troops from Seville to link the town up with other Nationalist-held territory. In the meantime, the besieged city would have to deal with threats from within.

One of the first to be arrested was Manuel Fernández Montesinos, the socialist mayor and husband of Lorca's sister, Concha. The news caused consternation in the Lorca household, where Manuel and Concha had been living with their three children. Lorca went to visit his brother-in-law in prison, but was so affected by the state in which he found him that he had to take to his bed in shock.[6] The torture suffered at the hands of the Nationalists led many to suicide.

Amid fears for Manuel and a growing sense of helplessness, the Lorca family was becoming increasingly worried that the gunmen would soon come for Federico as well. Falangists had arrived at the house to conduct a 'search', presumably for a secret radio which, according to a rumour running at the time, Lorca was using to contact 'the Russians'; but they had left, unsurprisingly, without finding anything. The message was clear, though – the poet was in their sights. Lorca himself had a nightmare during this fraught time where he dreamed of being threatened with crucifixes by a group of women dressed in black. He told a friend he felt certain it was a bad omen.

On the night of 7 August an architect friend, Alfredo Rodríguez Orgaz, arrived at the house looking for a place to hide. The Falangists were after him and he was trying to escape to Republican territory. As the Lorca house was on the edge of the city, sanctuary was only a couple of miles away down the road. But Lorca refused to go with him, convinced that the coup would soon be crushed. It was his second mistake. Hours later Alfredo would be safe, while his enemies were closing in on Lorca.

A few days later the Falangists returned to the Lorca house, this time to look for the caretaker, Gabriel. His brothers were wanted and the Falangists thought they might find them there. When Gabriel refused to give them any information, they dragged him out into the garden, tied him to a tree and, in front of his mother and the horrified Lorca family, began whipping him. Lorca, never a violent man and greatly fearful of physical pain, stepped in to try to stop them, but the Falangists simply knocked him to the ground and began kicking him instead.

'We know very well who you are, Federico García Lorca,' they said.[7] And before leaving, they informed him that he was now under house arrest.

Lorca was becoming alive to the danger he was in and decided to act. If he stayed where he was he would almost certainly be arrested, perhaps worse. He would have to move, but where? He decided to call a friend of his among the local Falangists – Luis Rosales, a fellow poet – to ask for help. Luis went to the Lorca home and discussed the options with the family. There were three choices: smuggle Lorca over the lines into Republican territory; take him to the house of Manuel de Falla – no one would touch him in the home of such a respected figure; or take him to live at the Rosales household itself. Luis's brothers were also Falangists and powerful in the city now – as Lorca's friends they would be able to protect him. It was decided that he should take the third option. It was his third and final mistake.

The Rosales' home was a large townhouse near the centre of the city. The brothers themselves spent little time there during that period as they were busy at the front, but their mother and sister were at home, along with an aunt who lived in a flat at the top of the building. Lorca was to move in with her.

For eight days he lived at Number One, Angulo Street, never venturing out, reading books from Luis's library and playing a piano that had been brought specially for him. But the violence outside was increasing by the day. The city's new masters had put in place their system of control through fear, and lorry-loads of their enemies were being driven up the Alhambra hill every night, beyond the Moorish castle, to the cemetery. There they were shot outside the walls and later dumped in unmarked pits. So many were being killed that they had to expand the grave-yard, and the grave-digger was rumoured to have gone mad from having to bury so many people. Everyone from left-wing politicians to union leaders was being hauled away to be shot – either at the cemetery, or outside the little village of Víznar near the front lines. For daring to hold out against the Nationalists, the Albaicín quarter suffered heavily: men were dragged from their homes to be shot in retribution. It didn't take long for those wanting to save their own skins to point out who their left-wing neighbours were.

Some of the executions were reported in the newspapers and Lorca sensed what was going on. 'I've never been involved in politics,' he lamented one day at the Rosales' house. 'I'm too afraid for that. To take sides you need a kind of courage I lack.'

The Rosales brothers' positions in the local Falange party might have offered Lorca some protection, but there were other forces at work in Granada at that time. On 15 August, gunmen went to the Lorca family home looking for Federico. In a moment of panic his sister let slip that he was staying with Falangist friends in the centre of town, perhaps mentioning the Rosales by name.

At dawn the next day, Lorca's brother-in-law, the mayor, Manuel Fernández Montesinos, was shot along with a group of other prisoners outside the walls of the city cemetery. By five o'clock that afternoon some forty men had encircled the Rosales' house in a large-scale operation to arrest Lorca. The man at the head of the group, driving a requisitioned Oakland convertible, was the former CEDA parliamentarian Ruiz Alonso, acting on the orders of the new civil governor. It seems that Ruiz Alonso, or someone backing him, had a grudge against the Rosales and wanted to discredit them – perhaps one of the squabbles between the various factions that made up the Nationalist movement now controlling the city. Whatever the details, it would explain at least how the Rosales were able to do so little to help their friend once he was arrested.

None of the brothers was at home when they came for Federico, and at first Señora Rosales stood up to Ruiz Alonso, refusing to let him take her guest away. Finally one of her sons, Miguel, was located and he came to the house immediately. Lorca was officially – if ludicrously – accused of being a Soviet spy. Convinced there was nothing else he could do, Miguel persuaded his mother to let Lorca go, promising to accompany him in order to sort everything out. Lorca came down from his attic flat to be taken away, horrified at what was happening and close to breaking down.

But once they had driven the short distance to the civil government building where Lorca was then imprisoned, Miguel was able to do very little. He tried in vain to contact his brothers, particularly José, who had the most authority in the Falange. Miguel became very concerned – a policeman had beaten Lorca with his rifle butt during the journey and he was worried that one of the sadists then operating in the civil government might subject him to an interrogation session. He did manage, at least, to ensure that Lorca was locked up in an office rather than a cell, and to extract a promise not to do anything to him until the civil governor arrived. Meanwhile, Señora Rosales contacted Lorca's family to tell them what had happened. Already in mourning for his son-in-law, shot earlier that day, his father felt helpless: the authorities had frozen his assets and he was only allowed to withdraw small amounts for living expenses. They sent a housekeeper round to where Lorca was being held, taking him some food and cigarettes. Frightened for their own safety, it was all they could do.

That night, when the Rosales brothers returned to the city from the front, they were outraged to discover what had happened. Gathering some friends, they stormed round to the civil government building and confronted Ruiz Alonso, but were unable to have their friend released. José Rosales even spoke to José Valdés Guzmán, the civil governor, but was stonewalled and warned that if he wasn't careful he would have to watch out for his brother Luis as well, for having taken Lorca in in the first place. Other friends tried to secure his release, including Manuel de Falla, but to no avail. Although no one knew for sure at this point, the order had been given to have him shot; the green light was probably given by the Nationalist general in charge of Seville, Queipo de Llano, with whom Valdés Guzmán was in nightly contact by radio.

Some days later, Lorca was taken from his cell in the middle of the night and handcuffed to a primary-school teacher with a false leg called Dióscoro Galindo, who was accused of being a communist by the Falangists. The two were pushed into a car and then driven out of town towards the village of Víznar. They were taken to a country house on the outskirts of the village that the local authorities were using as a holding centre before prisoners were dragged out to be shot. A group of Freemasons and university professors was forced to act as grave-diggers, many of them later meeting the same fate. Lorca was held there overnight, he and Galindo sharing a cell with two anarchist bull-fighters who had demanded arms for the people during the early days of the uprising. When they were called out in the early hours of the next morning a priest was on hand to give them the last sacrament. At first Lorca, never particularly religious, was reluctant, but he eventually asked to be confessed.

The priest, however, had left by this point, and a young police assistant at hand had to help him through prayers barely remembered from childhood.

The men were taken from the country house further along the road towards the next village of Alfacar, the view stretching out northwards over the sierra where, just a mile or two away in Republican territory, the four of them would have been welcomed as heroes. It was a favourite spot for the Nationalist assassins. The exact date of the execution is still uncertain, but it was about 19 August 1936. Lorca was thirty-eight years old.

Some hours later a young communist was forced to dig a large grave, and the four corpses were thrown in one on top of the other: four among thousands of Granadans whose remains lie to this day on that mournful mountainside.

Despite Spain's official silence over what had happened, the international community continued to call on the Franco government to release Lorca from prison well into the 1940s. Some clung to the legend that grew up which said he had somehow managed to escape the death squads, hitting his head as he ran away and forgetting who he was.

> *Si muero*
> *dejad el balcón abierto.*
>
> *El niño come naranjas.*
> *(Desde mi balcón lo veo.)*
>
> *El segador siega el trigo.*
> *(Desde mi balcón lo siento.)*
>
> *¡Si muero,*
> *dejad el balcón abierto!*

If I die,
Leave the window open.

The child eating oranges.
(From my window I see him.)

The reaper harvesting the wheat.
(From my window I sense him.)

If I die,
leave the window open!

7

Víznar

*T*he taxi-driver mumbled as we stuttered our way through the late-afternoon traffic and out of the city. Everyone in Granada seemed to have got into their cars at that very moment, pressing against one another in their steel boxes in the crushing, choking heat as they struggled in vain to move around the city. Stressed and frustrated, the *taxista* shunted and braked his way through, hurling me from side to side and poisoning me with a venomous cloud of halitosis whenever he opened his mouth to curse the other drivers. '*¡Me cago en tu puta madre!*' In the rear-view mirror I caught his fat-swollen eyes scanning me suspiciously. Beads of sweat were coagulating in the creases in the back of his neck.

'There's a bus out to Víznar, you know. Be easier than going by taxi.'

He might have been right, but I was convinced he was lying, preferring to dump me on the outskirts of town than to take what he assumed to be a *maricón* out to the site of Lorca's murder. I'd be paying him well, but it seemed he wanted the security of a quick batch of fares in town rather than a lengthy ride out into the country. Besides, I'd sensed him bristling when I'd told him I wanted to go to Lorca's gravesite.

'Another fucking queer. They're all obsessed with him.'

I knew it was somewhere between the villages of Víznar and Alfacar, just a few miles northeast of the city. Taking the bus would mean a long ride, with no guarantee of finding the spot when I got there. And at this point in the day there were only a couple of hours of sunlight left. I didn't want to have to wait till tomorrow. A taxi it would have to be, whatever the man's prejudices.

The road out to the site of Lorca's murder was a slow winding trail hugging the contours of the hillside, brushing past pine forests, meadows of dry wild grass and occasional fields cut into the slope – countrymen's allotments yielding tomatoes, courgettes, with some beans and a patch of parsley in the corner. It was a quiet spot, over the valley on the northern side of the Granadan horticultural plain, the *vega*: a place to take a Sunday stroll, perhaps, pick wild flowers, and bring children to play in a safe yet still semi-wild landscape. As we rolled on in silence, the driver sulking in the front, the chattering of birds blew soothingly through my open window, my eyes captured by the view as I stared out towards the horizon.

In the first few months of the Civil War this area had been close to the front line: Víznar and Alfacar, about five miles out from Granada, were among the last villages under Nationalist control before Republican-held territory. Granada had been encircled in those early days, an island of fascism in a sea of red. Every morning fighters from the city – policemen, soldiers, Falangists – would ride out to do battle with the enemy before returning to rest. It was a time for heroism and courage. The coup had not met with the success its leaders had hoped for, being neither crippled nor delivering a knock-out blow against the government in Madrid. A civil war, perhaps a long one, was looking inevitable. And Granada was on its own.

The gentle hills around the villages had become an arena of conflict. In the past, Moorish poets had written eulogies to the beauty of these surroundings, particularly the Ain al-Damar spring close by – a teardrop-shaped well of spring water whose name, an Arabic play on words, translated both as 'spring of tears' and 'eye of tears'. It was an apt name for so melancholy a place. For the Nationalists in Granada were not only concerned with defending their oasis against assaults from the outside; they were also keen to cleanse the area under their control. And they did so with a fervour and energy unusual even in those blood-thirsty days. The Víznar–Alfacar road, peaceful, secluded, ironically undisturbed through its proximity to the front lines, was the ideal spot for the systematic slaughter of the enemy – unionists, workers, left-wingers, even school teachers: anyone deemed 'liberal' and therefore seen to be a threat to the new authoritarian dawn. Hundreds, possibly thousands, met their deaths at the hands of firing squads here, many given a coup de grâce in the back of the head as they lay bleeding on the ground. A beautiful location for a violent end.

I noticed, as the light softened and began to caress the land-scape with shades of orange and gold, that the peace of this verdant corner was even now under attack. Where once the earth had been stained with blood, cement and concrete were now leaving their scars, housing estates and villas springing up like mushrooms in white and brown batches over the rolling hills. Not the violence of the past, perhaps, but with their uni-form balustrade balconies and built-in brick barbeques, it felt like a form of violence nonetheless.

The taxi came to a stop next to a graffiti-daubed wall, slogans condemning the government in scarlet scrawl. I waited for the driver to explain, but he said nothing.

'What's this?' I asked.

'You wanted to see where Lorca was shot, right? This is it.'

I looked up through the open window, breathing in the pure air. Weeds were growing out of a shabby flight of brick steps, with bits of litter caught on the brambles invading from either side. At the top, a memorial plaque in dark lettering declared the site to be 'The Federico García Lorca Memorial Park'.

I opened the door gingerly.

'Hey! You've got to pay,' the driver said.

'I want you to wait for me here,' I said. 'To take me back into town.'

'You pay for this trip first. You might just run off.'

I looked around: there was nothing but a few houses, forests and fields. Where was I supposed to run off to, exactly? I handed him the money.

'Wait for me, though.'

He grunted and I took it as a yes.

I climbed the steps and passed through the gate into an open empty space. On the far side, plaques had been placed on a wall quoting extracts from Lorca's writing, while the floor had been laid with stone and more brick to form an ugly design. I tripped over the awkwardly laid pieces in the failing light, twisting my ankle.

Cursing, I limped on. The place felt abandoned and unloved. The hillside rose above me with a thin covering of grass, mere twigs of occasional trees breaking through the soulless earth on this strangely bare and barren patch of land. It reminded me of the attempts developers made to lay out 'gardens' or 'land-scapes' when they finished constructing a new town, with thin artificial-looking grass. There was a feeling of desolation in the park, perhaps not entirely due to the barbarous acts that had once been carried out on the same spot. It was a sorry, pathetic memorial, unworthy of either Lorca or the people who had died here with him.

Pushing on and trying to ignore the pain now gripping my lower leg, I scampered down a path towards some trees. There, by a gate leading on to the road, was an olive tree. It was taller than most olive trees in Spain, which were zealously pruned to produce the best fruit. This one had been left to grow. It was, I recognized immediately from Miguel's description, the marker for one of the possible sites where Lorca's remains lay.

I had met Miguel Botella, professor of physical anthropology at Granada University, earlier that morning to talk about the mysteries surrounding Lorca's death and the moves being made finally to uncover his remains. The poet's body, dumped with three others in a ditch on this hillside, was, according to the papers, soon to be dug up, formally identified and given a 'proper burial'. Miguel, a forensic scientist, was the man charged with identifying his remains when they were found. It was often difficult to get to talk to people in positions of authority in Spain, a country where it was usually necessary to have a personal contact – a friend, or preferably a relative – to break down the barriers of suspicion between officials and ordinary members of the public, but Miguel was an exception, and had very kindly agreed to give me some of his time.

His offices were in the basement of the Faculty of Medicine, down narrow institutional steps in what felt like a forgotten corner of a labyrinth, tucked away among pale smooth walls and low ceilings. I had the sense of entering a secret bunker, a place where you might disappear and never be found again. In the hallway leading to his rooms, glass cabinets displayed an ossuaric chamber of horrors – skulls barely recognizable after years of deformation through leprosy and syphilis, joints fused together from arthritis, trepannings that had gone terribly wrong. I began to feel uneasy about meeting a man who collected such things, who spent his working life surrounded by death.

Miguel was a small elderly man with a long grey-white beard and an air of industriousness. As soon as I entered, his mouth opened into a wide embracing smile and he gave me a pale delicate hand to shake. We sat down amid piles of papers, assistants bustling in and out holding forms and mobile phones. On the walls were gruesome diagrams of partially dismembered bodies. I was slightly wary at first – the man appeared joyful and friendly, yet all around I could see signs of pain and mortality. Cautiously, I began to ask about the Lorca case. How soon was the body going to be dug up? I asked.

He paused before answering, and as he did so I shuddered slightly. His expression, or perhaps just his air – the smile remained genuine and warm – made me feel there was something morbid about the question. Lorca had been written about so much, had become such a symbol, almost like a character in one of his own plays, that it was easy to lose sight of the fact that he had also been a human being.

Miguel's reply, when it came, was measured and detailed. In his calm, steady voice he told me dispassionately how the families of two of the men buried with Lorca had agreed that their relatives' bodies should finally be exhumed.

'This, you understand, will entail the exhumation of all four bodies in the same grave, one of which will be Lorca's.' From within the depths of his beard, his mouth opened and closed like a blinking eye while he spoke.

It was this that had brought everything to a head. Descendants of the one-legged school teacher Dióscoro Galindo, and the plumber and part-time bullfighter Francisco Baladí, both of whom had been shot and buried with the poet, had now asked for the exhumation process to begin. It seemed that almost seventy years after their relatives had been shot in cold blood, the sons and grandsons of Republican victims of Nationalist terror were finally intending to recover their remains and give them a proper burial. Under Franco, Miguel explained, this had been impossible. Then, after his death in 1975 and the subsequent transition to democracy, the watchword had been 'forgetting': the success of elected governments depended on memories of the recent past being blacked out, hence the *pacto del olvido* or 'pact of forgetting'. Now, though, this was changing, and groups were springing up who were determined that the suffering endured during the war and under Franco should not be forgotten.

I thought for a moment about the graves I'd seen near our farm. Perhaps this was why Begoña had shown them to me. Perhaps even up there in the mountains she had been touched by this growing collective sentiment.

'The problem,' Miguel continued, his hands resting on the desk in front of him, fingers touching at the tips, 'is that Lorca's family is not really interested in exhuming his body. They feel it would only open up old wounds and problems, and want him to remain where he is.'

The day before, Pepa, a young curator at the museum that now occupied the Lorca summer house, had told me that the family wanted the grave to remain untouched because the local council were trying to develop the hillside where he lay and build more villas and estates on it. As things stood they could only do so much. The best way to remember Lorca was for him to remain where he was. That was, after all, where he had been shot.

'This has created a division among the lawyers,' Miguel said. There were those who argued that if only one person was against the exhumation then their wishes had to be respected. Others said those who did want their relatives' remains to be dug up had rights too.

'We would have to exhume and identify all the bodies, as they are almost certainly lying one on top of the other, so to exhume some and not others would be impossible,' he said with a shrug. 'So now the case is before the regional Andalusian government to decide.'

'It's not imminent, then?' I said. From the newspapers I'd understood it might take place any day.

'We are expecting a decision within the next few weeks, but sometimes these things can take time.'

I knew from experience that anything that reached the hands of bureaucrats in Spain could take a *very* long time. It might be years before a decision was made.

'We want to maintain the dignity of these people, not bring about a rise in viewing figures or circulation for the media,' Miguel said, after pausing to sign some more papers an assistant had brought in. 'Several channels have already asked to be there to film everything, but we're not going to let any cameras in. We'll have to put up some sort of tent to ensure privacy. The work must be calm, discreet and rigorous.'

He got up and closed the door to the office to make sure we weren't interrupted again, and began telling me about the techniques he would use if and when they got the go-ahead for the dig.

'It will be easy to identify Lorca,' he said, looking me in the face. 'Of the others, one had a wooden leg and the other two were young men. It will be just a matter of identifying the pieces.'

I asked if they would be using DNA testing.

'That's another department. They will do it, but only for final proof. The identity will be clear once we get him inside this laboratory.' I had no doubts. He spoke with such assurance: surely such a respected and authoritative figure couldn't be wrong.

'But there are people who want to know exactly how he died,' I said. 'Did he, for example, receive a coup de grâce to the head?'

'Yes, I know.' His expression, though steady, betrayed a

certain distaste. 'Some people, you know, they seem just a little obsessed by the whole thing. I had one in here the other day and the only thing he wants to know is if Lorca got shot in the backside for being homosexual, as somebody once claimed.' He paused. 'All this will come out. It is inevitable, but . . .'

I asked if he thought that too much attention focusing on just one man was a bad thing. Might people forget the thousands of others who had also been killed?

'Lorca's death helps people to remember, but it also, as you suggest, takes people's minds away from the other victims,' he said. 'This goes very deep. There was a great injustice carried out here in Granada during the war. Per capita it was one of the worst affected cities in the whole of Spain.'

I told him how on the previous day I had walked up to the town cemetery, beyond the tourist buses above the Alhambra hill. This, along with Víznar, had been one of the main execution sites during the early months of the war. Truck-loads of people were driven up during the night and then shot against the walls. The pock-marks were still there in the late 1940s, when Gerald Brenan had returned looking for clues to his friend Lorca's death. But now, when I'd asked a guard to show me where the graves of these victims were, she had pointed me to a corner of the cemetery where soldiers from Franco's forces were buried. 'No,' I said when I went back to find her. 'I want to see the graves of the Republicans shot here during the war.' The young woman looked confused; she didn't know what I was talking about. Seventy years on and the victims were on the verge of disappearing from collective memory altogether.

'The things that happened here should never happen again,' Miguel said. 'If I can help that in some way, that's all I can ask.'

The scale of the repression, he said, was staggering, all over Spain. And the problem was that it was still unclear quite how many had died under Franco's regime. This was one of the reasons why it was so little known about around the world.

'How many people do you think died in Pinochet's coup in Chile?' he asked me.

'Three, perhaps four thousand?' I said.

'One thousand, four hundred and eighty-nine,' he said. 'I worked on the investigating forensics team. The dead were all communists, their names written on lists and then tracked down and killed. We know exactly who and how many died.'

I was surprised. Not so much at the figure being lower than I'd thought, but at how precise knowledge of the repression was, and yet how seldom you heard this mentioned. It was so much easier and more emotive to talk in large round figures.

'Yet here in Spain it was chaos,' Miguel continued. 'People were shot just for being in the wrong place at the wrong time. In many cases old scores were being settled. It wasn't organized. Directed, yes – the orders came from the top for terror to be used to control the people and frighten the enemy, but there wasn't the organization you had in Chile in '73. We're talking about tens, possibly hundreds of thousands. But the exact figure will almost certainly never be known.'

I could understand why this work was so fulfilling for him: a compassionate, inquisitive man like himself could not fail to be drawn to trying to solve some of the mysteries of the Civil War.

He asked me why I was interested in all this.

'Things are finally beginning to change, slowly,' he said when I explained to him about the graves, about Begoña and my great-grandfather. 'Perhaps you should go to Extremadura. There's much to be found there relating to all this. The region suffered terribly under Franco, as they're just discovering.'

Extremadura had been one of the main battle grounds during the early weeks and months of the war in the summer of 1936, as Franco's troops crossed over the Strait from Morocco and then marched up the west of Spain to link up with General

Mola's army and launch an attack on Madrid. Some of the worst atrocities in the conflict had taken place in this poor, under-developed and arid region.

He scribbled down the names of some people to contact and places worth visiting.

As I left, news came in of an autopsy just starting on a woman who'd been run over by her husband. Miguel shook my hand again as he led me to the door.

'As you can see, I'm busy,' he said with a smile. Death seemed to surround him.

I stood by the olive tree in the Lorca park, remembering our conversation. There were three or four possible sites for Lorca's body, and this was one. Next to the tree, a body-sized rut in the ground seemed to show that someone at least had been buried here. But as I looked across at the new villas nearby, this whole area seemed little more than an impromptu graveyard. You could barely stick a shovel into the ground, someone had said, without coming across a pile of bones. Who in their right mind would want to build a house out here? Yes, the views were nice, but it was a tragic, haunted place. I sympathized with Lorca's family. Ugly though this memorial park was, at least it marked in some way what had happened to the man. Better than a conscience-easing plaque and marble tomb lying next to his killers in Granada city cemetery.

The sound of a car in the direction from which I'd come jerked me from my thoughts: the engine revved and then gradually died away as the vehicle disappeared round a corner. My heart sank: I knew instinctively what had happened, but needed to see it before I could actually believe it. Limping back up the path and down to the gate, I confirmed that the taxi had gone. The more generous side of me wondered whether he had gone to find a more convenient place to park. But when I caught sight of his gleaming white car hurrying away on the far side of the valley, I knew the bastard had abandoned me.

To the west the sun was already touching the jagged lines of the horizon, the light fading quickly. A few street-lamps were flickering into life down in Alfacar. If there were any buses out to these villages they would probably have packed up for the day by now. The only thing to do was retrace the way I'd come in the taxi and see how far I got. Somewhere further along, perhaps, I might get a lift.

Sparrows were flittering from branch to branch in the dusk air, while the heat of the day seemed to rise from the ground, allowing cooler breezes to blow in from the hillsides. The hairs on my body lifted slightly in expectation of the cold. My limbs heavy with anger, I pushed off along the road, grabbing a stick lying by the side to take some of the weight off my ankle. It would be a long walk. I had no choice but to continue in the dark.

8

Propaganda

'*Y*ou already know my system: for every supporter of order who dies, I will kill ten extremists at least. And let not those who run away think that by escaping they will be free. I will dig them up from the earth if necessary, and if they are already dead I will kill them again!'[8]

At ten o'clock every night during the first year and a half of the Civil War, Spaniards would turn on their radios to listen to the ranting from Seville of the Nationalist General Gonzalo Queipo de Llano, ruling his territories in the south like a wicked medieval warlord. Shouting, whispering and even singing his way through his dinner-time broadcasts, he became, in a pre-television age, a symbol for many around the country of the military uprising, of its cruelty, bravado, self-belief and contra-dictions. Every radio station in the Nationalist zone would connect with Radio Seville in order to hear the general's words; restaurants and bars would fall silent as the people listened in, while in the morning papers the following day his talks, *charlas*, would be reprinted word for word. Simultaneously rousing his supporters and placing fear in the hearts of his enemies, this bombastic character with his coarse manner, simple macho language and repetition of key phrases was one of the first broadcasters to make radio a key factor in a modern coup.

'The Marxists are ferocious beasts, but we are gentlemen . . . Señor Companys [the president of Catalonia] deserves to have his throat slit like a pig.'

Queipo was an unlikely hero for the rebellion. A tall, striking man with a neatly clipped handlebar moustache, he was a known supporter of the Republic, having been Master of the Military Household to its first president, Niceto Alcalá Zamora, who was also a relative by marriage. He had been a sworn enemy of the dictator Primo de Rivera in the 1920s, had plotted against the monarchy and was a Freemason – a group particularly hated by Franco for their associations with republicanism. None of this made him likely to join the military coup, but Queipo was a vain man, bent on self-promotion, obsessed with medals, and always with an eye for a chance. Alcalá Zamora, an intriguer disliked by both sides of the political divide for his handling of the various political crises since the birth of the Republic, was ousted by the Left as president just before the uprising and replaced by Prime Minister Manuel Azaña, a move Queipo took as a personal slight as well as a major setback to his career prospects. Although no one in the government suspected him, joining the rebellion now became a natural step for one so ambitious.

Few among the conspirators either admired or trusted him, however. As the plans for the coup were being drawn up, General Mola assigned him the city of Seville, thinking it a relatively unimportant place to secure in the expectation of a swift victory in Barcelona and elsewhere in the country. As things turned out, though, not only did Queipo take Seville for the uprising in a spectacular fashion, he also secured the only safe foothold in the south, which would enable Franco to transport his vitally important Army of Africa to the mainland. Without Queipo, the Nationalists might never have won the war.

The story of how he single-handedly captured Seville, the capital of Andalusia and, with a large working-class population, home to many natural supporters of the Popular Front government, has become legend and has no doubt been subject to Queipo's self-mythologizing.

Queipo arrived in Seville as the uprising was starting in Morocco, driving into the city in his plush Hispano-Suiza car, claiming he was there to inspect customs posts. He went to military headquarters accompanied by three other officers and his aide-de-camp. There they set themselves up in an office which had been abandoned owing to the summer heat. At around lunchtime he walked down the corridor and entered the office of General Villa-Abrille, the military commander, and offered him a choice: either the general joined him in the rebellion or Queipo would have to remove him.

'Listen,' he told Villa-Abrille when he received a negative response, 'I've got an order from the military council to blow the top of your head off. But don't be frightened. As a good friend I'm not going to resort to violence. I'm still confident you'll repent of your ways.'

'I can assure you,' the general replied, 'your jokes do not scare me. I am and will always be with the government. It is my duty.'

Queipo took a step backwards, looked around at his colleagues behind him, then turned back to Villa-Abrille.

'I'm sorry for you,' he said. 'I can do one of only two things: kill you or imprison you.' He paused for a moment. 'I'll imprison you.'[9]

Queipo ordered Villa-Abrille and his staff into the next room, but there was no key to lock the door, so he placed a corporal outside and ordered him to shoot anyone who tried to get out.

He then went down to the infantry barracks with his aide-de-camp, where he found the men already on parade and armed. Without batting an eyelid he went up to the colonel in charge and congratulated him for joining the rebellion. 'I am with the government,' the colonel answered. Queipo gave a look of surprise and then suggested the two of them discuss the matter in private. Once inside, he arrested the colonel as well. No other officer would replace him, however, as they were all worried about the consequences should the rebellion fail. Finally Queipo found a captain to take charge of the men. All the other officers were imprisoned. At this point a handful of Falangists showed up, but with only 130 soldiers and now fifteen volunteers, it was going to take a lot to overcome a city of some quarter of a million people.

As luck would have it, at this point the artillery barracks agreed to join the rebellion. The civil government building, full of Assault Guards loyal to the government, was quickly surrounded and the governor handed himself in. Queipo promised the Assault Guards their lives would be saved if they surrendered, then had them shot once they gave themselves up. The Civil Guards now threw in their lot with the rebels and by that night the airport was in their hands. All that remained was to take control of the working-class districts, an operation which was carried out with bloodthirsty ruthlessness over the following weeks. The city was under Nationalist control.

As Queipo himself would later describe: 'At quarter to two on the afternoon of that day frankly there was no one involved in the uprising except Major Cuesta, my ADC and myself . . . and one or two other officers. By two o'clock, two generals, two colonels, a lieutenant colonel and two majors were our prisoners. At half past two a state of war was declared. By three many government agents with their combat elements were in our hands. At five the artillery started firing. By six all the central government offices were under my command . . . At midnight Tablada aerodrome surrendered without a shot being fired. Seville woke up on the morning of the nineteenth completely Spanish and authentically Nationalist.'

Queipo's account makes for a great story, but the fact remains that he was aided in his capture of the city by the weakness of his opponents, feuding between anarchists and other left-wingers, and the indecisiveness of the officers he arrested at the city barracks. The unions had few weapons with which to fight him, and once Radio Seville was in his hands he was able to control the information reaching the public about the outcome of the coup, denying claims from Madrid that the rebels had been easily crushed.

Queipo went on to rule his southern territories through a system of fear, terrorizing the people into a state of submission through violence. Mass executions and torture were the norm, soldiers often dragging men out of their homes and shooting them in the street or bayoneting them to death. At night the sound of gunfire ricocheted around Seville as small groups of union leaders, left-wingers or people caught in the wrong place at the wrong time were taken to the outskirts of the city to be shot. Simply having a callus on your hand or a sunburnt face (which suggested you were a manual labourer or a farm worker), or had a tattoo or your shirt undone were reasons enough to be imprisoned. Even by the standards of the war, where the killing of opponents behind the lines was widespread on both sides, the bloodshed was rife.

With Seville captured for the rebellion, what kept Queipo in the public imagination was his nightly radio broadcast, a weapon as effective as any gun or artillery battery on the battlefield during the confused early months of the conflict, when people were desperate for information. Through a nightly barrage of rambling insults and threats delivered in his 'clear, flexible, rugged voice', as one listener described it,[10] he went a long way towards demoralizing the enemy, a group he invariably referred to as *canalla*, 'the rabble'. So famous did the phrase eventually become that Republicans were sometimes heard referring to one another jokingly as *canalla marxista* in imitation of the 'radio general'.

'Good evening, gentlemen,' he would begin, before launching into the topics of the day, which might be anything from rebutting Republican claims about the course of the war, to urging the rich to return their savings to the banks to ease the money flow, to calling on men to help fill the ranks of the Legión, or simply trying to scare people out of their wits. Always delivered in his macho street-talk style.

'I hereby order that if you find any Nancy-boy or poof spreading alarmist lies or false rumours about our glorious Nationalist movement you must kill him like a dog.'

Or on another occasion: 'Our brave legionaries and Regulares have shown the Reds what it means to be a man. And in passing, they've shown the wives of the Reds as well, who at last have known real men, not just castrated militiamen. Kicking and screaming will not save these women.'

As the Nationalist troops moved closer to Madrid, Queipo promised the women of Madrid to the Moroccan soldiers of the Regulares. These men, who would often gang rape women before killing them, were later to be made into 'honorary Christians' for their part in Franco's 'crusade'.

Sometimes the threats or references to the violence of his troops came in almost throw-away lines: 'Eighty per cent of families in [the Seville district of] Santa Lucía are already in mourning. We will not hesitate to take even more rigorous measures to assure our victory.'

This was at a time, during the early months of the war, when victims of Nationalist repression were often left dead by the side of the road to rot, and mourning for the victims was officially banned. Wives of militiamen often had their breasts cut off after they'd been raped.

Sometimes the threats were personal, for example against the Republican governor of Huelva: 'Oh, Cordero Bell, I'm going to flay you and use your skin to make something!'

At other times Queipo's discourses concentrated on demonstrating the fearlessness and ruthlessness on the Nationalist side: 'They don't know that when we win, I have plans that for certain crimes the words "pity" and "amnesty" will be removed from the dictionary. After what has already happened in Seville, I have agreed to suppress in my own personal dictionary the word "surrender".'

Often he made fun of the enemy and threats coming from Republican radio stations: 'Oh Sevillanos, be afraid! Prepare to die of fear! They're saying a powerful military column is moving towards Seville and that soon it will capture the city . . . We haven't seen any military movements at all and today it has been relatively quiet in that area – not even any planes coming over to bomb the people . . . This column marching to Seville – which will reach us very quickly if we take into account its progress from Andújar where it's been entrenched for the past two days without taking a single step forward – I calculate it will reach Seville in about forty or fifty years. So as I say: Sevillanos, be afraid!'

Queipo was fond of a drink and chasing women, much in line with the corrupt vice-regal style of his rule. Republican Radio Barcelona used to accuse him of being a drunk, but one evening he replied to their taunts with typical defiance: 'Well, why not?' he bawled into the microphone. 'The whole world acknowledges the superb quality of the wine and women of Seville. Why shouldn't a real man enjoy them?'

Some of his subordinates were known to take a similar

attitude. One official, Manuel Díaz, used to arrive at his office the worse for wear at six in the evening, where over the course of an hour and a half he would sign death sentences – about sixty a day – without bothering to take statements from or even hear out the defendants. 'It doesn't matter if I sign one hundred or three hundred: the important thing is to clean Spain of Marxists,' he used to say. Almost constantly drunk, he was surrounded by a group of lackeys, hanging out all night with flamenco dancers and singers. The only people allowed into his office were young women pleading on behalf of their loved ones. It wasn't unknown for him to give in to their appeals in exchange for sex.[11]

It was all part of a culture of machismo within Nationalist-controlled Spain, where any man who wasn't in uniform was taunted that he should wear a skirt. 'Young men of Spain,' went one of the phrases, '*o castrenses o castrados* – either you're a soldier or you've got no balls.' This was accompanied by faux-gentlemanly behaviour towards women, which led Queipo one night to surprise his audience by saying that from the following evening he would be starting his broadcasts half an hour later, because a group of pretty Seville girls had complained to him that they didn't have enough time with their suitors in the evenings before everyone had to go and listen to him speak. This was at a time in Andalusia when girls typically sat at the balcony of a low first-floor barred window of their homes in the evenings while young men walking the streets would court them. Queipo couldn't resist their request, and so the hour of his talks was changed. It only lasted a couple of nights, however: all the other radio stations in the Nationalist territories had to end their broadcasts and hook up with Radio Seville at ten to listen to the general, and his impromptu rescheduling was causing havoc among the networks.

His threats to the enemy continued. He warned the crews of

the Republican navy, which sometimes shelled Nationalist-held towns from the sea: 'Tired of asking them in vain not to carry out such attacks, I have ordered – despite it going against my instincts – the detention, in Huelva, San Fernando and the ports, of the families of these piratical sailors. For every victim that an attack of that kind produces, five of them will die. Perhaps this is what they want. In Badajoz a loathsome communist boss went to embrace his wife and stuck a knife in her heart. They say that because their wives smell so bad they want to be with younger girls . . . I repeat, the words "pardon" and "amnesty" will be wiped from the dictionary. I will pursue them like beasts until they all disappear.'

Meanwhile, leading figures on the Republican side – many of whom had been friends and colleagues of his, campaigning and plotting against the monarchy during the 1920s – came in for more personal attacks. President Manuel Azaña was always referred to as 'Little Miss Manolita', Queipo affecting a high girly voice whenever he mentioned his name in reference to Azaña's rumoured homosexuality. Indalecio Prieto, the socialist leader, was ridiculed for being fat: 'I already told you, Indalecio – leave now. We're going to get you and the price of lard is going to tumble!' General Miaja got the same treatment: 'No matter where he hides we'll pull him out like an insect, because if we squash him Spain will be awash with grease.' The French prime minister Léon Blum was dismissed as 'the Jew Blum', while the British journalist Noel Monks was accused of being drunk when he wrote in the *Daily Express* that the Basque town of Guernica had been flattened by the Germans.

Queipo wasn't averse to levelling criticism at his own colleagues either, particularly Franco, for whom he was to remain a thorn in the side for the duration of the war. Answering more taunts from Radio Barcelona about being a turncoat, he said that he had been a Republican until he had seen that the leaders of the Republic had taken a wrong turn and therefore should be overthrown. The future of Spain now lay in Franco's hands, he said. But should he see one day in the future that the Caudillo was not acting in the country's best interests, he would not hesitate to fight Franco for the sake of Spain as well. It is not clear how Franco reacted to this, but he certainly took measures to sideline Queipo as the war progressed.

Despite all his threats and boasts about the violent acts of his troops, in Queipo's twisted mind cruelty only ever came from the Republican side. 'The school of Marxism is murder, looting and theft. It is shameful that countries like England and the United States, and other countries so advanced they have organizations for the protection of animals, haven't busied themselves as they should have done in prohibiting the very real hunting of men that the Marxists have been carrying out since 18 July . . .' This from the mouth of a man who had overseen some of the worst atrocities of the war, including, in one instance, the stabbing to death of every man who could be found in the San Julián district of Seville.

How effective were his broadcasts as a tool of war? At the very least he was an easily identifiable figure on the Nationalist side, almost from day one. At a time when Franco was still stuck in Morocco and was then busy fighting his way up to the top of the Nationalist tree, Queipo was the public face of the rebellion, a character who could charm his audiences as well as terrify them. Apart from breaking into song on air, he would often finish off with a random personal message for friends or family: 'And now if my wife and daughter, who are in Paris, happen to be listening I'd like to say I hope they're well and to assure them we here in Seville are thinking of them.'

During the uncertain early days and weeks of the war, Queipo's broadcasts became a rallying cry and morale booster for Nationalists, helping the advance of Franco's army as it pushed northwards through Extremadura. On many occasions the defenders simply downed their weapons and fled on hearing that the Moroccans were on their way. Queipo, with his nightly barrage of vitriol and hyperbole, depicting in graphic terms the horrors that awaited them if they were caught by the Regulares, undoubtedly contributed to the levels of fear on the Republican side.

In January 1938 the radio broadcasts suddenly stopped, a year and a half after they had begun. By then his lectures had become, according to one English listener, 'as familiar as the nine o'clock chiming of Big Ben'. Queipo simply informed his audience one night that he would no longer be continuing and disappeared from the airwaves, giving no reason for his decision. Nationalist Spain, it was said, became a much duller place as a result. As ever with Queipo's changes of heart, the answer lay with his vanity: it later emerged that Franco had formed a cabinet and left Queipo out. Queipo had coveted the job of minister for war.

Militarily, his main contribution in the latter part of the war was to launch a successful campaign in the summer of 1938 against eastern Extremadura, but politically he made little impact after he went off the air. His moment of glory had passed. After he had fallen into disfavour his career reached a stalemate and he lived out the rest of his days building up the myth of his exploits in the war, hankering after more medals and honours. He finally received his much coveted *laureada*, the highest honour in the Spanish Army, in 1944. He died in 1951 and was buried in the Macarena church in Seville.

While Nationalist propaganda dominated the airwaves, the Republicans concentrated more on visual images, driven by a desire to persuade the governments of Britain, the USA and France to come to their aid in the fight against fascism. Films could easily travel abroad and be shown to large audiences, who in turn would pressurize their representatives to come to the aid of the Republic. Ernest Hemingway was one of the prime movers of this trend.

Hemingway arrived in Spain in the spring of 1937, after he was invited to become the war correspondent for the North American Newspaper Alliance. It was the first of four trips he made to the country during the conflict and he spent a total of nearly eight months covering events there. The Spanish Civil War had become a rallying cry for the Left in the USA, much as it had across Europe, and Hemingway was immediately drawn to the Republican side, alive as he had become over recent years to the political and social developments of the 1930s. Even before he arrived in Spain he had written the commentary for the pro-Republican film *Spain in Flames*. His most noteworthy contribution to Republican propaganda, however, came once he got to Spain, where he worked with John Dos Passos on the script for the documentary *The Spanish Earth*. The fifty-minute film was narrated by Hemingway himself (Orson Welles was due to narrate but was replaced when he wanted to change some of the text; he and Hemingway came to blows over the issue, but were later reconciled) and premiered in New York at the 55th Street Playhouse on 20 August 1937. Later it was given a private showing at the White House, where the Roosevelts were involved in raising funds for a Republican ambulance fund. While the president's natural sympathies lay with the Republic, there were many powerful interests in the country supporting Franco, not least the oil industry, and they applied pressure to ensure that no US aid ever reached the Spanish government.

The Spanish Earth showed bucolic scenes of Spanish country folk living a romantic if hard-working life, scratching a living off the land and now fighting to keep what little they had from the hands of the military rebels. Women wearing black were pictured walking through the dusty streets of whitewashed villages, while little boys rode on donkeys through the fields in quasi-biblical images that evoked the Holy Land and the time of Christ. Shattering this idyll, though, was the war, and the sight of artillery and explosions as the peasants defended their land broke rudely into this Arcadian world.

These were the doors of houses that are empty now, Hemingway solemnly intoned over scenes of doors piled in the streets. *Those that survived the bombardment bring them to reinforce the new trenches.*

From the countryside the story moved to Madrid, showing dramatic, if staged, pictures of the front line during the Nationalist assault on the city, with lingering shots of the devastation caused by the fighting: homes broken in pieces; dead bodies lying unattended on the floor. Then, returning to the countryside, the film focused on what was perhaps the greatest fear of the time: aerial bombardment and its possible use in future wars. The wreckage of a German Junkers shot down by a Republican fighter is shown in a field – this at a time when the Germans and the international community at large denied there were any foreign troops in Spain. *I can't read German either*, Hemingway intoned ironically as the camera focused on Gothic-script writing on the fuselage of the downed plane.

After more battle scenes, the film returned to images of peasants tilling and irrigating their land, making the dry soil fertile once more, while a Republican soldier fired his rifle in defence of his people.

The men who never fought before, who were not trained in arms, who only wanted work, and food, fight on.

The sparse, emotive commentary combined with strong images of the war was a powerful tool, but while supporters of the Republicans were moved by it, giving large sums to private charities working on the Republican side, government policies remained unchanged, and in this the propaganda failed.

Hemingway, however, stayed on in Spain. An active backer of the government, he was sometimes to be seen teaching young fighters how to fire a rifle on the front lines, if staying out of the fray himself. His presence was generally welcomed: on one occasion when Hemingway paid a visit to the XII International Brigade, the general in command invited all the girls from a local village to a celebratory banquet. Hemingway wrote his only play, *The Fifth Column*, while staying at the Florida Hotel in Madrid, which was hit thirty times by Nationalist bombardment while he was there. He was also one of the last people to cross back over the River Ebro after the heavy Republican defeat there in November 1938.

Hemingway's experiences in Spain made a lasting impression on him, and his thoughts on the conflict were distilled in his bestselling work *For Whom the Bell Tolls*, written after the eventual defeat of the side he had done so much to assist. A new, much greater war was on the horizon, one which Hemingway, like so many others, could clearly see.

'They wrote in the old days it is sweet and fitting to die for one's country,' he wrote in his *Notes for the Next War*. 'But in modern war there is nothing sweet or fitting in your dying. You will die like a dog for no good reason.'

9

Castuera

*T*here was little to show now where the concentration camp at Castuera once stood. I walked out of town along a little dust track past the cemetery, past farmhouses guarded by large fierce dogs that ran and barked overzealously in the oppressive heat, until I reached an empty field gently rising in the foothills of a long, wave-like mountain. There, at the side of the road, sat the ruins of an old lead mine, now used as a dump by the towns-people. Stretching out to the horizon, the desolate landscape of Extremadura baked under the sun. Everything in sight was either a dull yellowy grey, from the acre upon acre of dry grass, or black, where the barren soil had eroded to expose the rock that lay underneath. The place felt empty, meaningless, lacking even the austere beauty of a desert or the promise and fear of an empty ocean.

The area had been held by the Republicans for much of the war. The town became flooded with refugees fleeing the nearby front line at the start of the conflict. The house of a local wealthy family had been turned into a hospital, while the church became a car mechanic's workshop. As time passed and the war dragged on, though, the town slowly emptied: there were barely enough supplies to keep alive the soldiers from the 37th Division stationed there, or the whores 'bearing their butter-white breasts' on the streets.[12] When the Francoists finally took control in the summer of 1938, they killed 183 Republican defenders and took one thousand prisoners. And to house them they built the concentration camp, just as they were doing at various points across the country.

It was difficult to find remains of Spanish concentration camps now. Franco had forbidden any photos of them to be taken, and all the camps were destroyed when they were abandoned. Very few Spaniards, let alone foreigners, were aware that concentration camps once existed in Spain. Yet at Castuera there had once stood one of the most barbaric camps – over seventy wooden huts housing one hundred inmates each. During the day the prisoners were taken up into the hills to find wood to build more huts to house more men: by the time the camp was dismantled, over twelve thousand Republicans had been brought here. Many of them never left.

Hot angry air blew over the plain as I stumbled through the dust and rocks looking for signs of the camp. Sloping away up the Castuera y Benquerencia hills, the field where the huts once stood was featureless, barely a ripple on its surface. Yet the small mine building which had stood on its edge, and where it was said the worst atrocities had taken place, was still standing, if half falling down.

The area around the dirty red-brick building was littered with broken bottles and smashed toilets, heavy white porcelain scattered over the scrubby little weeds that seemed to be the only thing that could grow here. From the graffiti I got the impression kids from the town used the place for drinking parties, spraying the wall in moments of drunkenness. But when

I looked more closely I realized that whoever came here knew exactly what kind of a place it was.

¿Qué es la guerra? ¡Los de aquí dentro lo saben! Muertes olvidadas.

What is war? Those lying in here know. The forgotten dead.

At that moment the wind changed direction and for a second I caught the unmistakable sweet sickly smell of rotting flesh. No one knew how many had been killed there. Dozens, perhaps hundreds. But that had all been seventy years ago. Surely there couldn't still be decomposing remains of the men who had died here? For a second, with the heat, the smell and the hollow silence, broken only by the buzzing of flies desperately trying to catch drops of sweat on my forehead and arms in the seconds before they evaporated away, I began to wonder. There was nothing to hold on to in a place like this. No terms of reference. The triggers that usually surround us, reassuring us constantly that the world functions as we know it to, and will continue to do so, were all removed. You could think anything here.

I skirted around the back of the ruined mine, looking for a way in. It was a small rectangular building with high windowless walls, open to the elements save for part of a roof covering a taller, tower-like section at one end. I tripped up a small grey slope over more broken porcelain. There was no door, but I found the origin of the stench: a dead sheep, its carcass melting into the ground, crushed more by the heat of the sun than by the flies and worms of ordinary decomposition. Survival even for them out here would be hard, you felt. Circling back round to the dirt track at the front of the mine building, it was clear I would have to scale the wall if I wanted to get inside, as there didn't appear to be any entrance. And it was the inside that I wanted to see.

For the months that the Castuera concentration camp was in existence, members of the local Falange party had come up from the village at night to murder the inmates. Many of the victims were political activists from among the Republican ranks. In public, Franco used to declare that Republicans with no blood on their hands would be spared. In secret, at Castuera many were murdered simply for having been on the other side. Grouping the prisoners into batches of ten, the Falangists would tie them together around the waist and then drag them to the mine just outside the camp. There they would line them up at the top of the shaft and push them over the edge. Some fell directly to their deaths, others smashed their limbs at the bottom but remained alive. The Falangists finished them off with grenades.

Although some historians referred to Castuera as Franco's death camp, there was still a veil of silence draped over what precisely had taken place here. Few of the people involved who were still alive were prepared to talk about their experiences, while Pablo Ortiz, a school teacher from the nearby town of Zafra who had recently published an article on the history of the camp, had received anonymous threats over the phone. In Castuera, most were still determined to forget, and to keep the truth buried along with the unclaimed dead.

I found footholds in the wall and began to climb. The wall was only eight feet high, and within a couple of steps I was peering over the edge at a kind of shallow pit. The stench of death, once again, was overpowering, and as I looked down I could make out more dead sheep – at least half a dozen of them. Puzzled, I wondered how they had got in there – the only way in was over the wall. Would a farmer have thrown them in like this to rot? They lay on their sides, white bones pushing through what was left of their wool, mouths stretched into permanent grins where their faces had all but gone. Some of them looked to have been quite young.

Even stranger, lying next to an assortment of plastic bags and other rubbish were three or four prosthetic limbs. Legs, for the most part, full-sized and designed to go right up to the hip, complete with socks and boots covering the foot. Although clearly made of plastic, at first sight they seemed real. Even when, after the initial shock, I'd worked out what they were, it was hard not to think of them as actually human, with their carefully moulded knee caps and calf muscles. Was this some kind of statement, symbolizing the horror of what had happened here during the war? Lambs to the slaughter, abandoned fake body parts, all shrouded in the smell of decay. But maybe it was just a tip, a place to discard what you wanted to forget.

Looking further into the mine building, I realized the shaft where the prisoners had been murdered was on the other side of the pit. There was no way through, as the ground was a sea of dead sheep and plastic legs, so I gingerly crept over the outer wall and skirted around the inside of it, gripping on to any gaps in the brickwork. The drop was no more than a few feet, but it was the thought of what I might land in that gave me pause.

On cue, the ledge I had committed all my weight on to gave way and I fell down the edge of the wall, landing with a crack in the middle of the pit. I looked down and saw my foot placed in the middle of a sheep's abdomen, the dry bones snapping under my weight. The smell of putrefaction hit me as flies rose up into my face. Looking down at my foot as I lifted it out of the animal's corpse, I expected it to be covered in what remained of the sheep's innards, but it was just dusty, and thankfully there were no scratches on my leg. I didn't want to think about what kind of diseases the thing might be carrying. The sheep seemed fairly dry. In these conditions you got the sense that once an animal died its body liquids would evaporate within a few hours.

I scrambled back up the wall, trying not to retch, and deliberately avoiding the ledge that I'd just fallen from. Shuffling along sideways, I eventually got to the edge of the mine shaft and looked down. It was dark and dank, a featureless grimy cavern not quite as deep as I had expected: perhaps a hundred feet. I assumed it had been partially filled in. Perhaps earth had been poured into it at some point to cover the bodies that lay at the bottom.

I stayed there for a few moments, the sun beating down on the back of my head as I peered into this hole in the ground, sensing the animal fear and helplessness of falling into its depths. The moment of panic, the fear, the rush. Then the crash, pain, and explosions as the grenades fell from above. I pictured the men who had done this enjoying themselves as they disposed of another dozen or so Reds, slapping one another on the back and lighting cigarettes as they walked away, satisfied with their night's work.

Clambering out and away from the blackness, past the sheep and limbs and over the wall again, I took another look at the crumbling old building, trying to absorb and understand what had taken place there. On the outside of the wall the Conscience of Castuera had scrawled more graffiti.

Puta hipocresía. Estamos vendidos.

Fucking hypocrisy. We've been sold down the river.

A sheep's skull was nestling among some rags and the remains of a rusting washing machine by the side of the road. It had been blanched by the summer light, back teeth half formed as they pushed down through the bone of the upper jaw.

What was it about this country, I wondered, that places like this could just be abandoned, as though the events that took place here might evaporate simply by forgetting they had ever happened? Standing there, the bleakness seeping into me, I remembered how Miguel had told me of the horrors that had been committed in this impoverished part of the country. I felt buried by the weight of all the anger and violence that had been a part of this landscape. Why had I come? I had wanted to explore the Civil War, but right then I just wanted to get out as fast as I could.

As I was turning to walk back into the town, I caught sight of something moving over the dry dead plains in the distance. A white figure was bobbing up and down in a crease in the hillside, its form half obscured by the colourless weeds and dry grass. I stood still in the burning air to make out what it was. Nothing out there felt familiar – it seemed more like the landscape of a choking dream than any real countryside I had ever known. As I flicked away in vain at the flies, I suddenly realized: this was one of the hottest and most barren places on earth, yet at that very moment I was being approached by a jogger.

Caught in a trance-like state induced by the eerie surroundings, I watched in amazement as the man paced across the fields, following a path which stretched the length of the foothills, eventually passing in front of me. His face was red and swollen with exertion, and a pink baseball cap covered his head, patchy dark stains growing around the sides where it had absorbed the sweat. His white T-shirt clung to his skin, flecked with spots of grime where the dust had been kicked up from his running shoes. I simply stared at him as he came closer, wondering how and why he should be carrying out such an exhausting activity in this heat.

Despite the bovine expression on my face, he stopped as he ran up to the old mine building and greeted me. Two lunatics in the middle of the Extremaduran desert, each wondering what the other was doing there.

'Are you from the town?' I asked after we had introduced ourselves. His face spoke of nothing but pain. I half wondered if he was going to drop dead on the spot from heart failure.

His wife was from Castuera, he said, but he was originally from Cáceres. I remarked how amazing it was seeing someone jogging at that time of the day.

'I only come out here in the afternoon,' he said. 'Don't like to come any other time.'

'Wouldn't it be cooler in the evenings?' I asked. 'Or early in the morning?'

His head turned to the side and he gave me a furtive look, hands on his hips as his lungs heaved up and down, catching his breath.

'It's good for running round here,' he said with a nervous laugh. 'But it's a bit . . . You know what happened here, right?'

He mentioned the concentration camp, and the killings that had taken place there. I told him I'd just climbed in to take a look.

'You think it's a bit creepy,' I said.

His eyes became intense and shiny, black with fear.

'I don't know whether to believe these things,' he laughed again, 'but they say there are ghosts here – men who were killed in the war.' He looked down and swallowed, lifting the baseball cap off his head and wiping his brow with his arm. Grey hairs were beginning to sprout around his ears. I guessed him to be in his forties.

'Have you seen them?'

'No. People in the village . . . I don't know. I just don't want to take any chances. So I reckon it's safer only coming here during the daytime.'

'What have they seen?' I asked. 'Tell me.'

'Just comments. You know. One of the old men in the village said he was walking his dog out here one night a few years back and he saw this blue-purple shadow – a young man dressed as a soldier. The dog went mad and he had to put it down.'

'The dog saw the ghost too?'

'It was never quite right, that dog. Vicious. But after that day it just went out of control. They had to shoot it, see. Might have attacked a child or something.' The man's eyes moved

114

from side to side in a flickering motion, never looking me in the face.

'And where was the ghost? Where did this man see it?' I felt a sudden fascination with the story, a feverish desire to find out everything I could. The place felt like a reflection of the Underworld. Perhaps the only beings that could survive out here were phantoms and shades. The skin on the back of my neck began to sting with the heat of the sun. I had been outside unprotected for too long and needed water and to cool down. Dizziness was creeping up my spine.

The jogger took a step back.

'It was here, right in front of the mine,' he said quietly. His face was no longer red and was turning grey. 'Right where you're standing now.'

10

The Siege

On 28 September 1936, General José Varela clambered over the ruins of the old Alcázar fortress in the central Spanish city of Toledo to claim one of the most important Nationalist victories of the Civil War. Inside, the survivors of a harrowing seventy-day siege were white-faced and frail from weeks living off hard gritty bread and horse fat. Around them the ten-foot-thick walls of the medieval castle that had been their home and refuge since late July lay broken into piles of rock and rubble, smashed yet not defeated by the ten thousand Republican shells fired at it since the outbreak of the war. Dead bodies rotted in cellars and hidden corners, the smell of decaying flesh and human dirt mingling in the crisp autumn morning air. Many of the nearly two thousand people inside were too weak to raise a cheer when Varela and his Moroccan troops arrived to relieve their torment, and the women refused to emerge from their underground bunkers for shame at not having washed or changed their clothes in months. But the man who had led this defiant stance against the besiegers from the beginning, Colonel Moscardó, was able to stand to attention in the presence of his superior and utter the most famous line of his life: '*Sin novedad en el Alcázar, mi general.*' Nothing to report from the Alcázar, sir. It was untypically phlegmatic for the usually bombastic and excitable colonel, but it touched the hearts of Spaniards all over the country – and not only supporters of Franco – after one of the most dramatic and heroic chapters in the history of the war. While Republican blood flowed down the streets of Toledo in the wake of the Nationalist victory, the Alcázar had been successfully relieved, its inhabitants saved. Franco, retracing Varela's steps two days later and hearing the same statement from Moscardó for the benefit of the news cameras, was able to say, 'Now the war is won.' It took him another two and a half years to make that a reality, but the relief of the Alcázar had a symbolic importance which powered the Nationalist forces to eventual victory.

The siege of the Alcázar began almost by accident. Moscardó and other conservatives in Toledo had never intended to lock themselves in the fortress and so were unprepared for the ordeal they had to go through. The plan had been to take the entire city for the uprising; only when this failed did the insurgents have to fall back on the castle. That they held out for so long bore testament to their determination as well as the ineffectiveness of the Republican forces trying to force them out.

Colonel Moscardó was a middle-aged officer known for his nervousness and volatility. People said his mother had died insane. After a career in Spanish Morocco, this keen football fan had been farmed out to Toledo to take charge of the army's school of physical education. The school was on the outskirts of town, although attached to the military academy which was based in the Alcázar, a vast square fortress that sat on the highest hill in Toledo, dominating a city that had once been the ancient capital of the Visigothic kings of Spain. Rebuilt by Charles V in the sixteenth century, it had been burned down by the British during the War of Spanish Succession, then again by the French during the Napoleonic Wars, finally being remodelled and strengthened at the beginning of the twentieth century, just a year or two before a young cadet called Francisco Franco arrived from Galicia for officer training. It was a dour and ugly building, unremarkable save for its size and imposing towers, one at each of its four corners.

The plotters of the military rebellion hadn't even bothered to inform Moscardó of their plans. He was an unimportant figure in the scheme of things, an old football coach to young artillery cadets. But when he discovered that the army was rising against the government, he knew instinctively which side he was on. The rebel leaders didn't have any plans for the capture of Toledo, being more preoccupied with taking control of the major cities. So it fell to Moscardó and a handful of fellow right-wingers to try to take the town for the uprising of their own accord. The local unions and worker organizations fighting against the military rebellion proved too strong for them, however, and after failing to secure the town, they fell back to the haven of the Alcázar. There they were joined by almost seven hundred Civil Guards from around the province, and a couple of hundred Falangists and other supporters. After a daring raid on the neighbouring arms factory, where they managed to get their hands on over seven hundred thousand rounds of ammunition for their Mauser rifles, Moscardó's men locked themselves inside the fortress.

Outside, the town was overrun with anarchist militiamen as central authority broke down. Dead priests lay rotting in the streets, desperate women and children vainly pushing bread and cigarettes into their mouths to try to revive them. One priest was even found with a crucifix forced into his rectum.

The siege began as the situation across the rest of country was still volatile. Things did not look good for the defenders: the Alcázar was cut off from the other parts of Spain held by the Nationalists. As the situation clarified in the first few days of the war, they realized that their only chance of survival would come from rapid advances by either General Mola in the north, or Franco in the south. But Mola got stuck in the Guadarrama mountain chain as he tried to move on Madrid, while Franco was still held up in Spanish Morocco at this point, busy trying to get his troops across the Strait. The Alcázar was surrounded and very far away from any outside help. They had a good supply of ammunition, but food stocks were low as it was the summer holidays and most of the cadets had gone home. They did have a supply of fresh water, though, contained in ancient cisterns in the depths of the castle. Optimistically, Moscardó expected to have to hold out for a few days, perhaps a fortnight at most. No one suspected just how long they would have to stay in there.

Expectations about the duration of the siege were woefully off the mark on the outside as well, however. The anarchists were the main force among the Republicans now controlling Toledo, but socialists and communists were also in the city. The rivalries between these factions meant coordination during the early days of the siege was pitiful, and in the absence of any coherent strategy men lurked behind barricades, simply emptying their cartridges into the massively thick walls of the fortress in the vain hope that something might get through. But they thought they had time on their side and could take it relatively easy, that the Nationalists would eventually be forced into surrender.

Shortly into the stand-off, the attackers managed to find what appeared to be a trump card – Moscardó's family, discovered hiding in the city during a house search. Moscardó's wife was left alone by the Republicans, but his twenty-four-year-old son Luis was another matter. He was of an age where he could fight – and die. Militiamen took him to the *cheka* of the forces now controlling the city. These were unauthorized political courts where people were 'tried' on suspicion of supporting the enemy. They had been set up across Republican Spain at the start of the war and thousands passed through their hands before being 'taken for a ride', in the language of contemporary gangster films – a short drive to a swift execution. The name came from Russian, after similar bodies set up during the revolution there.

The man in charge of the Toledo *cheka* was a lawyer named Candido Cabello. Cabello could barely believe his luck when the militiamen brought Luis Moscardó through the door. Only a few streets away Luis's father was holed up with some two thousand people inside the Alcázar and was quickly becoming a thorn in the side of the government. According to one version of events, Cabello soon had Colonel Moscardó on the phone, and made his position very clear.

'I'm giving you ten minutes to surrender the Alcázar. If you don't, I'll shoot your son Luis who is standing here beside me.'

'I believe you,' Moscardó replied without any emotion.

'So that you can see it's true,' Cabello went on, 'he will speak to you.' He handed the phone over to Luis.

'Papa!' the boy cried.

'What's happening, son?' Moscardó asked.

'Nothing,' replied Luis. 'They say they are going to shoot me if the Alcázar doesn't surrender. But don't worry about me.'

'If it is true,' Moscardó said, 'commend your soul to God, shout "*¡Viva España!*" and die like a hero. Goodbye, my son. A kiss.'

'Goodbye, father. A big kiss.'

Cabello took back the phone, but Moscardó was the first to speak. 'You may as well forget the period of grace you gave me,' he said. 'The Alcázar will never surrender.'

Luis wasn't actually killed on the spot but was taken away to be locked up, although he was shot before the siege eventually came to an end. Cabello's plan, meanwhile, had totally back-fired. The defenders were now more entrenched than ever, led by a man who was prepared to sacrifice his own son. Any doubters there might have been within the Alcázar were now silenced. There was no going back.

Some historians have doubted the veracity of this conversation; the story feels almost mythological, having a peculiar resonance, not only for its echoes of Abraham and Isaac, but within a Spanish historical context. During the time of the Reconquest, at the siege of the town of Tarifa on the very southern tip of the Spanish peninsula in 1294, the ruler Alonso Pérez de Guzmán had been given an almost identical ultimatum by the besieging joint Christian and Moorish forces, who threatened to kill his son, whom they'd kidnapped earlier, if he didn't surrender. Guzmán was from the same school of parenting as Moscardó, and famously replied that if they didn't have a knife on them to murder his boy they could take his. He was later nicknamed 'the Good' for his defence of the town. Moscardó was now a hero in this vein, a character straight out of the tales of the knights of old.

Meanwhile, time was moving on and people inside the Alcázar were adjusting to their new environment. A homemade newspaper, *El Alcázar*, was printed with snippets of news, appeals to keep up morale from Moscardó, and bulletins of events. The large inner courtyard began to resemble a town square in these quieter early days, with young girls taking an evening stroll, unmarried officers chatting to them and courting them in the traditional manner. A circus was held, two different magicians gave performances, and the band played as though it were an ordinary Sunday afternoon. But it wasn't long before the lack of supplies became evident. The day after the first edition of *El Alcázar* appeared, the flour supplies ran out and it became necessary to slaughter the horses for meat. It was even agreed which was to be the first: a bad-tempered animal called Pistolero, 'gunman', who'd managed to throw off anyone who'd tried to ride him. Aside from the meat, horse fat could be used for lamps in the cellars. The electricity was down and the only way to power the all-important radio was to use car batteries, but even then reception was bad and often failed altogether.

Conditions started to worsen dramatically shortly after this. On 1 August the Republican besiegers, impatient with trying to starve the Nationalists out, began to batter the Alcázar with artillery, hoping to smash their way in. On the same day, dysentery broke out. From the pages of *El Alcázar* Moscardó ordered people not to defecate outside the latrines, but often this warning was ignored. The place was slowly turning into a hell-hole and the question of food had to be resolved quickly. Whenever suggestions were made about scouting for supplies, Moscardó, ever trusting in divine providence, continued to maintain that God would take care of things. Previous raids into the town had proved unsuccessful, fatally so for some of the Falangists, who were always the first to sign up for any daredevil missions. Finally someone in the Alcázar remembered that sacks of wheat had been stored by a bank in some buildings just within reach of the defenders. It seems too crazy to be true, but after a midnight scouting party crept out and discovered there was indeed a large supply of unground wheat in the buildings concerned, sacks of it were brought back inside the Alcázar. A primitive grinder was made using a saw mill powered by a leather strap running round the back wheel of a Harley-Davidson, and eventually a crude gritty form of flour was produced. Baked into dark bullet-shaped loaves, this and the horsemeat was to keep the defenders alive until late September.

Outside, the attackers were getting more and more frustrated. The thick walls of the fortress were virtually impervious to their bullets and 75mm shells, so now heavier artillery firing 155mm shells was being brought in. In the meantime a strange kind of rapport was building up between the besiegers and the besieged, the two sides so close to one another they could trade insults, while personal rivalries between individuals on either side developed. The Republicans called the defenders *moscas*, or flies, a play on Moscardó's name. For the rebels inside, the Republicans were *abisinios*, Abyssinians, a pejorative reference to Mussolini's 'primitive' enemy during his recent African adventure. Yet despite the hostility, twice a day there was a brief unofficial ceasefire to allow a blind beggar to walk up the calle del Carmen – right in the middle of no-man's land – once in the morning and then back down again in the evening on his way home.

Apart from the shelling, the Republicans also tried a crude form of psychological warfare, blasting lectures on Marxism and music at the Alcázar through loudspeakers in the hope that they might wear the defenders down. One of the favourites on Radio Cigarral, as it was called, was Wagner's 'The Ride of the Valkyries'. But these tactics were not enough to force a surrender, although there were up to thirty-five Nationalist desertions during the course of the siege and a handful of those who held out went permanently insane as a result of their experiences.

Inside the Alcázar, people had to be inventive to deal with the harsh conditions. Apart from using a motorbike to grind flour, they found that the heavy leather-bound books from the fortress libraries could be quite effective at stopping bullets, especially if they were over four hundred pages long, and many were placed in windows for protection.[13] The men would scavenge around for dried leaves to smoke in lieu of tobacco. Acacia, eucalyptus, elm and mulberry were all used, although eucalyptus had a habit of making them ill. In the sickroom, the Alcázar 'surgeon' was Dr Pelayo Lozano, an expert on athlete's foot and acne, the usual complaints of the young cadets at the academy. Now he had to read up on how to amputate limbs injured by bullet wounds. Men who lost a leg were usually given a pair of broomsticks as makeshift crutches to hobble around on.[14] On one occasion the doctor's surgical saw broke down and he had to borrow the chef's cleaver from the kitchen instead. The chef was becoming used to this kind of thing, often having to prepare meals while bullets flew around him, one of them even knocking the spatula out of his hand as he was preparing another horse-meat special, seasoned with saltpetre off the walls instead of salt. He was lucky if he ever got to see what he was cooking, as he often had to crouch down behind the stove to stir whatever was on the hob for fear of being hit by something.

The atmosphere inside the fortress changed dramatically one morning in the middle of August when one of the defenders started screaming hysterically about hearing strange noises coming from underground. At first Moscardó dismissed the soldier as mad, but a team was sent off to investigate and came back with the harrowing news that the attackers were almost certainly digging a tunnel underneath them in order to blow up the Alcázar. Hence the muffled bangs as explosives were used to bore into the hard rocky foundations. The Republicans were in fact digging two tunnels, having brought in miners from the Asturias region for the job. Starting from a couple of houses on nearby Juan Labrador Street, they were working round the clock in four-hour shifts, burrowing their way towards the southwest tower and the west wall. Tired of trying to shell the defenders into submission, the Republican government had decided to take stronger measures as the stand of the Alcázar became an ever greater embarrassment for them. The siege had become something of a sport for Madrileños, who would motor down to Toledo on a Sunday to have a picnic in the shadow of the rebel-held castle before taking a couple of pot shots of their own and then heading back home by nightfall. Impressive as the Alcázar was, and stuck in the middle of Republican-held territory, it was starting to take on a symbolic significance – evidence of the tenacity of the rebels and the ineffectiveness of the government forces. Something had to be done.

But building the tunnels, both about seventy yards long, would take about a month, and as they progressed the shelling continued. On 4 September, after a concentrated effort, the northeast tower fell – the first breach in the massive walls had been made. Four days later the northwest tower was also toppled. Still the defenders held out. Odd bits of news were coming in, which kept their hopes alive that the longed-for relief was perhaps on its way. A Nationalist plane had dropped a few scanty supplies of food and a message of support from Franco. Then, on the day the first tower fell, Franco's troops, now well inside mainland Spain and pushing up the west side of the country towards Madrid, captured the town of Talavera, only seventy kilometres away from Toledo.

But the tunnels were getting closer, and the inevitable day of the explosion was growing nearer. On 9 September the government sent an envoy, Major Vicente Rojo, to talk to the defenders. Rojo was a former member of the academy who knew many of those inside. During a brief truce he crossed over to the Alcázar and was blindfolded before being taken up to see Moscardó. Despite Rojo's warnings of what was coming, the colonel rejected his appeal for a peaceful surrender, refusing even to let the women and children go safely. Instead he asked for a priest to be sent over as none of the town priests had joined them. Rojo agreed, and as he left repeatedly implored his former colleagues to keep looking for where the explosives were being laid. Deeply moved and with tears in his eyes, he crossed back to the Republican side empty-handed, the appeals from the rebel officers that he remain with them inside the besieged castle still ringing in his ears. That evening the first of the two babies born in the Alcázar during the siege came into the world. He was given the name Restituto Alcázar Valero.

Other attempts were made to persuade the defenders to give in, but to no avail. On 18 September, after weeks of growing tension which had led to a handful of desertions and even some suicides, the long-awaited explosion took place. The government had brought journalists from the world's media to watch the spectacular defeat of the rebel forces, and the blast was so loud it was heard in the southern suburbs of Madrid, forty kilometres away. The southwest tower flew into the air like a rocket before collapsing. On the ground, teams of Assault Guards were waiting to storm the building and claim victory. Yet even as the journalists watching from afar started to announce the fall of the Alcázar, the efforts to capture the ancient fortress failed. While some Republicans did manage to get inside – a red flag was even placed on the statue of Charles V in the main courtyard – the attackers had little idea of how many men they were actually facing: at one point an assault on a breach in the walls was fought back by only four Civil Guards brandishing pistols, the Republicans assuming in the confusion that they were up against a much larger force. Skirmishes took place all around the building, but the defenders, most of whom were unhurt by the blast after their successful calculations of where it would take place, knew the area far better and were able to use this to their advantage. By nightfall the Alcázar was still in their hands and the government's embarrassment deepened even further. The explosion did, however, bring forth another life – the second baby born in the Alcázar, who popped out with the force of the blast. Her mother was already in labour at the time, but nonetheless she named her daughter Josefa del Milagro in honour of the 'miracle' of her birth.

Time was running out for the Republicans. Franco's forces were inching closer by the day. Desperate now to take the

Alcázar, the Asturian miners started digging another tunnel, while government troops fired an ever greater number of shells at the wreckage of the once proud castle. On one day alone a total of 472 shells were sent crashing into the walls. Still the defenders held out. Then on 21 September Franco's men captured the nearby town of Maqueda. The general had to make a choice: either continue northeastwards and move swiftly on Madrid, thereby possibly bringing the war to a quick end; or turn round and head southeast and relieve the Alcázar, which would give the government more time to prepare its defence of the capital. Franco took the latter option, explaining to one of his supporters that it was necessary to convince the enemy 'that we will do what we say we will do'. For the defenders in the Alcázar it was a godsend. For the rest of Spain it meant another two and a half years of misery as the war dragged on.

Within days the defenders could see and hear Franco's troops pushing towards Toledo. But the fight was not over yet. The Republicans made a last-ditch attempt to take the castle before it was relieved, despite scores of militiamen abandoning their positions and running away. On the morning of 27 September another explosion rocked the castle, but again the follow-up attack failed to dislodge the besieged. It was now just a matter of hours before the Nationalist vanguard would reach the town.

General Varela, in charge of Franco's forces on the ground, turned the relief of the Alcázar into a competition between the Legión and the Regulares. Both these forces, based in Spanish Morocco, liked to think of themselves as the crack troops of the army. Now they could test themselves against each other. As they pushed through the town they ignored the promise by Moscardó inside the fortress that Republicans caught in the conquest of the town would be spared, and militiamen were shot dead or bayoneted on the spot where they were found. Their brains and guts 'sizzled like sausages' on the hot cobblestones, according to one observer. The massacre was horrific, the Regulares even killing a doctor and his wounded patients in the San Juan hospital with grenades. A group of forty anarchists, trapped in a seminary by the advancing troops, locked themselves in, got drunk on anise then set fire to themselves rather than hand themselves over. 'These men knew how to die,' was the admiring comment of the legionaries.

In the end the Regulares were the first to reach the Alcázar. The defenders could hear their high-pitched barking war-cry in the streets below before the vanguard got to the ruins, bringing the first decent food and cigarettes to pass their lips for months. General Varela arrived the following morning as the massacre continued in the town, officially declaring the end of the siege at ten a.m.

'*Sin novedad en el Alcázar, mi general,*' Moscardó told him. The rest of the defenders were silent, too weary to say anything.

As many had predicted, diverting forces to relieve the Alcázar almost certainly turned the war from a relatively quick affair into a long, drawn-out conflict, in which attrition often took the place of the swift campaigns of the early months. Madrid got the time it needed to build up its defences against the coming Nationalist assault. A strong defence was the government's main priority, as Republican forces – still largely made up of militiamen at this point – were no match in the field for the Nationalists' professional soldiers. Franco's forces, while claiming a great victory and securing a massive morale-booster for their cause, lost the momentum of their northward campaign on the capital. Not until the very end of the war would they regain such a pace, and then it would mostly be through the implosion of the Republican forces.

But the relief of the Alcázar was highly important for Franco personally. It was the crowning achievement in his rapid rise through the ranks of the Nationalists, turning him from a fence-sitting vacillator in the weeks before the rebellion into the undisputed head of the movement. Two days before he embraced Moscardó for the benefit of the cameras inside the ruins of the fortress – a great media coup set against the rapidly developing art-form of war propaganda – the 'saviour of the Alcázar' had been effectively named head of state on the Nationalist side and *generalísimo* – the supreme commander of its forces. He was to retain this position of absolute power until his death. Ever a savvy manipulator of people's emotions, Franco gained the maximum political capital possible from the drama of the siege. His first goal – taking complete control of the Nationalist movement – had been largely achieved. Now he could concentrate on winning the war.

Moscardó was promoted to general, but the former football coach was out of his depth commanding armies in a civil war. Franco made sure he was never placed in positions of crucial importance, although always treating the hero of the Alcázar with the respect he deserved. Eventually he was made a count and died in 1956, having spent much time in his later years taking visitors around Toledo and telling them the story of the most dramatic events of his life.

11

Burgos

*T*hey said the food in Burgos was so rich it could 'wake up a dead man'. The main square, pressing against the Gothic cathedral, was filled with bars to accommodate the visiting crowds – sandal-wearing pilgrims, mostly, making their way towards Santiago with uniform staffs, sun hats and expressions of holiness. It was very picturesque, the needle-sharp towers of the temple rising up into a cloudless sky, quaint postcard views in almost every direction. I headed out and away from the centre down the side streets looking for a place to eat. Crossing the Arlanzón, an uncannily clean river for one that flowed through a city, I found a grimy café down a blind alley and immediately walked in: when in unfamiliar Spanish towns in the past, a general policy of making for the busiest and dirtiest workers' bar had usually served me well. Beer crates had been left in the entrance and I had to climb over them to get in, but I was quickly greeted by a joyous smell of frying garlic and sour smoke filled my nostrils. The place was packed and the television was yelling from the corner. I found a free chair at the side of a shared table and sat down. A woman with greasy dyed-blond hair who had her back to me turned round and smiled, revealing black stains like caves between each yellowed tooth.

The bar was a dark cramped space with walls painted in odd colours – one blue, another purple, another brown – while miniature imitation street-lamps stood at angles in the corners as though they were about to fall down. Behind my back, a chimney stack had been covered in shiny 'brick-look' wallpaper. Down some steps at the back, underneath a minstrels' gallery, was a kitchen, from which steam and fatty odours wafted up and mingled with the nicotine and hot breath of the customers. Behind the bar stood a body builder looking like a model for Action Man, with protruding forehead and tight hips. There was so much bulk on his upper arms and chest it was a wonder how he could even turn round amid all the bottles and trays of food, but somehow he managed to slip through, wiping his hands on the dark-blue cloth sticking out of his front trouser pocket. Down in the kitchen, what looked like his mother and sister were clad in white aprons, their hair wrapped up in nets. I looked over towards the metal bar and the plates of food warming under the glass: boar stew, *tigres* – stuffed mussels, Burgos-style black pudding packed with rice, and *sopa castellano* – stomach-lining garlic and chorizo soup with egg. A few tapas and some warming red wine and I would feel like new.

Burgos was a surprisingly small place for somewhere that called itself a city. It had barely spread out from the constraints of its medieval limits and felt very much like a provincial town. Which is all it would have been had it not been home to one of Spain's most important Gothic cathedrals, a major stop-over point on the route to Compostela, and the capital of old Castile – the county, later a kingdom, which had so dominated the Iberian peninsula over the past thousand years. During the Civil War Burgos had also been a centre of the Nationalist campaign and, during the latter part of the conflict, Franco's headquarters. Few places symbolized better the tenets of the reactionary movement of which the Generalísimo was the head, being both devoutly Catholic and strongly centralist – insisting on all power in Spain being concentrated in Madrid to the detriment of the regions. It had been the polar opposite of anarchist-controlled Barcelona, which during the war followed a pattern well established throughout Spanish history of trying to break away or gain greater autonomy, only to be forced back into uneasy matrimony with the rest of the country. Spain had always been a patchwork of a place, divided by the Romans and later by the Moors, and seemed to swing every so often between breaking apart completely and being held together by force, as though two opposing laws of nature were battling it out over the centuries for the identity of the country. Whenever anything less than an authoritarian regime was in power in Madrid, the regions, particularly Catalonia and the Basque Country, began pushing for independence. This had been the case in the years of the Republic leading up to the Civil War and was a major factor in the start of the conflict, and today similar moves were being made under Spain's new democracy. Whereas in the past these tendencies had been stamped out mercilessly, it looked as though this time they might get somewhere. The age-old tension at the heart of Spain, which served to give the country a certain dynamism, was flaring up again.

But the threat of violence was still alive, too. The president of the northwestern region of Galicia, Manuel Fraga, a former propaganda minister under Franco who was still going strong in his eighties, had reminded the armed forces only months before that they had a duty to defend the unity of Spain under the modern democratic constitution. It seemed very old-fashioned language in the early twenty-first century, but it struck a strong chord with some. The newspapers had recently reported how a colonel in the army had been arrested for circulating 'coupist' literature on the Ministry of Defence intranet, calling on the military in the name of God not to stand idly by while the country was broken up in front of their eyes. The danger of Spain splitting into several smaller states still, today, had the potential to cause certain sectors of society to turn to violent preventative measures. Occasionally the spirit of Franco seemed alive and well.

All eyes were turned towards the television set, so I looked over to see what people were watching. A football match was under way and not a soul was aware of anything else. Even the barman had his eyes fixed on the match, filling the glasses on the counter in front of him by intuition. The blonde woman by my side was jumping up and down in her seat as events unfolded on the screen, while a man on the other side of our tiny table breathed out smoke through flared nostrils. He had the air of an actor: lean, with well-defined features, a large Adam's apple, short-cropped grey hair and a straight back. He seemed to be the intellectual of the group, making studied, informed comments on what was happening on the pitch in a heavy, slow voice. The others murmured in agreement when he spoke.

'Who's playing?' I asked.

The woman turned and smiled again. 'It's Barcelona–Madrid,' she said, before turning back to watch.

I squinted up at the screen, making out the familiar blue-and-red and white strips of the famous football rivals. A noise like a building collapsing was coming from the speakers. I tried to make out if there was any indication of the score.

'It's a draw at the moment,' the woman said. 'I'm Paula, by the way.' And she leaned over briefly to kiss me on the cheeks before taking her place once again. I was used to Spaniards being friendly and affectionate at unexpected moments, but this was exceptional. I put it down to the excitement of the game. From the other side of the table the football expert signalled to the barman and pointed in my direction: I was without food or drink and needed attending to.

I appreciated the gesture and began wondering what I would order. The *morcilla* looked good, as did the soup. I was starving and needed a good meal to lift my spirits. I had spent weeks on my own now. Salud was still touring around Europe, and on the few occasions when she'd managed to call me I'd either not had coverage for my phone or else the batteries had run out. Our inability to talk in this age of communications was almost comical. Now I wanted to feed off the energy and warmth of the atmosphere I'd unexpectedly found in the bar. Until I felt Paula's face pressed against mine, and picked up the smell of her day-old perfume, I'd forgotten how good it was to have some company.

Up on the television something had happened to stir up passions in the bar. One man near the front was on his feet and shaking his fist at the screen, while his companions jeered and swore.

'It's the same problem as always,' the expert said. 'Weakness on the left.'

The energy that a Real Madrid–Barcelona football match produced in Spain was extraordinary. Most fans across the country would support a local team, but would then always take sides when the great clash of the season came up between these two most important clubs. Betis or Deportivo might ordinarily be the object of their devotion, but on that day almost every Spaniard was either *del Madrid* or *del Barça*. Whereas in the past the Spanish had fought battles over whether the country was a single nation or a collection of nations, now the ancient conflict was played out by twenty-two men manipulating a leather sphere with their feet. It wasn't just a football match – the very tectonic plates that had moved under Spain throughout its history were at the heart of it. Real Madrid represented centralism, Barcelona the aspirations of the regions.

Franco had recognized this and had cannily poured huge amounts of money into the Madrid side during his dictatorship. A victory for the men in white was a victory for the regime, and the Madrid team was used for propaganda purposes as a symbol of all that was good about a centralized, unified country. A Barcelona win, on the other hand, was a poke in the eye – the only non-lethal form of opposition to Franco under his brutal rule. Needless to say, all attempts were made to prevent Madrid from losing. In 1943, during the semi-finals for the King's Cup, the major tournament in Spanish football, Barcelona went on to lose the second leg against Madrid 11-1, having won the first round 3-0. The only apparent explanation for the Barça players' sudden drop in form was a visit to their dressing room before the second match by Franco's head of state security. Threats were made, and the *azulgranos* – the 'red and blues' – duly handed the match over to their rivals by a score line that has never been matched since.[15] Some say it was Franco himself who paid a visit to the dressing room.

I looked around the bar and quickly realized that this was solid Real Madrid territory. I hardly expected anything less. Burgos, the birthplace of Castile, was centralist to the core. The Basque Country was only a few miles away to the north. A couple of days earlier, a woman kidnapped by the Basque terror group ETA had been found tied up in a car in an abandoned village not far from the city. Drunken revellers, looking for a late-night party venue, had stumbled upon her in the dark and been able to set her free, but the event was still all over the papers, serving as a reminder of the violence which still marred the division at the heart of the Spanish state. Hatred ran deep.

Back home in Valencia, the Basque problem seemed distant and only ever touched us when the gunmen brought their violence to the coasts to damage the tourism industry, bring attention to their 'cause' and leave broken bodies and lives in their wake. Here we were close to the front line: Burgos was the symbol of old Castile, the dominating centre of the country; Vitoria, the Basque capital with its ancient traditions and culture and language, was only an hour's drive away to the northeast. Attempts had been made to place *Euskera* – the Basque tongue – on pretty much every branch of the world's linguistic family tree, but without success. It was a thing apart, an icon of Basque otherness. Not all Basques wanted to break with Spain, but a committed, violent minority certainly did.

The problem was that for the last years of Franco's life, ETA had been the only real effective military group fighting against the dictatorship. The communists and other organizations from the Civil War had tried to continue the struggle in one form or another after defeat in 1939, but by the early 1950s had disappeared. The emergence of the armed Basque separatists in the 1960s was a new challenge for Franco, and one which managed to cause him much damage. Admiral Luis Carrero Blanco was the Generalísimo's right-hand man and prime minister during the latter years, and his appointed successor. In the early 1970s it was clear that Franco wouldn't be around for much longer; Carrero Blanco was due to step into his shoes to ensure his legacy and continued authoritarian rule. It was ETA that put a stop to this plan, blowing the admiral up in the centre of Madrid in 1973 with a bomb so powerful his car flew a hundred feet into the air and over the roof of the building it was parked next to. Opponents of Franco were so jubilant they even composed a song about the historic event.

But despite seriously hurting the dictatorship, ETA proved it was no friend to democracy once Franco died and a constitutional monarchy was put in place in the late 1970s. In response to a general amnesty when all political prisoners were released, the group embarked on the most violent period of its campaign, staining the newborn state with the blood of hundreds of its victims, demanding nothing less than full independence for the Basque Country. Ever since, a low-level warfare had continued, sometimes the authorities, sometimes the gunmen gaining the upper hand. During the Civil War, the Basque Country had gained a large degree of autonomy, only to be ruthlessly crushed and forced back into the Spanish fold, much as Catalonia had been. But whereas the Madrid–Barcelona rivalry was today mostly restricted to football and politics, blood still flowed from the Basque wound.

What struck me as most curious about the issue of regional tensions within Spain, though, was how vehement the arguments were for the country to stay as one, and the anger and loathing you found towards Basques and Catalans among many Castilian Spaniards. From the way you heard them talk sometimes, jumping up and down and swearing about Catalonia this or *Euskadi* that, you had the sense of an intransigent husband determined to punish an unfaithful wife he couldn't stand. Divorce was out of the question: he must make her suffer and stay with him by force.

Yet despite my feeling that each party should be allowed to go its separate way if it so wished, I was glad that Spain was still a united, if squabbling, family. It was the very richness of the place, the pluralism and diversity of its cultures, languages and peoples, that made it such a vast and fascinating country. Break it up and its regions would lose the special quality that made Spain greater than the sum of its parts.

The V-shaped barman twisted past the other customers to our table to take my order. Looking back up at the television as I decided what to have, it occurred to me that it was a very odd time of year for there to be a match on. We were in the middle of summer. The football season was over. Yet this was no B-team warm-up game or friendly during the holidays. The main players were all there, the stars of each team, and passions were running so high that nothing short of the eventual outcome of the League seemed to be at stake. It was only then that I realized it was a replay – a way of filling air time during the hot low-audience months, and of giving starving fans a fix before the new season started. This match had already been played, won and lost several months ago, yet people were screaming and shouting at the screen as though it were happening live, now.

'Why are you watching this match?' I asked the barman with a laugh as he scribbled my order. 'You must already know the result.'

Without moving his head up from his notebook he gave me a look.

'Who won?' I said, the smile draining from my face.

He turned on his heel and walked away. I wondered if he hadn't heard me over the cheering and shouting. But the severity of his expression suggested otherwise. This was a hard-core football bar. It was not an opportune moment to play the innocent, however inadvertently.

I turned back to the table in time to catch Paula and the expert exchanging a look and I felt the rattling of shutters being pulled down. Breaking away from the table at half-time, I headed up the stairs of the minstrels' gallery above the kitchen to the loo, ducking my head under a low beam and trying not to scrape a Real Madrid team poster off the wall as I squeezed round a tight corner to close the door behind me. As I pissed I heard shouts and mocking laughter coming from the bar. I was surprised no one else was using this opportunity to empty their bladders before the second half. Perhaps they were frightened of missing something. But what?

Back at the table I noticed the expert had moved his chair away, closer to the others, leaving me on my own with Paula. She looked up momentarily as I sat down, but this time she didn't smile. Neither my food nor the beer I had ordered had appeared. I was beginning to feel light-headed from hunger.

'Who do you support?' Paula asked me seriously once I was back in my place. She was sucking hard on a cigarette with thick red-painted lips, bony knotted fingers ringed with bright-gold bands. The veins under her tanned skin bulged a dirty blue, while her white blouse pulled tightly over her breasts.

'No one. I just enjoy a good game.'

'What?' she said, smoke streaming out of her mouth.

'Really,' I began earnestly. 'I don't care. It's good entertainment whoever wins.' Very slowly the particles cleared in the unmoving air of the bar. Her eyes were fixed on me yet she seemed to be looking elsewhere.

'It's just a game, right?'

What failed to register at that moment was that I was not talking to an ordinary human being as such, but a football fan, and one caught up in the climax of her hit. Only one language would make sense to her at that moment and I was not speaking it. How could I not support one of the teams? It was either Madrid or Barcelona. Nothing else existed.

'You're foreign, right?' she said finally. That was it, the only explanation she could deal with. And she drew again on her cigarette before turning her back on me to stare once more at the screen. The barman came over and handed her another drink. I tried to catch his eye and remind him I was still waiting, but failed, with the shrinking feeling of being deliberately ignored. From an unexpected outsider welcomed to the party, I was becoming an undesirable element in their midst.

The second half of the match began and I sat back to watch. This time the women from the kitchen stopped cooking and came up to see the action for themselves, their hands stuffed in the front pockets of their smeared aprons. Within seconds of the game restarting, though, disaster struck and Barcelona scored. A noise like a whirling, screaming high-pitched wind filled the bar, men and women covering their faces in shock and pain. The man who had earlier shaken his fist at the television was standing again and bellowing until his cheeks flushed purple and his eyes bulged. Obscenity after obscenity was hurled at the opposing side.

I shit on your father! I shit on your fucking mother! I shit on God!

The expert, too, was enraged, leaping up from his chair and pounding his fist into his hand. Yet the constraints of his position as intellectual of the group hindered any venomous outpouring. You felt he wanted to react just like the others, but couldn't allow himself to speak in such low terms. Finally he could contain himself no more and cried out above the din, 'Hermaphrodite!'

The others fell silent and looked at him. What the hell was that?

'Sexually inadequate pervert!' the expert screamed again.

There was a groan of gradual understanding. All eyes shifted back to the television and the images of the celebrating goal-scorer, now the object of so much hate in this distant Burgos bar. Paula said nothing and simply stared at the screen, motionless. I could only marvel at how something that had already taken place, and of which everyone knew the result, could arouse such strong passions. But for the people around me, at least, it was as if they were watching the match for the very first time.

Looking away from the television, I tried to catch the barman's eye once more, but he stared resolutely at the screen in a way that seemed to suggest he wanted nothing to do with me. One of the women from the kitchen, though, the younger of the two, saw me looking and signalled to me that she would bring my order in a few minutes. I smiled and thanked her, my stomach already rumbling at the thought of tucking into something hot and flavoursome. A drink would also be welcome, but it looked like I was going to have to wait a bit longer.

As the hubbub after the goal started to die down, the expert began to speak. Paula shifted her chair away from the table to hear him.

'The trouble is lack of commitment,' I heard him say. 'These players don't live and breathe Real Madrid. They're pampered and spoilt so they don't care. It's not in their blood.'

The usual murmurs of approval and understanding came from the others.

'Too many foreigners in the team, for example,' the expert went on. 'They cannot understand what this is all about. You spend millions bringing good players into the side, but what happens? This. A Barcelona match is just another pay day for them, win or lose. For us it's life or death.'

Everyone nodded in silent agreement.

'I blame the foreigners,' the expert concluded. 'Get rid of them.'

There was a cheer of assent and inwardly I groaned. I was being excluded from the group. But I had food coming and was hungry: I decided to sit tight.

The match restarted, Madrid trying hard to score an equalizer but failing. Finally a movement on the far side of the room caught my eye and I saw the young woman from the kitchen coming towards me with a bowl of soup and some bread. She placed them down in front of me, the smell of garlic and spicy chorizo rising up with the steam into my face. Although it was boiling hot outside, the air conditioning was on full blast in the bar and I was beginning to feel a slight chill.

Picking up a piece of bread, I was just about to dip it in the soup when the barman appeared from behind and lunged his thick arm down to grab the side of the bowl.

'That's not your order,' he said sharply. And before I could say anything he had lifted the offending article away from me and was carrying it back to the kitchen, scolding the girl as he did so. Perplexed, I stared at the one small piece of bread in my hand that I'd been left with.

The football match continued ever more frustratingly for the Madrid supporters as their team struggled but failed again and again to equalize. Then, in the dying minutes of the game, Barcelona scored once more and defeat was assured.

Real Madrid had lost. Just as they had when this match had originally taken place. Nothing had changed. For the people in the bar, though, the disappointment was as intense as it had been the first time.

From the counter the barman held out the remote control and with a flick of the wrist switched the television off, leaving a momentary hiatus in the noise level. People began to lift them-selves from their seats. Perhaps, I thought, now that it's over I might get my food. The customers started to leave, pushing their chairs back with a scrape on the ash-stained floor, barely bothering to say goodbye to their friends and companions, too depressed even to nod or smile. A few looks were cast in my direction as they plodded out, twisting past the crates of beer still blocking the entrance. I averted my eyes, sensing that in some way I was being blamed for their team's defeat. A non-supporter was in their midst: the fault was mine.

Among the last to go were Paula and the expert. After their initial warmth to me, I simply didn't exist any more. Fair enough, I thought – I'd only come in looking for a bite to eat. Friendly company – albeit brief – had been a bonus. But as they got up, a half-empty beer bottle sitting on the edge of the table went tumbling over, spilling its contents on to the table and over my lap. Jumping up, I started wiping myself down, reaching for the thin paper serviettes Spanish bars keep in plastic boxes on the tables. I looked up, expecting the incident to produce some kind of final interchange between us, but they simply walked away. No word of apology or regret. I watched them pass out of the door and into the street, then turn and head off in opposite directions. I was on my own. The bar was deserted.

'Come on, we're closing.'

The barman came over with a cloth and started wiping up the spilt beer, making me feel as if I was the one responsible for giving him this extra work.

I thought for a second about remonstrating, asking for my food finally to be brought to me, but decided against it. I was being pushed out – that was it. I would gain nothing but more hostility and perhaps the ignominy of being physically ejected. I picked up my beer-stained bag and walked to the door. The lights were already off, and the barman was hurriedly placing chairs on table tops to allow the girl to sweep. Outside it was still light and sunny, being no later than mid-afternoon, but here in this bar it seemed like five in the morning after a particularly long and busy shift. The girl with the broom stared at me as though querying why I was still there and I moved to the door, scrambling out as I had scrambled in.

Before I could adjust my eyes to the light, the door behind me was slammed shut and locked. I stood still for a moment on the pavement, hungry and lost. In the sky above, high winds were pushing the clouds into distorted forms, crashing into one another and stretching in odd, scattered shapes.

From an open window somewhere I could hear the sound of the old song about Spain and the costas, 'Y Viva España'. I tried to remember the words from my childhood that everyone used to sing, about how wonderful Spain was, how the people were so nice and friendly.

'*La la la-la-la-la lah,*' I sang along under my breath as the emptiness welled up inside me. And I walked away from the bar, away from the centre of the city and out, down the drab streets towards the suburbs and the country, not knowing where my feet would take me.

España por favor. España por favor.

12

Unamuno and Millán Astray

*F*ew countries in the world are made up of such a rich mixture of peoples as Spain. Iberians, Celts, Basques, Alans, Suevi, Phoenicians, Greeks, Carthaginians, Jews, Romans, Vandals, Visigoths, Byzantines, Arabs, Berbers, Persians, Slavs, Franks and Germans can all contribute to the genetic and cultural make-up of an average Spaniard. Typical of the contradictory nature of the place, though, the Spanish give great importance to the idea of 'Spanishness' – referring both to national character and ethnicity. The day set aside for its celebration is 12 October, the day Columbus (Genoese? Portuguese? Perhaps Ibizan, according to one of the latest theories) touched land on the far side of the Atlantic. Now they simply call it *El Día de la Hispanidad*. In 1936, just three months into the Civil War, it was more usually and bizarrely referred to as *El Día de la Raza* – the festival of the Spanish Race.

If Lorca, shot two months earlier, was the greatest poet and playwright in Spain at the time, Miguel de Unamuno was the country's greatest intellectual and philosopher: a Catholic and an admirer of Kierkegaard. White-haired, and with a clipped white beard, he looked not unlike the elderly Freud, with his small round glasses, elegant suits and hunched shoulders, hardened after a life spent with books.

In his early seventies now, he was at the tail end of his academic career, having been professor of Greek at Salamanca University and now holding the post of rector of this, one of the oldest universities in Christian Europe. A Basque, he had spent most of his life at Salamanca, where he was regarded as something of a national treasure: a renowned Spanish writer, admired internationally, who had often been at the forefront of the galloping intellectual evolution in Spain over the past half-century. He moved to the political centre after being a member of the Socialist Party when young, becoming a celebrated liberal in the 1920s during the dictatorship of Primo de Rivera, who exiled him to the Canary Islands for his attacks on the king and himself. Primo de Rivera finally gave in to pressure and pardoned Unamuno in 1924, but the proud philosopher took himself to Paris and then to the town of Hendaye, just over the border in France, refusing to set foot in Spain again until the dictator's fall from power in 1930.

Now, in the early days of the Civil War, the old man seemed to have completed his political journey from Left to Right by declaring in favour of Franco and the rebellion, believing the Nationalist movement would restore order to the Republic, an institution he had greatly supported at its birth five years earlier. Like many moderate Catholics at the time, the sight of churches being burned by anarchists while the Popular Front government appeared to stand by perhaps blinded him at first to the brutality of those he backed. But in the early days of Franco's rule in Salamanca, there was repression all around him which he could not ignore. His eyes were beginning to open.

There was great pomp surrounding the celebrations of

El Día de la Raza in Salamanca in 1936. Only days before, the city, beautiful and austere, home to the finest square in all Spain, had become the headquarters for Franco, now officially declared *generalísimo* and head of state by the other Nationalist generals. United behind one leader and courting recognition from abroad – principally Nazi Germany, fascist Italy and the Vatican – all attempts were being made to give an air of legitimacy to this rebel movement. The university ceremonial hall was used to provide some of the pageantry associated with past kings and rulers of Spain: ancient tapestries hung from the walls and the dons dressed in red, yellow, light-blue and dark-blue robes, representing the schools of law, medicine, literature and science. And a large photograph of Franco hung from the front wall where once a royal portrait might have been. The heavyweights of Salamancan society were there: professors, deans, judges, Unamuno presiding over the ceremony as university rector, with Franco's wife Carmen Polo seated beside him on the presidential dais along with the bishop of Salamanca. Sitting in the crowd were a number of blue-shirted Falangists, armed with machine-guns, and the founder of the Spanish Foreign Legion – and soon to be Unamuno's nemesis – General José Millán Astray.

Millán Astray was Franco's mentor, a hysterical, one-eyed, one-armed sadist who coined the unforgettable battle cry, '*¡Viva la muerte!*' 'Long Live Death!'. He'd founded the Legión back in 1920 on the model of the French Foreign Legion, taking on the young Major Franco as his second-in-command. The two had quickly transformed the rabble of ex-convicts who volunteered for the new force into the most ruthless section of the Spanish Army, brutally repressing any unrest among the local population of Spain's Protectorate in northern Morocco. Spanish legionaries were true *machos* Latin-style, their shirts open at the chest, never marching like ordinary soldiers but running in unison, laughing in the face of death and with scant regard for human life or suffering. A legionary was effectively married to the Legión and was pretty much expected to die in service: recruits were often referred to as *los novios de la muerte* – the bridegrooms of death – and were subjected to a system of violent punishments. Meanwhile, anyone who came in their way was given short shrift, the favourite way of despatching victims being to slit their throats. The men, women and children of Moroccan rebel villages were often given the Legión treatment, with many resultant massacres. In 1922 the duquesa de la Victoria organized a group of volunteer nurses for the Legión and was offered a tribute of thanks – a basket of roses, in the centre of which sat the severed heads of two Moroccan rebels. The dictator Primo de Rivera was once shocked while inspecting a battalion of legionaries to find them with severed Moroccan heads on the ends of their bayonets.

Much of the character of the Legión stemmed from Millán Astray himself, who formed the force in his own image – or rather a romanticized version of his own image. He was married to a woman who'd sworn a lifelong chastity vow, and there was more than a hint of eroticism in his obsession with death and manliness. Many of his ideas about soldiering came from a confused account of the samurai way of life found in a book called *Bushido: The Soul of Japan* by Inazo Nitobe, an international bestseller published in 1899 and one of the favourite books of President Teddy Roosevelt. Millán Astray claimed to have translated the book from English into Spanish, and he treated it like a bible that provided not just the inspiration for how to be a warrior, but a whole philosophy of life. What Millán Astray probably didn't know was that Nitobe was a Christian Japanese married to an American Quaker, who had been educated in English and, as one expert has put it, was 'in almost every way imaginable . . . the least qualified Japanese of his age to have been informing anyone of Japan's history and culture'.[16] Many of his ideas were a curious fusion of Christian and Japanese thinking, resulting from the distortion of ordinary Confucian values. But Millán Astray thought he was on to the real thing, and the Spanish Foreign Legion was the product of this twisted journey of samurai practice through the hands first of a Japanese Christian convert and then of a Spanish maniac. The result was a savage body of disciplined fighting men, their eye-patch-wearing founder, mutilated with the scars of his many battles, screaming at them to die like heroes.

At least that was the image they presented. However, in a highly critical report following a rare but devastating defeat by Moroccan rebels in 1921, a Spanish officer attributed the legendary bravado of the Legión to a cocktail of alcohol, morphine and cocaine, while their leader was described as a 'theatrical clown . . . who trembles when he hears the whistles of bullets and flees his post'.

In 1936 Millán Astray was no longer officially in command of the Legión, having been promoted to general. But as its founder, and as a sycophantic follower of his erstwhile subordinate Franco, whom he saw as an almost Christ-like saviour of Spain, he was still a prominent figure and was now head of the Nationalist propaganda department. There was a charged atmosphere in the Nationalist zone at the time – the disasters of the first few days of the rising had been forgotten in the wake of Franco's astonishing victories as his forces marched up through Extremadura and the west of the country to unify the northern and southern Nationalist-held territories. Blood flowed freely as political opponents – real or imagined – were despatched in their thousands. Almost anyone could fall under suspicion, the principal bogeymen being 'Reds' as a whole; Freemasons – for their perceived support of the Republic; and advocates of autonomy for the Basque Country and Catalonia – which usually extended to Basques and Catalans in general. But often the killers on the Nationalist side – as on the Republican side – were not even this discerning. Another propaganda official, Captain Gonzalo de Aguilar, boasted that he had shot six of his own innocent farm workers at the outbreak of the rebellion, *pour encourager les autres*. This from a man who thought all the country's problems were due to the introduction of modern drains – the usual illnesses weren't killing off the working classes as they once had.

Meanwhile this nostalgic harking back to the Middle Ages was taking a less violent but no less anachronistic form in the same building where Millán Astray's propaganda department was housed. There a Hindu alchemist called Sarvapoldi Hammaralt was beavering away in the university's chemistry labs, trying to produce gold for Franco, having persuaded the authorities that he had the formula for making the precious metal so long as it was for a good cause. He did help the propaganda department read messages written in invisible ink, and carried out experiments on the bodies of dead Moroccan soldiers, but never produced the promised gold and eventually had to escape after accusations of spying for the British.

It was against this backdrop, in October 1936, that the 'play' of Unamuno's clash with Millán Astray was enacted in the Salamanca University ceremonial hall on *El Día de la Raza*. It was witnessed by a man called Luis Portillo, a lecturer in law at the university and a poet who would later flee to Republican Spain and eventually settle in Britain, where he would father a future leading member of the Conservative Party. His account of the clash was later published in London by the magazine *Horizon*, edited by Cyril Connolly.

After Unamuno opened the ceremony, a couple of speeches were made on the current situation, about how the Civil War was a purifying experience from which the gold of pure Spain would emerge, having cleansed itself of the enemy or 'anti-Spain', as the Republican side was often characterized. Then Millán Astray, thin and battle-scarred, got up from the public benches to speak, to the cries of '¡Viva la muerte!' from his cronies. After branding all supporters of the Republican government as criminals guilty of armed rebellion and high treason, he started warming to his theme.

'The Basque Country and Catalonia are two cancers in the body of the nation,' he boomed. 'Fascism, which is Spain's health-bringer, will know how to exterminate them both, cutting into the live healthy flesh like a resolute surgeon free from false sentimentality. And since the healthy flesh is the soil, the diseased flesh the people who dwell on it, fascism and the army will eradicate the people and restore the soil to the sacred national realm.'

Perhaps shocked to hear the armed forces so blatantly given a role as oppressors and murderers of ordinary civilians, the public remained silent. From his presidential chair, Unamuno, who had not been planning to speak, began scribbling notes.

'Every socialist,' Millán Astray continued, 'every Republican, every one of them without exception – and needless to say every communist – is a rebel against the National government, which will soon be recognized by the totalitarian states who are aiding us, in spite of France – democratic France – and perfidious England.

'And then, or even sooner, when Franco wants it, and with the help of the gallant Moors, though they wrecked my body only yesterday, today deserve the gratitude of my soul, for they are fighting for Spain against the Spaniards . . . I mean the bad Spaniards . . . because they are giving their lives in defence of Spain's sacred religion, as is proved by their attending field mass, escorting the Caudillo and pinning holy medallions and Sacred Hearts to their burnouses...'

Carried away by his own rhetoric and contradictions, the general floundered.

'*¡Arriba España!*' came the cry from the Falangists around him.

Clinging to this lifeline, Millán Astray took up the call.

'*¡España!*' he shouted.

'*¡Una!*' the crowd answered in mechanical response to the Nationalist rallying cry.

'*¡España!*' he repeated.

'*¡Grande!*' came the reply.

'*¡España!*'

'*¡Libre!*'

Inspired by the general and responding to the heightened atmosphere in the hall, the Falangists rose to their feet and, holding out their right arms in fascist salute towards the photo on the wall, cried out, 'Franco! Franco! Franco!'

There was a lull after this commotion, and as people sat down again attention turned, perhaps with a little embarrassment, to the elderly philosopher sitting on the dais. How would the great man react to this very unacademic behaviour in his sacred university? Very slowly, Unamuno rose to his feet and began to speak.

'All of you are hanging on my words,' he said. 'You all know me and are aware that I am unable to remain silent. I have not learned to do so in seventy-three years of my life. And now I do not wish to learn it any more. At times to be silent is to lie. For silence can be interpreted as acquiescence. I could not survive a divorce between my conscience and my word, always well-mated partners. I will be brief. Truth is most true when naked, free from embellishments and verbiage.

'I want to comment on the speech – to give it that name – of General Millán Astray who is here among us. Let us waive the personal affront implied in the sudden outburst of vituperation against Basques and Catalans in general. I was born in Bilbao in the midst of the bombardments of the Second Carlist War. Later I wedded myself to this city of Salamanca which I love deeply, yet never forgetting my native town. The bishop, whether he likes it or not, is a Catalan from Barcelona.'

Unamuno paused for a second. The bishop at his side appeared uncomfortable at being reminded of his place of birth.

'Just now,' the philosopher continued, 'I heard the necrophiliac and senseless cry *Viva la muerte* – long live death. To me it sounds the same as *Muera la vida* – death to life. And I, who have spent my life shaping paradoxes which aroused the uncomprehending anger of others, I must tell you as an expert I find this outlandish paradox repellent. Since it was proclaimed in homage to the last speaker I can only explain it to myself by supposing that it was addressed to him, though in an excessively strange and tortuous form, as a testimonial to his being himself a symbol of death. And another thing: General Millán Astray is a cripple. Let it be said without any slighting undertone. He is a war invalid. So was Cervantes. But extremes do not make the norm. Unfortunately there are all too many cripples in Spain today. And soon there will be even more of them if God does not come to our aid. It pains me to think that General Millán Astray should dictate the patterns of mass psychology. That would be appalling. A cripple who lacks the spiritual greatness of Cervantes – a man, not a superman, virile and complete in spite of his mutilations – a cripple, I said, who lacks that loftiness of mind is wont to seek ominous relief in seeing mutilation around him . . . General Millán Astray would like to create Spain anew – a negative creation – in his own image and likeness, and for that reason he wishes to see Spain crippled, as he unwittingly made clear.'

As he paused, Millán Astray exploded. Jumping to his feet he screamed, '*¡Muera la inteligencia!*' – Death to Intelligence!

A fascist poet and journalist in the audience, José María Pemán, tried to correct him. 'No. Long Live Intelligence! Death to bad intellectuals!'

With tensions quickly rising, the armed Falangists around the general took up the cry, unholstering their pistols amid the shouting. One pointed his machine-gun at Unamuno's head. A number of the university professors in their colourful gowns moved to protect him. Arguments flared up around the hall over academics who had disappeared or been shot over the previous months. Above the din Unamuno spoke once again, back straight and arms folded.

'This is the temple of the intellect and I am its high priest. It is you who are profaning its sacred precincts. I have always, whatever the proverb might say, been a prophet in my own land. You will win but you will not convince – *vencereis pero no convenceréis*. You will win because you possess more than enough brute force, but you will not convince because to convince means to persuade. And in order to persuade you would need what you lack – reason and right in the struggle. I consider it futile to exhort you to think of Spain.'

His arms falling to his sides, his voice lowered to a more resigned tone. 'I have finished,' he said.

The apoplectic Millán Astray was unable to counter with any eloquence and merely pointed to Franco's wife, shouting, 'Take the Señora's arm!'

This Unamuno did, and the two walked out of the hall and the hullabaloo, the philosopher dignified and pale, the dictator's wife stunned and silent. Had she not been there Unamuno might not have left the university alive.

When Franco heard later what had happened he wanted Unamuno to be shot, but embarrassment over the disappearance of Lorca was still high and in the end the elderly academic's international reputation probably saved him. Nonetheless he was sacked as rector and placed under virtual house arrest at his Salamanca home, where he died two and a half months later of a stroke, on the last day of 1936. Paradoxical to the last, this former sympathizer of Franco, now an implacable enemy of the brutality of the Nationalists, was hailed at his funeral as a Falangist hero.

As a result of the clash, however, Franco became aware of the danger of having such a volatile character as Millán Astray as head of propaganda. He kept him in place for some time afterwards, but eventually had him replaced. It was the beginning of Millán Astray's gradual fall from grace. By the time he died in 1954, Franco refused even to attend his funeral. For both the philosopher and the legionary, men obsessed in their own ways with death, the confrontation between them proved to be their last great performance.

13

Saragossa

*F*rom his accent, the little man with the white hat seemed to be from Cádiz, just like the woman who had asked me the same question moments before.

'What time is the Madrid train leaving?'

I assumed they were together, having caught sight of them hanging around at the back of the queue, and put the repeated question down to nerves about travelling or fear of missing the train. As before, I turned and pointed to the screens on the other side of the ticket hall where the departure times were clearly shown and indicated the information he sought. He gave a brief smile and then hurried off, rather nervously, I thought. With hindsight I seemed to be partially aware of a shadow passing behind me as I spoke to him, but perhaps my mind was filling in the gaps afterwards.

After a few more minutes' waiting in the queue it was my turn at the counter. I wanted to see if I could change my ticket and travel that evening to Madrid rather than wait till the following day. I had come to Saragossa to visit nearby Belchite, a small town in the Aragonese desert destroyed in the Civil War and whose ruins had been left untouched ever since. Now, though, I didn't want to spend the night here: Saragossa was an ugly, dry place with little charm, although, in my experience, the people were friendly.

'There'll be a charge,' the girl behind the counter said. It was then that I noticed something was wrong. The bag on the trolley – it looked like mine, but wasn't it slightly rougher-looking, and paler? These thoughts flashed through my mind at the speed of a camera shutter – a second later I realized that it wasn't my bag, just one that looked a bit like it. Even then I still took time to register what had happened. Perhaps I'd picked up my neighbour's bag instead of my own. I looked behind me to see a portly, sweaty man in a business suit holding a black briefcase in his left hand. No, not that. I looked to my left and right. Nothing. Understanding finally dawned. I opened the bag I'd thought was mine: it was completely empty. Someone had done a switch and robbed me of everything: credit cards, passport, wallet, cash.

'My bag,' I said, almost swallowing the word in shock. The girl behind the counter looked impatient. I was holding up the queue. 'I've been robbed,' I said. 'They've stolen my bag.'

There was no response. She didn't deal with robberies, only selling and changing tickets. Like grinding rusty machinery, my mind started piecing together what must have happened. The Cádiz couple, who were now nowhere to be seen, had been distracting me, turning my attention momentarily away from the bag on the trolley while an accomplice behind my back swapped it for one that looked similar. Annoyed by the old man's question – I'd already explained to his wife – I hadn't noticed a thing, my mind wandering back and forth from what had happened during the day to where I was hoping to be that night. Anywhere but the present. And now the bag was gone.

The businessman was scowling at me for holding things up. I looked desperately around the ticket hall for a sign of the little couple. For an awful moment, though, anyone and everyone might have been guilty. I felt I was surrounded by thieves, all trying to take something from me.

'Didn't you notice anything?' I said to the others in the queue. No one stirred. They were all lost in their own thoughts and worlds, just as I had been.

'Please,' I said, turning back to the ticket girl, 'call security.'

As though the effort might kill her, she lifted her arm and pointed sleepily to the security guards' office on the other side of the hall. I should go and report to them myself if I thought there was something wrong. But in the meantime I was keeping people waiting, so if I didn't mind . . .

I sprinted across the hall. There might still be time to catch the thieves if we hurried. They couldn't have got far. For a second I oscillated between looking for them myself and getting help from the guards. But I might not be able to answer for myself if I did manage to find them on my own.

The guards' office was closed and no one responded to my pounding on the door. Looking around, I caught sight of someone in a blue uniform with handcuffs and a gun hanging from his belt.

'Please,' I said, running up to him. 'My bag's been stolen.' And I explained what had happened.

Far from bursting into action, though, the guard – a young man with a premature paunch and thin beard meant to make him look older – pulled out a small clipboard from inside his jacket and started jotting down some notes.

'What are you doing?' I said, exasperated.

'I'll need to write a report,' he said.

Suppressing an urge to strangle him, I wondered aloud if going after the criminals might not be a better idea.

'No chance of catching them now,' he said with a cynical, knowing smile. 'They're professionals.'

And did part of their scam involve buying him off? I wondered.

'Come with me,' the guard said. 'The office is just over here.'

I knew I was going to need his pieces of paper if I wanted to report any of this later on, but images of the Andalusians scrambling away with my things, then raiding my bank account, selling my credit-card details and identity to the mafia – whatever – flooded my mind. I needed to get out there and run after them. Or just run, burn off the anger coursing through my body. Not sit quietly in a smoky office while someone looking like a heavy-metal fan in a uniform took down my details.

Without saying a word I took off, leaving him behind with his clipboard as I ran to the main entrance, ignoring his calls for me to return. There was just a chance I might catch sight of them. But the late-evening rush hour was in full force, people streaming through the main doors to catch their commuter trains to the outlying towns, or the last AVE to Madrid, and I could barely move through the crush. My eyes darted in all directions as I scanned the crowd. If only I could catch sight of that stupid white hat again.

Outside, the evening lights were coming on, determined bodies pushing forward against me in a tidal wave of end-of-work stress. I was going in the wrong direction, I was in their way. Rage flared as I brushed heavily past bulky shoulders and linked arms, handbags and laden trolleys. Feet pattered past me like an army of ants. No way through, no one to help. I knew the Cádiz couple had gone by now. Out of the building and away, slipping down side alleys, squeezing on to a bus, counting my money. Only an hour before I'd been to a cash machine and taken out a larger amount than usual to invite Kiki for dinner once I arrived in Madrid. Now someone else would be feasting at my expense.

I crouched down against a wall as the crowds passed me by, rushing and charging while I sank into a quiet hole. In the end I knew none of it really mattered: the credit cards could be cancelled and new ones sent out, a new passport could be issued, and the money – well, the money was gone. There was no way of getting it back now. I felt exposed, though, and cheated, cursing myself for being so unaware that I could be robbed from under my very nose. My guts churned as I repeatedly played out how I might have caught them had I only turned round at the right moment.

I began to realize there was something more pressing to be dealt with, though. I had my train ticket for the following morning – there was no chance of changing it now – but apart from loose change, I had nothing to get by with that night. No money and passport meant no hotel and nothing to eat. I was stranded, and facing a hungry night in Saragossa.

For a moment I thought of calling friends for help. Perhaps someone could wire some money to me – but the credit had run out on my mobile phone and the banks would be firmly closed till the morning. I knew no one in Saragossa, not a single contact there, nobody I could call on in an emergency. Salud was abroad and out of reach, most of my friends were away on holiday. Even if I could get in touch with them they would be unable to do anything. I had nothing but what I was standing in, a small leather rucksack filled with dirty clothes, and four euros sixty-six in my trouser pocket.

A few moments later most of that, too, had gone after a quick call to the bank from a phone box. This time the man on the other end had wanted to offer sympathy but I had to cut him short, fearful that my change would run out before the cards were stopped. I stepped out into the oven-heat of late evening, the last light of day fading behind faceless buildings. Still the rush, still the crowds.

I drifted away from the station towards the centre of the city, as if a solution might be found by the act of moving. My legs ached as I came down from the adrenaline rush, my senses aware of little more than the heavy pacing of my feet on the pavement.

Energy seemed to drain from me as though from a leaking tap. It wasn't the money, or the thought of sleeping rough. Rather, it was that I'd been picked out as a target; I felt vulnerable and alone. I longed to slip, ghost-like, through the streets and houses and disappear.

Headlamps scrambled in my vision into a mesh of streaming fireflies. As I inhaled the exhaust fumes I felt a tightening, dipping sensation in my stomach, my lungs objecting to the foul hot air. Without thinking I turned off the main avenue and into the dark, shadows leaping out from the gaps between the cars parked in tight rows down the length of the tunnel-like street.

An elderly man stepped out of a doorway, and with dulled reactions I crashed into his side as he turned in my direction. With a start I looked up to catch his shocked white-haired head glaring up at me indignantly.

'*Pero ¡bueno!*'

'I'm sorry,' I stammered after an embarrassing pause. Wires crossing in my head, my Spanish deserted me momentarily, a twisted combination of other half-forgotten languages trying to pass through my lips.

'I'm sorry.'

'What, are you blind or something?'

'I just—'

'Look where you're fucking going!'

And he charged off in a huff, staring back at me hatefully as I stood motionless, rubbing my arm where it had crashed into his shoulder. I could still smell the sweat on him, the sharpness of tobacco on his breath.

I walked on, down and away from the noise of the main drag,

my eyes glancing up at the dirty, cracked blue and white tiles beneath rusty iron balconies jutting out from the buildings above. Strips of posters that had been eroded from the walls by the sun and wind criss-crossed in white and multi-coloured lines, half an eye from a politician seeking re-election, or the corner of full painted lips seductively selling kitchen bleach, just visible against the grimy coating on the stone walls. A young boy held a felt tip against one of the houses and tried to scrawl a word or a design, but threw the pen down into the gutter when it failed to make a mark. In the shadows of scaffolding erected against the facade of one of the buildings, a couple of bearded men with bloodshot eyes wearing smeared grey vests arranged pieces of cardboard and paper beneath them to provide a comfortable space in which to drink and spend the night. They laughed as I passed by, with forced retching cackles.

Smells drifted out of open kitchen windows from dozens of dinners being prepared, the steam lifting the promise of fried garlic, fresh bread and thick red wine into the early night air. I jingled the three inadequate coins left in my pocket and sighed, trying to push from my mind the fantasy of some stranger pitying me and taking me in for the night. Perhaps, I thought, I should just knock on someone's door. I remembered how one night in England, years before, a young man had done just that to me. It was late – gone two o'clock – and he was walking back home from a night out with his friends. But, and this was the problem, he had no money for a taxi and desperately needed to go to the toilet. I let him in and showed him the bathroom, then went and made him a cup of tea, amused at the surreal situation of having a stranger shitting in my house in the early hours of the morning.

'You're a life-saver,' he'd said into his mug before rushing back into the dark. I'd been on the point of offering him a lift home.

The problem was, at that moment I lacked his nerve.

The streets and buildings came to an abrupt end and I found myself next to a wide avenue and park area that lined the banks of the River Ebro, shadowy trees stretching along the road in the pale-pink street-lights. A stone bench beckoned and I sat down. There were fewer people here: the occasional jogger, women walking their dogs. I placed my rucksack beneath my head and lay down, careful that the few remaining items in my pockets didn't fall out, trying to ignore the increasing complaints coming from my empty stomach. My limbs felt heavy against the rough stone, and my eyes flickered, unable to close properly as the robbery replayed itself ceaselessly inside my head.

The visit to Belchite earlier in the day seemed distant now, but the memory of the ruins returned to my mind: a littered landscape of destruction untouched and unrepaired in order to serve as a permanent reminder of the sweeping chaos of the Civil War. The shattered windows, pock-marked walls and crumbling roofs had been left as they had stood almost seventy years earlier, when Franco's men gave up their defence of the little Aragonese town and tried to break through the circle of besieging Republican forces and get back to Nationalist territory. Out of six hundred, only around two hundred made it; the others were hunted down in the bleak desert landscape.

Belchite was one of the more visible remains of Spain's fratricidal conflict, a reminder of the power of bullets, bombs and artillery against ancient stone and human life. The battle which had led to its destruction was one of several launched by the Republic against Franco as a means of diverting his troops away from the north coast, where over the spring and summer months of 1937 he had been steadily and methodically capturing territory that was cut off from the main Republican areas in the east and centre of the country. Madrid had held out against Franco after a lengthy and bloody siege at the end of 1936 and was still in Republican hands, although pressed against the front line in a tense stalemate. Nationalist forces, meanwhile, their energies now concentrated in the north and with considerable assistance from German and Italian troops, had successfully taken first the Basque Country, then Santander, and were soon to capture the remaining Republican region on the northern coast, Asturias.

Brilliantly thought out though the Republican diversionary offensive in Aragon was, the assault had been blighted by chaos and lack of coordination: artillery weapons couldn't be fired because the wrong-sized shells had been sent; infantry columns had to stop dead in their tracks just miles from their objectives through insufficient back-up; lines were stretched; communications broke down. And as with most of these assaults, Franco's forces were able to launch a strong counter-attack after initial defeats. By the end of August, the Republicans' attempt to conquer Saragossa, once an important centre of anarchism, had got bogged down in the small town of Belchite, just over thirty kilometres from the Aragonese capital. Belchite had to be taken at all costs, more for reasons of morale than strategic importance, and Republican dignitaries would come up to watch proceedings from a safe distance as street by street and house by house their soldiers inched forwards.

The church of San Martín had once been a fine example of Mudéjar architecture. Complex geometric patterns in brick had wound up its octagonal bell tower and horseshoe arches had lined the nave. This place of worship became a fortress during the siege, however, being the strongest point from which to defend the town's northern approach. The Republicans pounded it relentlessly. It had never been touched since.

From a distance it looked as though the elements had worn it away. Walking towards it through the rubble and smashed, deserted streets, I'd noticed a battered cone sitting on top of the tower like a child's party hat, falling to one side as though the festivities had gone on too long and tiredness was beginning to set in. But as I got closer, I realized that the almost fuzzy effect came from the number of bullets that had been fired into the brickwork. It had been shot up to such an extent that it seemed to be melting in the heat, its edges losing their sharpness as it slowly disintegrated. Except that the process had been frozen, captured in the moment before collapse. Only odd glimpses of the original design work were visible, the rest shattered by the thousands of bullets and mortar shells sent hurtling into the walls. At the entrance, great wooden doors leaned precariously as though about to fall, the studded iron plates that covered them now peeling with rust. On one door someone had painted a homage: 'Old town of Belchite, young boys no longer walk in your fields, nor shall we hear again the *jotas* that our fathers sang.'

Trade-union flyers were stuck to the walls, while on the outside of an old shop opposite you could still make out the words of advertisements painted in strong bold letters. Belchite had obviously been a pretty place once, a quiet little town caught in the front line of civil war. The mayor had been killed on one of the first days of the attack, a mortar blast knocking him dead as he held a rifle in his hands. Only days before he'd written to Nationalist troops in Saragossa that there was no hurry in coming to relieve them. 'If death reaches us before you do it will be welcome.'

The colours now were all ochres, oranges and greys. Wooden beams that had once supported ceilings and floors leaned forlornly out of sighing walls. In the desolate silence, the only sound was the bells on the flocks of sheep grazing in the nearby fields of dry grass. Some houses were shattered or were just empty holes, others still retained a pristine and elegant facade but with the rest of the building missing, like a man with the back of his head shot off. Occasionally you caught a glimpse of scraps of faded blue wallpaper on the inside of what had been a bedroom or parlour – rare sparks of colour in a largely monochrome world. Beyond the town, at the end of a broken street, the flat Martian landscape of the Aragonese desert stretched for miles. In the overgrown central square the old village fountain still stood, dark paint flaking off its rusty heart. This would once have been a congregation point, a place of life. Now the ruins were mostly used by kids from the new town half a mile away, vodka bottles, empty cigarette packets and the smell of piss bearing witness to their late-night parties, despite warnings that the place was unsafe.

And so I had walked around for hours, hot and salty, the sound of a distant afternoon funfair in the new town blowing in on the wind. There were no other visitors to the ruins that day: Belchite was both a reminder and a symbol of forgetting.

Lifting myself up from the bench with a swirling head, trying to grip something that might give me balance, I wondered about going home, back to the farm, leaving all this, the downward path I seemed to have set myself upon. But thoughts of return left me just as empty. I would have nothing but questions and doubts if I went back now. Besides, I had a ticket to Madrid for the following day. That would be my next destination. After that, I would see.

With the setting of the sun the temperature had dropped rapidly, and I felt a chill about my upper arms as I sat in the dark. The atmosphere of the riverbank had changed as well – it was now populated not by the joggers of earlier but by single men walking alone, casting hurried, nervous glances at one another in the shadows with a curious mixture of fear, desire and aggression. As I watched, one of them, a short, elderly man, walked over and sat next to me on the bench. He let out a deep breath, then, staring out across the river, shuffled on his backside towards me and, before I could react, roughly placed his hand on my crotch. I stood bolt upright and looked down at a horrified face, dark whiskers sprouting from plump greasy cheeks.

'*¡Subnormal!*' he shouted at me before I could say anything. I picked up my rucksack and walked away, heart beating with a weary thud.

I wandered aimlessly through the streets for another couple of hours until I found myself unexpectedly in the centre of the old quarter, in the alleyways surrounding the city's imposing cathedral. Bars were already starting to close, the main square deserted now. For a while I stood still, watching the emptying scene from a shady corner of an abandoned building. As in Belchite earlier in the day, there seemed to be piles of rubble everywhere where houses had once stood, only here it was neglect, not bombs, that had brought destruction. As the finely dressed of Saragossa headed off to their flats and country villas for the night, a different population moved in to fill the vacuum: men with large boots, long hair and skin-tight black trousers, their shoulders hunched as they swung bottles by their sides, talking in low voices. The sharp sweet smell of dope drifted in the air. Hidden by the darkness, I felt unable to move, my nerves vibrating like a tuning fork.

From across the square came the sound of shutters being pulled down over the doors and windows of restaurants and bars, their metallic echo like rattling chains. In the distance, occasional cars drifted down barren avenues. From the street I could see lights going off, curtains being drawn across open windows to let the cool air in and keep the night out. I pulled a dirty shirt from my rucksack and put it on over my T-shirt. But still I stayed in my spot, immobilized and fearful, unable to decide where to go or what I should do. I was tired – the idea of walking all night seemed less attractive now. But if I was to rest it would have to be somewhere safe. There was an uneasy air of threat and danger about the world I was watching.

I leaned my head against the broken plaster of the wall that was supporting me, half closing my eyes as I tried to find the energy to move on, a childish hope telling me that if I wished hard enough everything would be all right again. I ignored it, resolving to stay where I was until I fell asleep. There was no point going on any more.

'*Buenas noches.*'

A voice spoke behind me. Wearily I turned and saw two policemen standing in the shadows, peering at me inquisitively. Long truncheons hung from their hips, black leather holsters wrapped around their pistols. One of them had a torchlight and was shining it around my face.

I sensed that in their minds I was likely to be either a dealer or a buyer. At that time of night in the city centre there seemed to be few other categories of people about. I had no passport, so if they asked for identification I was going to be in trouble. Memories flooded back of being arrested by the Moroccan soldiers near Ceuta.

They stared at me for a moment, trying to work out what type of a person I was: a pause before either striking down or letting me go.

Perhaps through tiredness, or a feeling of not really caring what would happen, I did something I might not ordinarily have done – I took a chance; I simply turned and walked away from them without a word, around a corner and down a narrow street in as relaxed a fashion as I could. For a second I could hear feet behind me as they took a few steps to follow me, still undecided as to what or who I was. Would they pounce? I was betting on them assuming I was a lost tourist. I tried to blot them from my mind, all the while looking for corners to turn into and ways of losing them. Eventually I reached a street lined with trees. Crossing into it I started to run, not looking back, but in my mind's eye watching the two policemen doubling back on themselves as they decided I was not worth the chase and heading off to seek a larger kill. Still I ran, just to make sure: running from everything that had happened that day.

I sprinted through the streets, but my body could only go so far. Breathless and sore, my chest heaving and the clammy taste of physical exertion on my tongue, after a few minutes I came to a stuttering halt, leaning against a lamppost as I tried to catch my breath. Black spots flashed across my eyes, and my veins pulsed like thunder. I already knew the police were not behind me, but checked just in case: the road was empty. I was the only person there. I looked around: the buildings were in better condition here. Geraniums poured over railings on upper balconies, while in a corner of the street a large overhanging tree stood next to a collection of large municipal dustbins. I stumbled towards it. Bits of old wood had been left out, broken wardrobes and chests of drawers, to be picked up by rag-and-bone men. There was also, I saw, up on the pavement and placed under the veiling branches of the tree, an old sofa, dragged out of the way of the street and pedestrians. It had tears down the sides and the cushions had gone, but it was long and wide. I walked towards it, doubting what I was seeing. There was no one around; the sense of danger lessened. The sofa was perfectly placed underneath the tree. If anyone did pass by they would have trouble seeing me anyway. I sat down slowly, testing it for hidden surprises. It smelt dusty and smoky. Its floral pattern would have been at home in some overly decorated flat belonging to an elderly couple, I thought. And I imagined all the thousands of times it had been sat on, the conversations it had witnessed, the lives that had been lived on it.

My head sank down on to the arm rest while my feet moved up at the other end. Curling my legs slightly I could just fit, my rucksack placed under my cheek for comfort and security. For a while I kept my eyes open while my body rested, until at last they closed. It was dawn before I realized I had fallen asleep.

14

Death of an Anarchist

On the afternoon of 19 November 1936, shortly after lunch, a group of leading anarchists left their headquarters in Madrid to drive to the front lines on the outskirts of the city for a tour of inspection. Franco's troops were in the middle of a concerted but frustrated bid to take the capital by force. With determination and a certain amount of luck, the Republican defenders were holding them back. *¡No pasarán!* – They shall not pass – went the defiant cry, and in Madrid, at last, the rebels' seemingly inexorable advance was encountering its first serious setback. Despite claims by Nationalist generals that they would be drinking coffee in the city's bars by the following day, Franco wouldn't take Madrid until the very end of the war, almost two and a half years later.

On that afternoon, the anarchists drove towards the University City, the large campus district to the northwest of the centre, built only a decade before and now the focal point of the war. Among the heavily damaged faculty buildings, General Millán Astray's battle cry 'Death to Intelligence' must have had a particular resonance. It was a sunny autumn day and the large black car sped through the streets until it reached the area near the Hospital Clínico, at that point the scene of fierce fighting against Moroccan Regulares. Near the Dentistry Faculty, the anarchists in the car saw a group of their own militiamen walking in the opposite direction, away from the front line. The vehicle stopped and the occupants got out. One of them, a large man with a barrel chest, powerful neck and delicate, almost deer-like features, with small almond-shaped eyes, started haranguing the men in his typically direct way. They shouldn't be deserting their positions, but fighting the enemy. The forces of fascism were on the attack. Here in Madrid they would be defeated and buried for good.

His words seemed to have an effect, and the weary men turned round and started trudging back towards the front. But then a shot rang out. The anarchist leader fell, wounded and bleeding. His companions, seeing what had happened, quickly hauled him back into the car and raced off towards the Ritz Hotel, now being used as a hospital for the Catalan militias. There, doctors examined the wounded man and deliberated. After a while, another doctor was called over from the Hotel Palace nearby, at that point an anarchist hospital. After he had performed an examination, the medics decided there was nothing to be done. The man was seriously wounded – a nine-millimetre bullet had entered his body just below the left nipple and passed out through the back. He would almost certainly not survive. He was also an important man. Better he die from the bullet wound than under the knife of a surgeon trying to save his life.

A few hours later, in room twenty-seven, situated on the first floor of the hotel, at around four o'clock in the morning, the anarchist leader breathed his last.[17] Two days later, in Barcelona, hundred of thousands of people attended his funeral. One of the most popular and charismatic leaders of the forces lined up against Franco had gone. His name was Buenaventura Durruti.

Spain is the only country in the modern Western world where anarchism has ever had mass appeal and where something approaching an anarchist revolution has ever taken place, leading many to speculate on an inherently 'anarchist' aspect to the Spanish psyche. This, combined with a strong and sometimes violent reaction to the strictly authoritarian and hierarchical regimes that have ruled the country for so much of its history, can perhaps explain some of anarchism's appeal.

The movement's beginnings in Spain had not been particularly auspicious. Anarchism was introduced by the Italian Giuseppe Fanelli in 1868, on a trip organized by Mikhail Bakunin to recruit Spanish members to the First International. Fanelli was a deputy in the Italian parliament who was officially domiciled on the state railway system, taking advantage of the free train pass that came with his job. After he had failed to meet anyone in Barcelona, a group of radicals in Madrid eventually arranged for him to give a lecture to some members of a printing organization. Fanelli spoke in French, not having any Spanish. Only one member of the audience understood anything he was saying.

Nonetheless anarchism subsequently spread rapidly across the country, finding a natural constituency among Andalusian peasants living in oppressed, semi-feudal conditions who were attracted to the ideas of a stateless society and redistribution of wealth. Intellectual anarchists would spend time with them to propagate their ideas, teaching them to read and write, and, reflecting a common puritanical streak in the early days of the movement, converting them to vegetarianism, weaning them off alcohol and tobacco, and preaching the virtues of being faithful to their wives.

Anarchism in Spain never lost a certain quasi-religious romanticism, but by the outbreak of the Civil War it had moved on. The movement had its own trade union – the CNT – with about a million members, and had become particularly strong in Catalonia and Aragon. The CNT was the largest single workers' group at the time, larger in number than the socialists or the communists. The communists were still a tiny minority, but were soon to grow rapidly in number and importance. General strikes had been the anarchists' main weapon in their struggle for better working conditions, and, more importantly, in trying to bring down the apparatus of the state. But faced with the prospect of a fascist government being set up, they had chosen the lesser evil of supporting the more mainstream left-wing parties involved in the Popular Front coalition that won the February 1936 elections.

There were problems, though. By definition the anarchists were not a centralized, well-organized body, which goes some way to explaining their eventual eclipse by the communists and socialists. The Republic needed them to help defend itself against the military revolt, but at the same time was frightened of them. Much of the prevarication about handing weapons out to the masses at the start of the war – a move which might have stopped the rebellion in its tracks – came from the fear of what would happen once these radical groups took control. In the end the anarchists did take to the streets, and in Barcelona brought about a revolution once they'd put down the military coup there. But loath to have anything to do with governments and state organizations, they failed to 'consolidate' their power as other groups might have done. The anarchists were idealists and libertarians who believed that revolutions and change came from below, not from above, and that it was not their place to impose their will. More ruthless parties, particularly the communists, quickly took advantage of this political gap.

The romanticism of the anarchists was the cause of some of their greatest weaknesses. In battle they tended to rely heavily on passion and belief in the cause, with the result that many of their members were needlessly killed in 'heroic' charges against the enemy. This method had worked quite spectacularly in Barcelona, where the anarchists had played a major part in thwarting the military coup and keeping the city out of Nationalist hands. Afterwards, though, particularly during the siege of Madrid, it failed as an effective mode of attack. It is not entirely clear how much the anarchists' image as a disorganized fighting force is due to subsequent communist propaganda aimed at discrediting them. Even before Durruti died in Madrid, the talk among Republicans had turned to 'discipline'. The communists and socialists were all in favour. For the anarchists it was anathema. Durruti had led a group of some three thousand anarchist militiamen, the 'Durruti column', out of Barcelona in the early days of the war to help capture the rebel-held Saragossa, almost two hundred miles away. Flushed with success and flying their red and black flags, they had marched for over two hours before they realized they had forgotten to pick up even basic supplies. The anarchists had no formal officials or salutes, orders were often discussed by soldier councils before being acted upon, and men were theoretically free to leave and head back home at any time. Belief in their cause was what held them together. To have behaved in any other way would have been to lose their very identity. On what other basis could an anarchist fighting force be formed?

Another problem was the apparent cruelty of many in the anarchist ranks. One of their members, for example, murdered the postman in the coastal town of Altea with a hatchet for over-charging on stamps. Believing that the 'crimes of society' were responsible for people ending up in jail, on occasion anarchists released scores of murderers and thieves who then affiliated themselves with their liberators and carried on as they had before. Priests and nuns in particular bore the brunt of their rage. Although, in a strangely typical anecdote of the times, the French writer Saint-Exupéry told how he once saved the life of a monk who was about to be shot by the anarchists, by telling them it was a bad idea. The militiamen were convinced by his arguments and instead of shooting the monk went and shook him by the hand, congratulating him on his escape.

If everyone in Spain at that time had friends elsewhere, the anarchists had none. The socialists could look to similar parties in France and Britain, the communists to Moscow, Franco to Germany and Italy. Almost nobody, though, liked the anarchists, this uncontrollable rabble blamed for many of the atrocities carried out on the Republican side during the early months of the war. They were one of the reasons why assistance was not forthcoming from the other democracies around the world. Travellers to Barcelona at this time found a city where everyone wore workers' overalls (*el mono azul*), tipping had been abolished and it was forbidden to utter the overtly religious *Adiós* when saying goodbye (the standard greeting became *Salud*). Abortions, divorce and 'free love' were all the norm. Meanwhile, in the countryside controlled by the anarchists, whole villages had been collectivized and private property and money abolished. The notion that the conservative-led governments of Baldwin or Chamberlain in Britain would support anything like this was absurd. The anarchists were well aware of this. The Republican government, though, was constantly hoping for London and Paris to help them in their struggle against Franco. One of the things that stood in their way, in their eyes, was the spread of anarchism.

Although a charismatic leader of the anarchists, Durruti was less an ideologue and thinker than a man of action and, for many, a terrorist. Born in León in 1896, he had trained as a metal-worker before being thrown out of the socialist UGT trade union for being too radical. He then embarked on a life as an anarchist agitator that saw him spend a great deal of his adult life behind bars. While free men, he and his best friend Francisco Ascaso had, among other things, managed to rob the Bank of Spain at Gijón – to give money to the workers; made an attempt on the life of King Alfonso XIII during a royal visit to France; and murdered the corrupt casino-owning Cardinal Soldevila of Saragossa. (Shortly before his death, Soldevila had made a promising young student in Saragossa, José María Escrivá, a prefect at the San Carlos Seminary. Escrivá would go on to form the secretive and controversial Opus Dei movement, which much later, in the 1960s, would play a significant role in Franco's government.)

For several years Durruti travelled through Latin America and Europe, fomenting revolution where he could, often struggling to survive, and condemned to death in four separate countries. At one point he ended up in Paris, where he scraped a living as a musician and ran a bookshop.

When the military launched their rebellion and the Spanish Civil War started, Durruti was in Barcelona, at the heart of what turned into an anarchist revolution. The city was a major stronghold of anarchism, thanks in part to the immigration there over the years of Andalusian workers seeking employment in textile factories. The zeal of the anarchists along with the decision of the Civil Guard to remain loyal to the Republic were the main reasons for the Nationalist coup failing in the city. General Goded, who had flown in from the Balearics to lead the revolt, was arrested and later shot. Durruti at this time was a leading member of a secret organization within Spanish anarchism, the FAI – the Iberian Anarchist Federation – which campaigned to keep the movement 'pure' and truly revolutionary.

People who knew Durruti described him as a 'primitive' kind

of man, passionate and a natural leader, but not one for complex or subtle thought.

'From his elemental way of passing judgement on things,' one former cellmate of his said, 'what was good was good, and what wasn't, wasn't. There was no middle ground, no reasoning, no subtleties which might lead him to see things in another way. In his view, the world belonged to the workers and to no one else, although a minority had taken possession of what really belonged to others.'[18]

This prisoner, who shared a cell with Durruti for eight months, described him as 'a man made out of a single piece of cast iron, with no air bubbles or fault lines in him: solid'. He was intelligent but had little 'culture'.

'There was no possibility of sexual relations with women in jail. Whenever his body demanded it, Durruti would suddenly walk up to the sink and, right in front of me, would simply turn on the tap and place his testicles under the cold water.'

This earthy man, with his steel will, proved to be one of the few great characters fighting Franco. While many Republican politicians were overweight intellectuals, Durruti had the combination of single-mindedness, violence, charisma and physical energy that was characteristic of some of the leaders on the Nationalist side.

The Durruti column grew in numbers as it marched across Aragon in the summer and autumn towards Saragossa, but the city stayed stubbornly in Nationalist hands. By November 1936, however, a more pressing situation had emerged in the Civil War. Having marched up the western flank of the country and relieved the Alcázar in Toledo, Franco's Army of Africa was poised to take Madrid. All attention was focused on the capital. For the Nationalists, victory was in their grasp. For the Republicans, the enemy had to be kept back at all costs. The government of socialist prime minister Francisco Largo

Caballero, in an act of bare-faced cowardice, abandoned Madrid and set up a new capital in Valencia. They almost didn't make it, being stopped en route at the town of Tarancón by anarchist militiamen who wanted to shoot the lot of them for 'desertion'. Manuel Azaña, meanwhile, now president of the Republic, had simply disappeared to Barcelona. Foreign dignitaries followed suit, reducing their staff in the capital or decamping altogether. The British ambassador, Sir Henry Chilton, left the country for the French border town of Hendaye, where he set up a new embassy in a grocer's shop.

The defence of Madrid was left in the hands of General José Miaja and his brilliant chief of staff, the newly promoted Lieutenant Colonel Vicente Rojo – the man who had previously tried to negotiate on behalf of the Republic with the defenders of the Alcázar in Toledo. Miaja and Rojo were left with a few soldiers who had stayed loyal to the Republic, along with thousands of militiamen belonging to various trade unions and political factions who until a few months previously had been trying to kill each other in a political turf war. They were facing the best troops in the entire Spanish Army. The odds were not looking good. A number of factors, though, were in their favour. First, Franco's soldiers, despite their run of success, were beginning to tire after being on the go non-stop since July. Second, the Regulares were particularly good over open ground, but were weak in urban warfare. Third, most of the militiamen had nowhere to run to if they decided to abandon the front line – their wives and children were waiting at home only a short distance behind them. Their backs, as it were, were against the wall, and the Nationalist troops were already notorious for carrying out gang rapes and massacres of civilians.

The enemy was closing in and Miaja and Rojo were desperately trying to build up defensive lines. The question was, where would the attack come from? At this point there came a stroke of luck. During one of the early vanguard strikes on the city, Nationalist forces attempted to get across the Toledo bridge in a mini Italian Fiat Ansaldo tank. One of the Republican *carabineros* defending the crossing crept up to the machine, taking advantage of its blind spot, and disabled it with a grenade. When its two occupants got out to escape they were gunned down. In the pockets of one of them, Captain Vidal-Cuadras, the Republicans discovered the Nationalists' attack plans.[19] Within an hour they were in Rojo's hands. The Nationalists were going to come in from across the Casa de Campo, a large park area to the west of the city.

With only twenty-eight thousand fighters at his disposal – including one women's battalion – Rojo went about fortifying the positions of the defenders. There weren't enough to close up any breaches in the lines, but one other factor was in his favour: at that point the attackers only numbered eighteen thousand men.

Behind the trenches the city braced itself for the onslaught with a growing spirit of defiance. Posters were daubed on the walls urging men to fight and wives to take their husbands' lunches to them at the front line rather than at the factory.

'We will not abandon the trenches!' declared La Pasionaria, the great communist orator. 'We will resist until the last man, until the last drop of blood!' Dressed in her widow's black, she would become something of a mother figure for soldiers on the Republican side.

They were tense times, though. Many feared that hidden anti-Republican sympathizers within the city might rise up to assist the attackers. General Mola, when asked which of the four Nationalist columns bearing down on the capital he thought might eventually take Madrid, declared that a 'fifth column' of supporters from within would emerge victorious, thus, according to some, coining the phrase.

But such talk possibly did his side more harm than good. Paranoia took hold and, in the power vacuum left by the rapidly departing government, the communists and their newly arrived Soviet advisers – some posing as correspondents for *Pravda* – took control of much of the running of the city. They were ruthless in their dealings with perceived opponents. Unofficial *chekas* had already been set up around the city since the start of the war, where suspected Nationalist sympathizers were hauled in for questioning and later 'taken for a ride' – a short car journey accompanied by a bullet to the head. These acts of violence now increased, however. One pressing issue was what to do with political prisoners in the city's jails who had declared their support for the rebellion. If they were liberated they would greatly strengthen the enemy. The communists decided to have them killed. As Franco's troops moved closer to the city, hundreds of army officers, right-wing politicians and priests were loaded into double-decker buses and driven to the village of Paracuellos, some twenty miles up the Barcelona road. There they were shot and buried in mass graves. In total around 2,400 people were killed in this way. It became the most notorious single act of repression carried out by the Republican side during the war.

The Nationalists were still supremely confident, though, not least because of the recent arrival in the country of some 6,500 German soldiers in the newly formed Condor Legion. Although mostly airmen and technicians, they would play a decisive role as the war dragged on.

The main Nationalist assault on Madrid began on 7 November 1936, and came, as expected, from across the Casa de Campo. The defenders, travelling up to the front lines on trams, were able to hold the attackers off. Aerial bombardments continued as the Nationalists hoped to spread panic among the populace. There was particular interest in the effect incendiary bombs might have. Then, on 8 November, the first of the International Brigades arrived. Responding to a cry around the world to halt the rise of fascism, thousands of volunteers were arriving in Spain from France, Germany, Hungary, Italy, the United States, Britain, and a host of other countries – even some from China. The majority of these were formed into the communist-dominated International Brigades, and they were to suffer some of the heaviest casualties of the war: around a third of the forty thousand who saw action were killed. Their arrival in Madrid at this time gave a massive morale boost to the defenders as they marched up the Gran Vía towards the trenches, singing the 'Internationale' to the cheers of onlookers.

As the days passed and still the city didn't fall, the Nationalists began to realize that the conquest of Madrid would not be as easy as they had expected. After numerous attempts had been beaten back, they eventually managed to get a foothold across the River Manzanares and take the Garabitas hill, from which they could bombard the rest of the capital. But the main fighting was now taking place in the University City, where the faculty buildings were being fought over floor by floor. Enterprising soldiers would place grenades in the lifts to explode when the doors opened on the enemy on the level above, while some of the Regulares fell ill after eating laboratory animals which had been inoculated with typhus for experiments.[20] From his headquarters, General Miaja urgently wired the government in Valencia for more ammunition. In reply he received a counter-order from the prime minister telling him to send down the cabinet's table silver, which had been left behind in the rush to get away.

It was at this point that the Durruti column, now with some four thousand men, arrived in Madrid, having left the Aragon front. Durruti immediately asked to be given the most difficult sector of the Madrid fighting in order to show the bravery of his men. Miaja assigned him to the Casa de Campo and the recapture of the Garabitas hill. But armed with Swiss rifles dating from 1886, and in the face of the enemy machine-gun fire, the anarchist lines collapsed.

The Nationalists inched forward again. The anarchists were ordered to hold them back, but faced with an attack by Regulares and legionaries, they once again turned to run. General Miaja himself had to harangue them to return.

'Cowards! Come and die with an old man! Come and die with your General Miaja.'

The militiamen returned to the fray, but Rojo had to lead the general away lest he get killed too. Back at headquarters, they seriously considered disarming the anarchists: they were too liable to give in. Durruti was adamant. His men, he assured them, would show what *cojones* they had.

Two days later, when he stepped out of a car in the campus area to persuade fleeing anarchists to return to the front line, he was shot, dying in the early hours of the following day in the Ritz Hotel. He was forty years old. Not long afterwards, direct assaults on Madrid ceased as the two sides reached a stalemate. From now on most of the fighting for the capital would take place around the city in various outflanking manoeuvres.

The mystery surrounding Durruti's death has never been cleared up. There are many theories regarding what happened. One is that the bullet that killed him came from the Hospital Clínico, where Nationalist troops had been fighting the anarchists through the day, gradually working their way up the building. This is doubtful, as the hospital was about a kilometre away from where Durruti was standing at the time and the nine-millimetre bullet that hit him couldn't have been fired that far. The other main theories centre on either a conspiracy or an accident. The conspiracy theories are that he was shot by the communists as a political rival, or deliberately shot by one of his own anarchists, who felt he was getting too close to the communists. The accident theories are that one of his colleagues inadvertently shot him with a sub-machine-gun that went off when he placed the butt on the ground or when it hit the side of the car; or that Durruti accidentally shot himself with an automatic rifle.

Little evidence has emerged to support either of the conspiracy theories, and an accident seems more likely – possibly the first suggestion, as Durruti, according to some, was more in the habit of carrying an Astra pistol than an automatic rifle or *naranjero*, which had no safety catch.

The only possessions Durruti had with him at the time of his death were a notebook, a pair of glasses and some dirty clothes. They were handed to his widow, Emilienne Morin, a ticket girl at the Goya Cinema in Barcelona. He also left behind a five-year-old daughter, Colette.

Two hours after Durruti died, in an unrelated incident, José Antonio Primo de Rivera, the dapper, aristocratic founder of the Spanish fascist party, the Falange, was executed in an Alicante jail. Imprisoned the previous March during the violent build-up to the war, he had been transported to Alicante shortly before the coup for fear that he might try to escape from his Madrid cell. Found guilty by a jury of rebellion against the state, he was led out at six-thirty in the morning of 20 November and, standing with his arms crossed, was shot by a Republican firing squad. His last request was for the patio to be wiped clean afterwards, so that his brother Miguel, also being held prisoner, would not have to walk in his blood. Attempts by leading members of the Republican government to spare him and commute the sentence came to nothing: the local left-wing authorities had taken matters into their own hands and would not be dictated to by central government. Ironically the anarchists were against his execution, regarding José Antonio as a 'Spanish patriot in search of solutions for his country'.[21]

With José Antonio's death, Franco lost a potential rival as leader of the Nationalist movement, and was simultaneously handed a martyr figure around whom he could develop a cult of devotion. The Falangist ranks had swollen enormously over the previous months, in some cases with men joining as a means of saving their skin when caught up in Nationalist-controlled areas. Franco, however, did not agree with many of the policies of the party, which, despite being authoritarian and nationalistic, called for radical social reforms. Franco needed the Falange's support, but was himself a conservative, trying to stop change in the country and even push it back. Now, with the leader of the Falange dead, Franco could bring the party under his direct control, while at the same time turning José Antonio into a mythical and symbolic figure at the head of the Nationalist cause, a martyred saint of the 'crusade' against the Reds. The fact was that on the few occasions they had ever met, Franco and José Antonio had not got on.

Durruti and José Antonio are two of the great 'what-if' characters of the Spanish Civil War. What if neither of them had died when and as they did? It's tempting to think the whole war might have changed. Durruti might have been the only man capable of preventing the eventual eclipse of the anarchists by the communists, and the stifling of the revolutionary spirit of the war's early days as the Republic tried to put on a more respectable and bourgeois face to the rest of the world. Based on his writings from jail during the last months of his life, some have speculated that José Antonio might have been able to curb some of the violence of his followers had he lived and escaped jail, as well as acting as a brake on Franco's rise to supreme power within the Nationalist ranks.

It is doubtful, though, if either man would have made such a great impact had they lived. The world was changing very quickly around them and they were both being left behind. With its leader behind bars, and with thousands of new members, the Falange had turned into something larger than and quite different from the small group of fascists that José Antonio had originally created. Had he been back in charge, he might have reformed it more to his own liking, but it is probable that Franco would have marginalized and neutralized him as he did so successfully with his other potential political opponents. As for Durruti, with the Soviet Union being the only serious backer for the Republican side, the communists were in the ascendant and becoming increasingly powerful. Stalin, in his attempts to increase his appeal in London and Paris, would have had little patience with a genuine revolutionary like Durruti having a leading role in the war. Again, as with José Antonio, you feel he would either have been absorbed or removed. As it was, both men were destined to become semi-mythological characters for their respective sides.

15

Kiki and Moa

*T*here was a specific moment when Kiki became a woman: not when she put on her dress or her high-heeled shoes; not even when she applied her make-up: these things were superficial, requirements for her to play the part, to step into character, but nothing to do with the essence of who she became in those moments. From the dirty white sofa in the living room of the tiny attic flat I watched her transformation as she fixed herself up in the bathroom. She talked incessantly to me about work, life at the club, the last time she'd been back in Vigo to see the family – or at least those of them who still spoke to her – about the new condom shop round the corner, about the cold she'd had the week before. And all the while she waxed and plucked and painted, padding where there should be something, strapping down where there should be nothing – all with an efficiency of movement and care which made it clear this was a routine she knew well and had been practising for many years.

No, all this was just the outer layer, barely skin deep. The transforming moment came in a split second when all this was done and she was staring into the mirror, putting on her earrings, leaning closer to see better what she was doing. Beneath her black cotton skirt her hips rolled out in traditional female form, her waist held tight by a thick black belt, modest sponge breasts pressed against the fabric of her blouse, her slim calves taut from her heels. The instant when the energy she gave off subtly changed, when she ceased being a man dressed as a woman and simply became a woman, was with an almost imperceptible glance at herself in the looking glass, as though casting something out and catching something new from the reflection, like a magic spell. That was when she truly became Kiki, the greatest *transformista* I have ever known.

'Well,' she said, pouring us both a glass of wine in the kitchen, 'are you ready to go?'

I had been in her flat for two days, sleeping and hallucinating in a cold, pale, wrinkled shell as a high temperature caught hold and pushed me into a world of illogical form and distorted shape. I had arrived in Madrid with nothing but a virus that made my body shake as it worked its way around inside. On the train I had become feverish, banging into the walls and slow-sliding doors as I rushed to the toilet. Kiki had been waiting for me at the station, and after a short, perilous taxi ride I had reached the sanctuary of her flat. There I collapsed, vaguely aware of cool hands brushing against my burning brow, my head being tilted as I was given water to drink. Now my temperature was beginning to come down, my body purged, but I felt weak and light-headed.

'Do you want to borrow some of my clothes?' Kiki had asked. It felt like the first time I'd laughed in weeks. She'd gone down and bought me a couple of new shirts, lending me money until I sorted myself out.

The flat was tiny and cramped, but done in such a way that you felt deeply relaxed, as though you never wanted to be anywhere else. Everything about it was of a pale, soothing quality. A reindeer skin stretched across the floor on top of white-painted floorboards, while the beams of the sloping attic roof were also white, except for one at the far end which was painted pale pink. A quiet extravagance, very Kiki. There was no television or music system, but a few newspapers dotted spare patches of floor. 'Noise and entertainment come from life,' she had said to me when I pointed this out. 'I don't need them here in a box.' The flat was her refuge, her world, her place to be. Although being her*self* was no simple matter. I sometimes wondered what agonies she had been through inside this tiny space: the serenity she showed to the outside world, I felt sure, had not come without a struggle.

'Come and stay whenever you're in Madrid,' she'd said. She was an old friend of Salud whom I'd met four or five times in Valencia and Madrid. They'd worked together years before, doing cabaret shows in villages across Spain, travelling with twenty others in a cramped bus from one corner of the country to the other over the hot summer months, appearing at fiestas where the locals danced for two days before drinking themselves into a coma. Salud did the flamenco; Kiki did the drag-queen bit. But that was when things were tougher and she did any work she could get. Now she had a job at the club and had refined her act. The drag queens who shared the stage with her were clowns by comparison: none could change so completely from one sex to another as well as Kiki. She didn't want to be a freak, didn't want to appear as a mere *travesti* – a word she never used for herself. Her aim was to pass completely for a woman, and she managed it – only the regulars and people who knew her were in on the secret. Even then I'm not sure they didn't see a woman anyway, as I always did.

There had been complaints – brutish businessmen telling the waiters they didn't want to see a female singer performing: it was supposed to be a drag club. When they were quietly informed of the facts, they would fall back in their chairs, open-mouthed, incredulous and amazed. A few would leave at this point, as though something about Kiki disturbed them at some deep level. Others would return the following night, and the next weekend, bringing friends and wives to see this extraordinary performance.

'No, really,' they whispered to their unbelieving companions. 'I swear. They told me so last week.'

Kiki loved it, but you could tell her act was less to do with entertainment and more to do with reinforcing her self-identity. The attention was wonderful, but while she enjoyed it she always laughed about it too: she knew what it meant to feel blind hatred for what she was. Adulation was just as extreme and perhaps more dangerous, though less disagreeable. It was all based on ignorance – no one had penetrated the real person, so no one could really judge.

'Pío Moa's giving a lecture tonight,' she said, handing me a glass of Ribera del Duero. She was trying to get me back on my feet, and I'd been telling her about my interest in the Civil War. 'We'll have to go.'

I had come across Moa a few times in newspaper articles and magazines. A former leading member of a communist terrorist organization and now a right-wing commentator, he had written two or three best-selling books on the Civil War with a hard-line anti-left interpretation, 'revising' the accepted truths of the conflict to paint Franco and the Nationalists in a more sympathetic light. For a while historians had mostly ignored him, but the high volume of sales of his books meant people were having to take him seriously, and already works targeting his 'inaccuracies' were being published. His bugbears were the mainstream, often left-leaning historians who had done much to shape the commonly held ideas of what had happened in the conflict. Moa seemed to be on a one-man mission to change things, and from the success of his writings he certainly seemed to have an audience.

My curiosity was immediately piqued. I wanted to know what kind of a man he was. Someone who could shift so firmly from one extreme to the other might be quite interesting, even if I didn't agree with what he said. I was also interested in what Kiki's reaction to him would be. She seemed strangely enthusiastic about going to his lecture. I had no idea what her politics were, but in the largely tribal world of affiliations in Spain, I expected her, if anything, to be left-leaning. Thanks to Franco, the Right was associated with austere authoritarianism. It was hard to imagine Kiki identifying with that.

'It'll be enlightening, believe me,' she said.

We took a taxi to the hotel where the lecture was taking place. The large mirrored room was already full ten minutes before it was due to start. Unusual for the Spanish to be so punctual, I reflected. We stood against the back wall, hemmed in by well-dressed men in suits accompanied by pearl-wearing wives. Most of them, it seemed, were over fifty, although there were a dozen or so younger people with keen angry expressions in their eyes. People smiled and chatted to one another, but with a certain serious intensity I was unused to. For a second I saw them as a group apart, not the 'real' Spaniards of my experience. The Spanish I knew and loved were a much looser bunch of people. But at the same time I could see how they had always been there: I had just ignored them. Stiff and rather hard-looking, they had a set look of disgust and disapproval in their eyes, as though quick to condemn or to speak a sharp word.

Kiki pulled me out of this dark reverie by treading on my foot and pointing at the arriving speaker. Moa was a slight, balding man with a grey walrus moustache and glasses. Not quite how I had imagined him.

'What were you expecting?' Kiki said when I whispered down into her ear. 'A man in a balaclava helmet swinging in on a rope?'

I laughed while the audience applauded Moa's arrival. Kiki's gloved hands pressed hard against one another in unashamed admiration. She lifted herself up on tiptoe, darting her head from one side to the other to look over the shoulders of the crowd standing in front of us. No one had given her a second glance – or at least not in any quizzical way. Men looked her up and down appreciatively, but her discreet attire ensured she slipped by almost unnoticed – except for the occasional more discerning eye. She didn't want to be a star, or stir things up. What could be a more disturbing spectacle than a drag artist showing up at a meeting of the far Right? With a slight shudder I imagined what the reaction of these lusty elderly men would be if they discovered that the woman they had been eyeing up had a few surprises hidden inside her skirt. But this was really just idle imagining. No one there suspected anything at all, and as Kiki proved, physical gender and real gender were not always the same.

Moa was having his photograph taken as he stood on the dais: he had removed his glasses and was staring at the camera with a fixed, determined expression. An expensively dressed woman bustled around, pouring him a glass of water and fiddling with his microphone. Men in shiny leather shoes shuffled on the carpeted floor expectantly. One of them, catching sight of Kiki, invited her to stand in front of him so she could get a better view. She accepted his kind offer, standing with her back as straight as an arrow, hair pulled up in an Italian-style bun, delicate silver necklace glimmering around her breastbone in the creamy light issuing from the candelabra above our heads. Her Japanese silk blouse hugged her torso tightly.

The lecture began. Moa hunched over the microphone and spoke in a clear, deep voice, his physical slightness slipping away as he moved into performance mode and quickly captured the audience's attention. It was remarkable to see the change – one minute a relatively nondescript middle-aged man, the next an orator of not inconsiderable skill, carefully and calculatingly hitting the buttons of his public. The talk was ostensibly about new ideas he was putting forward, blaming the Left for the outbreak of the Civil War, arguing that the conflict had really begun not in 1936 but in 1934, when left-wingers had staged an unsuccessful rebellion across the country. This seemed to be the main preoccupation of this second phase of his life – blaming everything on a group he once thought had all the answers. Spain in the 1930s, in his view, had been a hotbed of Marxist revolutionaries and Franco had merely stepped in at the very last minute to prevent the country falling to the Reds.

It was what the audience wanted to hear, being essentially the view the Right had had of the Civil War since the beginning. '*They* caused it – we had no choice.' And for it to come from the mouth of a former communist and founder member of the left-wing GRAPO terrorist organization seemed to give the theory extra weight and authority: if Moa could see the error of his ways and that the Right had been 'right' all along, then so could everyone else; for years the only view of the war you heard was from the Left, and it was all lies. Someone – Moa – had to come along and rectify things. And he was angry – angry that few historians took him seriously, angry that people insulted him rather than properly debating his theories, angry that the Left's view of the war always prevailed. For a moment I had to pinch myself. Who won the war in the end? Wasn't it Franco? From the way he talked you'd have thought it was the Right who had suffered persecution and terror all these years.

What was most striking about the lecture, though, was the emotionalism of it. Moa talked as though the Civil War had only just taken place, as though the causes of the conflict were still alive, as though bloodshed could start again at any minute. This was not a lecture by a historian discussing some interesting but now distant period of the past. It was almost like a political rally. He spat out the names of some of the politicians of that time – President Azaña, or Indalecio Prieto, one of the main socialist leaders – as though they were alive today and still damaging the country, not men who had died fifty years previously. For a moment I felt I was back in the bar at Burgos, submerged in the seething, unthinking rage of the football fans: the energy that was beginning to circle in the room was disturbingly similar. Moa seemed under the spell of some deep-seated anger and ready to vent his spleen against anything. And the more he spoke, the more he pushed the buttons, the higher the emotional pitch rose among the audience. Here was a fallen angel who had seen the error of his ways and was now redeeming himself by preaching the gospel of the Right. They loved him because his change of political spots evoked their sympathy, while his messianic fervour excited their passions. It was strange that such an apparently unremarkable man could do all this, but he had the three-hundred-strong crowd in the palm of his hand. I could only marvel. From over her shoulder I saw Kiki applauding whenever the others clapped, nodding from time to time. The only difference was that while everyone else had serious scowls on their faces, I could make out a smile on her lips. She was enjoying every minute.

After Moa ended his lecture, a pale-looking man in the audience stood up to ask a question. He was younger than most of the people in the room, his hair was ruffled and his clothes hung awkwardly from his body, but he was clutching a copy of Moa's latest book under his arm and had a youthful cockiness about him. Why, he wanted to know, wasn't he being given Moa's books to read at university? All students were fed was the Left's interpretation; it was time they started teaching 'the truth' about the Civil War. Thankfully people like Moa were doing their bit, but his lecturers ridiculed him for reading Moa's books.

There were cries from the audience, a wave of anger, this time with sympathy for the poor lonely student, bravely taking a stand against the establishment. Moa simply smiled and shrugged. It was, he said, to be expected, but things were slowly changing. He didn't say it explicitly, but implied that one day – and you felt he longed for nothing so strongly – his books would be on the curriculum at universities around the world. They were right to be angry, but this anger would eventually lead to better things, like a golden dawn just waiting for them over the horizon.

Another member of the audience stood up to ask a question about the recent general election. After a massive bomb attack at Atocha train station just three days before the polls, the socialists had been voted back into power, to everyone's surprise. Everyone had expected the right-wing Popular Party to win. Now, months on, the Right was still reeling from an election they had thought was in the bag. It was perfect material for the strange victim complex that seemed present in the room. I couldn't help drawing parallels with what I'd read of the atmosphere in the 1930s, when a similar paranoia had pushed the Right to the extreme. It had been a more polarized time – anarchists were burning down churches and convents, land-owners were starving their peasants to death – but I had the feeling of being back in a world where everyone was talking and no one was listening.

The question solicited a predictable response from Moa. All the anger and rage that had been building up until that point blew up. They had been robbed. The socialist victory had been written in blood. And he went as far as he could, without actually saying so, to suggest that the Left had been behind the attack. 'Who benefits from this?' The paranoid conspiracy-theorists lapped it up. The Basque terror group ETA was named; people were standing up and shouting; a furious hubbub filled the room. Outside, the rest of the world was convinced some Al-Qa'ida group had planted the bombs. But here they could only understand the political language of the 1930s, of Left and Right, revolutions and dictatorships. The country was falling apart: time for another Franco, law and order.

I had often watched the old black and white newsreels of Hitler's rallies, with their massed ranks of party faithful, flaming torches, huge flags and the little man standing on the platform whipping everyone up into a hateful frenzy, and wondered what it actually *felt* like to be there. Atmosphere doesn't really come across in the moving images captured on film. That evening, with just a few hundred people crammed into a conference room, I came as close as I ever want to to experiencing it. Moa was no Hitler, and the wealthy old people making up most of the audience were not SS storm troops or officers from the Gestapo, but the hate, anger and self-righteous indignation that I sensed flowing from the audience, somehow coagulating around us until it almost had a life of its own, was something I never wanted to feel again. The echoes of what for me was a past age, with its fascist salutes, jackboots and the name-calling that could precede persecutions and shootings, were deeply disturbing. The people here were a minority, and they were mostly elderly romantics dreaming of a glorious past that had never really existed. But the energy they produced was electric, unpredictable and menacing. Multiply that a few times, inject it with youthful vigour, and it gave cause for concern.

'The government and the forces of "progress" are nailing condoms to the mast as their penultimate Jacobin flag against the Church!' Moa proclaimed, meandering momentarily away from the events of the 1930s to another of his pet subjects.

'AIDS goes hand in hand with sexual promiscuity and this is almost always linked to drug use.'

Bland truisms were handed out and the audience loved it. I had the sense not only of witnessing a mass hypnotism, but also of living a dream myself. This kind of power and energy was always running just beneath the surface. We went about our lives, eating, shopping, working, playing, and this kind of thing seemed a million miles away. It belonged in history books or in faraway countries, but would never happen now, here. But wouldn't it? For the first time I began to feel less certain about things I had taken for granted, about assuming that peaceful democratic life would carry on for years to come. It might not be these OAPs who gave us a shock, but others could easily stir up passions that were clearly all too ready to ignite. I found my thoughts turning back to the fist fight in Valencia.

After the questions had ended and the crowds had gone, we left the hotel to have a drink at a bar a couple of streets away. Kiki ordered half a litre of beer while I asked for an anise.

'I try to go against people's expectations,' she said when I questioned her choice of beverage. 'It's so obvious to order a glass of wine or a sherry. They'll think I'm a rather strange girl who likes beer, not a man in drag. *You're* the one they're probably worried about, ordering a little glass of anise before dinner. Very odd.'

It was all thought out, yet also so natural. Like her voice: she never changed it from male to female, just something subtle perhaps in the intonation. Yet close your eyes and listen to her speak – I had tried it a couple of times now – and you really couldn't tell if she was a man with a light voice or a woman with a deep one. It was at some perfect midway pitch that could be either. Many Spanish women had deeper voices than hers anyway, brought on, you imagined, by heavy smoking. It was an ideal country for her.

'God forbid!' she'd said once when I'd asked how she avoided the falsetto whining of other transvestites. 'What do you think I am?' Although that was exactly the question: what, or who, was she? With time I found myself asking the question less and less. She was Kiki, unique, a one-off. Why try to define her any other way?

We didn't talk about the lecture for a while. After rousing rather disturbing emotions in the audience, Moa had brought things to a close, swarms of admirers circling round him like bees. There stood this seemingly unremarkable middle-aged man at the centre of buzzing, nervous attention. I had hesitated for a moment, wondering whether to try to talk to him, but had decided against it. There was nothing more I really wanted to know. The event had left an unsavoury taste in my mouth and I had wanted to leave as quickly as possible.

'You don't look very happy,' Kiki said after a while. Her pale lipstick had left semi-circular marks on the edge of the giant glass on the table in front of her. In the gloomy light of the bar she had taken off her gloves.

'I found it rather uncomfortable in there,' I said. 'All that hatred.'

'Yes,' she said thoughtfully. 'But Moa's wonderful, you have to admit.'

I looked her in the eye. She was being sincere.

'What the hell do you mean?' I said. 'He was the one whipping it all up, all that stuff about the war, about how Franco had no choice, it was all the Left's fault.'

'What – you think they were blameless?'

'No, of course not. But that's my point: you can't just dump all the blame on one side. Left, Right, they were all involved, all responsible. Or are we to think the thousands Franco had shot were the Left's fault as well?'

'I can see,' she said, taking another swig of beer, 'that you weren't unaffected by the emotions in there yourself.'

I sat back and sighed. She was right. I was angry – if not as angry as Moa himself, then angry at him and what he'd said.

'OK, you're right. But "wonderful"? What's wonderful about him?'

'Moa has reinvented himself,' she said. 'All right, it's superficial. He was an extremist, now he's still an extremist. He's simply swapped one extreme for another. But he made the change. He used to be a member of GRAPO, now he's standing there in front of people saying *mea culpa* and singing a different tune. One must always applaud someone like that, no matter how small the step.'

I said nothing, but could see she was serious. And there was more than an echo of her own self in what she was describing.

'Moa's living his own Civil War, his own version of it. That's what's important. The war has ended – it ended seventy years ago. It no longer exists. He takes that material and casts it in whatever form he chooses, and casts himself and recasts himself in the process. When Moa's talking about the war, he's really talking about himself. And the way he sees it goes to the heart of who he considers himself to be.'

'Aren't you being just a bit too generous to a miserable old fascist?' I asked.

'He's reinvented himself; he's made his own image of himself. That takes balls.'

I put down my drink and closed my eyes.

'My head's spinning,' I said, getting up. 'Let's go and find a place to eat.'

16

Guernica

'*I* arrived at Guernica at four-forty in the afternoon. I had barely got out of the car when the bombing started. People were terrified . . . five minutes did not pass without the area turning black from the German planes. The planes flew very low, destroying the roads and woods with machine-gun fire, men, women and children in piles lying on the ground in the ditches by the side of the road. After a short while it was impossible to see more than two hundred metres for the smoke. Fire wrapped around the city. Cries of pain were heard from all sides.'[22]

It was a market day in the Basque town of Guernica, just twenty miles from Bilbao, when Father Alberto Onaindía witnessed the most notorious event of the Spanish Civil War. As Madrid still held out stubbornly against the Nationalists, Franco had opened up a new front against the strip of Republican territory along the northern coast made up of the Basque Country and the regions of Cantabria and Asturias. By conquering the area, the Nationalists would gain a significant number of arms factories and centres of heavy industry, as well as taking over a handful of important ports. The Basques were the first to come under attack. Catholic and largely conservative, they might have been Franco's allies under different circumstances, but they had, in Franco's eyes, committed the gravest sin of entertaining hopes of independence from Spain. They would be given no quarter and Basque Catholic priests were among the thousands of victims of Franco's 'crusade'.

Spearheading the air campaign for the Nationalists was the Condor Legion. Hitler had already rescued Franco at the start of the conflict when he had sent planes to Morocco to help airlift the Army of Africa to the Spanish mainland. German advisers had been with the Generalísimo ever since. But when the Madrid front ground to a halt, Hitler decided to send more German troops in an attempt to speed up the war. The Condor Legion was formed towards the end of 1936. Initially it comprised some five thousand men, but this would later increase to over twelve thousand. At its head, reporting directly to Franco alone, was General Hugo von Sperrle, and below him Colonel Wolfram von Richthofen, cousin of Manfred, the Red Baron. Sperrle had demanded high-performance aircraft from the Luftwaffe and was supplied with Heinkel He111s, Junkers Ju87s (Stukas) and Messerschmitt Bf109s. In contrast to the slow-paced, old-fashioned Spanish style of campaigning, Sperrle preferred swift, concentrated attacks with high firepower. Later he was to play an important role in German Blitzkrieg tactics on the Western front in the Second World War.

The Condor Legion took part in many of the important battles of the Spanish Civil War, during which it lost more planes in accidents (160) than to enemy action (72). Spain was a testing ground for new military ideas: it was here that the Germans invented 'carpet bombing'. The unit had some colourful people flying for it – one pilot, recovered from the wreckage of a shot-down Dornier 17 near Bilbao, was found to have plucked eyebrows and was wearing lipstick and ladies' pink underwear. He was lucky to die in the crash – many who survived were lynched by angry mobs. The Condor Legion's most infamous act, however, occurred at Guernica.

General Mola had begun the Basque campaign on 31 March 1937 with a statement promising to raze the province of Vizcaya to the ground if the enemy did not surrender. 'I have the means to do so,' he said, and to demonstrate this he destroyed part of the town of Durango in an aerial and artillery bombardment, resulting in the deaths of some three hundred civilians, including fourteen nuns and several priests who were celebrating mass at the time. Although the Condor Legion was answerable only to Franco, liaising through his office in Salamanca was slow, and so Franco had given Sperrle the go-ahead for direct communications with Mola. Almost a month on, though, Nationalist troops were not advancing as quickly as hoped.

On 20 April they started the second phase of their campaign with heavy bombardment of the Republican lines, which now broke. Basque fighters fell back in disarray, many ending up in Guernica. With refugees also flooding in from the surrounding areas, the town's population had risen from seven thousand to almost ten thousand people. But despite the Nationalist advance, and the attack on Durango just a few weeks before, the people of Guernica had little notion of how much danger they were in.

Aerial bombardment, although used as a military strategy before this point, even within the context of the Spanish war – Durango was a case in point, as were earlier Republican bombings of Córdoba and Saragossa – had failed to register in popular consciousness. So much so that when Picasso was told about the method of destruction of the emblematic Basque town, he asked, 'What's an aerial bombardment?' Previously, Western powers had experimented with the technique to control their distant colonies. The Italians had first dreamed up bombing from the air in the autumn of 1911 when Lieutenant Giulio Cavotti, flying a Taube monoplane, had dropped four 4.5lb bombs from a height of some six hundred feet on rebel positions in Libya. No one was injured and little damage was done, but a precedent was set. Since then the British had carried out systematic aerial bombardment in Somaliland in 1920, but Guernica was the first bombing of civilians to enter the world's collective imagination, and the first town to be systematically razed to the ground in such an attack. The line from Guernica to Hiroshima passes through Coventry, London and Dresden, and while the Basque and Japanese experiences barely compare in scale, the underlying concept is still the same.

Perhaps the only part of the Guernica story that has never been contested is the fact that the town suffered great damage from explosions. Everything else, from how it happened to who was responsible, why it was done and how many people were killed, has been the subject of intense argument at some point or another. And the debate still goes on.

One version of events goes something like this:[23]

At around half past four on 26 April 1937, a German Dornier 17 – later dubbed a 'flying pencil' during the Battle of Britain – flew over Guernica and dropped a handful of bombs around the bridge crossing the River Oca, failing to hit the target and destroying a number of nearby houses. Although perhaps strategically unimportant for the Nationalist advance, the town was home to a couple of small-arms factories, and soldiers from some four Republican battalions were stationed there. It was also the spiritual home of the Basque people, being the site where traditionally the Spanish king, or his representative, swore to uphold the Basques' traditional rights and culture. An old oak tree marked the spot where the ancient ceremony took place, next to the Casa de Juntas.

A few moments after the Dornier's bombs were dropped, three Italian planes – Savoia-Marchetti SM.79s – passed over, dropping thirty-six 50-kilo bombs. These, too, fell on houses around the bridge and in an empty plot near the train station. A little while later more German planes arrived, Junkers Ju52s carrying 50-kilo and 250-kilo bombs, as well as 1-kilo incendiary bombs with aluminium tips. These caused considerable damage – with their delayed explosion they penetrated the old wooden houses and quickly set them on fire. The blaze spread easily to neighbouring areas.

At around six o'clock that afternoon a Republican plane flew over the town on the orders of the Basque president, José Antonio Aguirre. The pilot did not report any significant damage. But the bombardment was far from over. Half an hour later, nineteen Junkers Ju52 bombers accompanied by four Messerschmitt Bf109s returned to Guernica for the final assault. While the bombers concentrated on the centre, the fighters strafed the roads leading away from the town, which were now crammed with men, women and children trying to escape. In one pass alone twenty tonnes of bombs were dropped. By seven o'clock they had finished. Guernica was ablaze. Over 70 per cent of the town was destroyed. The bridge, the arms factories and the train station, however, were all still standing.

Foreign journalists on the Republican side were sitting down to dinner in Bilbao thirty kilometres away when the news came through that Guernica had been bombed. They rushed off and arrived to find the place in the grip of a firestorm. 'We tried to enter, but the streets were a royal carpet of live coals; blocks of wreckage slithered and crashed from the houses, and from their sides that were still erect the polished heat struck at our cheeks and eyes.' Reuters were the first to tell of what had happened, but George Steer, writing for *The Times*, captured the world's imagination with his account, later retold in his book *The Tree of Gernika*. 'Some of the witnesses were quite dumb. They were digging them out of the ruined houses – families at a time, dead and blue-black with bruising. Others were brought in from just outside Gernika with machine-gun bullets in their bodies: one, a lovely girl. The militia cried as they laid her out on the ground in the broken hospital: they could give no reason for their tears – they just cried.'

The scene was apocalyptic. Many people had been crushed as they sought shelter in cellars too weak to withstand the intensity of the bombardment, while witnesses described cattle and sheep running around the town on fire, set alight by thermite and white phosphorus from the incendiary bombs.

The flames had not been extinguished before the claims and counter-claims began as to what had actually happened. For the Republicans, outrage was mixed with a desire to elicit the sympathy of democratic countries and perhaps push them into assisting in the battle against Franco. Accounts were soon circulating that many thousands of people had been killed in the bombing. The Nationalists realized the event could potentially be very damaging, and Franco's propaganda teams, after briefly denying that Guernica had been attacked, quickly shifted to insisting that the 'Reds' had blown the town up themselves as they were retreating. Anxious to minimize the bad publicity, they peddled their account to journalists accredited to their side, who reported it back to London, Paris and Washington. Catholic supporters of Franco around the world dutifully clung on to this version of events.

But the raid was a disaster for Franco's image abroad, and there are reports that he was furious with the Germans when he learned of the consequences of the bombing. Guernica lost the Nationalists a lot of support, and *Time* magazine, *Life* and later *Newsweek* took the side of the Republic. Franco continued to insist that the enemy had destroyed the town until the 1940s. Only then did he concede bombers from the Nationalist side had been responsible. But according to this new official version, the Germans had been acting without his knowledge, so he still managed to avoid blame or responsibility.

The question of whether Franco did know that the attack was planned is still unclear. There is nothing to show he gave the definite go-ahead for it, yet he had made no complaint following the Durango bombing a few weeks earlier. If anything, the bombing of civilians fitted in with his ideas about 'redeeming' Spain through bloodshed. What he didn't want was a swift victory which would leave him with problems on the home front. The enemy had to be beaten down and subjugated.

The reasons why Guernica was targeted are, likewise, unclear. Strategically, the destruction of the town in this fashion was far from necessary. Goering, at his trial at Nuremberg, said the attack had been an experiment by the Luftwaffe.

'It's a shame, but we couldn't act in any other way,' he said when the prosecutor pointed out that women and children had been present. 'At that time these experiences couldn't be had anywhere else.'

Like a test tube, Guernica was a way of examining the effect on the enemy's morale of aerial bombardment.

Goering committed suicide in his cell, but the man more directly responsible for what happened, General – later Marshal – Sperrle, head of the Condor Legion in Spain and one of the men subsequently behind the bombing of Coventry, died a free man in Munich in 1953.

Another theory regarding the bombing is that the Germans carried it out in order to show General Mola how to conduct a rapid campaign. The Spanish Civil War was costly for Berlin, and German commanders tried on numerous occasions to speed things up or persuade their Nationalist allies to go faster.

Franco, however, preferred a slow, steady conquest that caused as little damage as possible to infrastructure. Guernica was one way of showing him how the campaign might otherwise be conducted.

More recently, though, historians have found evidence that the destruction of Guernica was an act of revenge by the Luftwaffe for the lynching of one of its pilots shot down over Republican territory earlier that year. Many who escaped their planes by parachute met the wrath of local people before the authorities could get to them.

Whatever the cause, the Germans and Italians – and the world in general – learned much about the effect of mass bombardment of civilians through the attack on Guernica, and the clock was set ticking for the future air raids that would so mark the Second World War. As one British Foreign Office official scribbled in a note at the time, Guernica 'told us what to expect from the Germans'.

The question of how many people died on that day in 1937 still seems to depend, as does so much about the Civil War, on your political persuasion. No one now talks of three or five thousand casualties, a figure claimed by some soon after the attack. The Basque government eventually gave the official figure as 1,654 killed and 889 wounded. Most now regard this as too high. Nonetheless, many historians today insist around one thousand people died. For right-wingers, though, the figure is as low as 120, or even less. Although a tragic and bloody event, now this is perhaps the least important part of the story: Guernica exists beyond the events of 26 April. In his despatch, Steer wrote: 'In the form of its execution and the scale of the destruction it wrought, no less than in the selection of its objective, the raid on Guernica is unparalleled in military history.'

Even today it is a symbol of our power to destroy.

17

Valley of the Dead

I had slept deeply the night before, and when I woke it took some minutes for the memory of where I was and what I was doing to seep back into my mind. Kiki's flat, the smooth wooden floor, hot summer light streaming through the upper window. I had sweated profusely again, skin clammy and thin. Staggering to the kitchen for a glass of water I almost fell over, my legs like rubber, head spinning. It seemed the virus had still not left me entirely.

Kiki was almost annoyingly jolly.

'We're going for a drive into the mountains. You need some mountain air.'

A couple of hours later, after I'd slowly showered, eaten and put on some of my new clothes, I was slumped in the passenger seat of an orange 2CV, wearily watching the miles of towering chocolate-brown suburbs shift gradually into dry countryside. I tried to rise above the din of the tiny engine to connect once again with where I was. Some part of my brain was aware that today Kiki was dressed most definitely as a man. Perhaps it was a disguise in order to step out of the protection the city gave him.

We stopped to pick up some newspapers and magazines, and I glanced at a photo report on Picasso's famous painting *Guernica*. Commissioned by the Republican government for its pavilion at the World Fair in Paris in the middle of the Civil War, this huge black and white depiction of the bombing has become one of Picasso's most celebrated works, a violent, chaotic scene of destruction that fits well with the painter's fragmenting, distorting style. Inspiration for the work had come after a million people took to the streets in Paris, where Picasso was living, to protest at the news of the Basque massacre. Photos of the bombed city were soon circulating. The work got mixed reviews when it went on display – the Germans and the Soviets in particular found it displeasing – but went on to become perhaps the most famous painting of the twentieth century, touring the world from its eventual home in New York. Although he had bestowed it on the 'Spanish people', Picasso had insisted it could never be shown in Spain until democracy was restored. It finally reached the country in 1981. Today it hangs in the Reina Sofía museum in the centre of Madrid.

'Picasso makes the same mistake as everyone about the Civil War,' Kiki said.

'What's that?'

'He can only see it in black and white.'

My concentration locked on to the screaming horse with its arrow-tongue, and the light-bulb eye in the sky, like a mechanical, soulless god. Try as I might to absorb other aspects of the picture, I couldn't move my gaze from these two central motifs, my eyes moving in and out of focus in a fog-like drift. A voice somewhere inside me was speaking with solid assurance, saying how natural it was that there should be no colour in such a scene. Such wilful destruction and wrongdoing could only be depicted in shades of grey. Colour would be inappropriate here.

I found myself nodding silently, taken in by the strength of the argument. But from the other side of the car came a different voice.

'It's simplistic,' Kiki said. 'If life is as complicated as it is, imagine what war must be like.' His voice hadn't noticeably changed, but it seemed subtly different from before in a way I couldn't quite pin down – more suited to one wearing 'male' dress. Perhaps it was the style of speaking more than a blunt shift in register.

'Do you think it's possible there were good guys and bad guys?' he said.

I remembered coming across a comment by Stephen Spender, who'd served on the Republican side with the International Brigades. He'd said that according to his tutor at Oxford, the Spanish Civil War was the only conflict in his lifetime where there was an absolute and clear choice between good (the Republic) and evil (Franco). Perhaps in the Europe of the 1930s it was easier to make such bold statements than it is now. Certainly I couldn't come down on one side like that myself.

There seemed to be very few people who could treat the Civil War simply as history. As with so much in Spain, emotion and passion played a large role in the matter, so much so that the echoes of the conflict still resounded today. Would they ever fall silent, I wondered?

'What happened to your family in the war?' I asked. I could hear the words coming out of my mouth in a tired slur.

'They were up in Galicia,' Kiki said. 'Not much. That whole area was under the Nationalists from the start. My grandfather had a shop and was too old to fight; my father was still a boy. An uncle on my mother's side was enlisted into Franco's army and got a bullet through the stomach at Brunete. But no one talked about the war too much. It was always there, like a headache that just won't go away, but you try to get on with things. When I was sixteen I asked my uncle about what happened, but he broke down. I didn't bother after that.'

The Battle of Brunete, in July 1937, had been one of the biggest battles of the war, an ultimately unsuccessful attempt by the Republicans to break out of the circle the Nationalists were slowly trying to draw around Madrid. Casualties were high on both sides, with around 42,000 men lost in total.

I sat back and closed my eyes, happy for a short while to be driven around, sickness inducing a childish desire to withdraw into a secure space where responsibility rested on another's shoulders. The temptation to be led, to hand yourself over to one who seemed or claimed to have all the answers, was a constant threat. Wasn't that, after all, how people had been lulled into the sleep of political extremes of the thirties? As I drifted into a dream-like state, I had visions of the Civil War turning into a battle between religious sects, Franco morphing into a tambourine-wielding Hare Krishna while his opponents lined up in the lotus position, levitating their way to the front lines and attacking their enemies with nut roasts.

I felt a hand on my arm.

We were on a country road, climbing up a hillside clad in thick pine forests, glimpses of light and spectacular views over the valley below coming into sight through breaks in the foliage. It seemed fresh and unusually green for Spain in the middle of summer, and I felt the rich dark colours washing over my senses like a cool shower.

'How long have I been asleep?'

'I want you to see something,' Kiki said.

There was something bleak and unattractive about the crosses erected under Franco's rule, as though they had all been cut by machines or cast in their thousands in some grey foundry on the edge of a once-beautiful town. Made of iron or concrete, they were to be seen dotted around the country, marking the scenes of Nationalist victories or paying homage to Franco supporters who had lost their lives to the 'Reds'. Their inscriptions often followed the formula of the Falange, saluting the founder of the fascist party, José-Antonio, before giving a list of the fallen 'heroes' from the local area, with an unintentionally ironic ¡PRESENTE! proclaimed at the bottom. How the dead were supposed to be 'present' was anyone's guess. Perhaps in spirit. But they were uniformly ugly monuments, the iron crosses rusted and overly ornate, the concrete versions cut along austere, utilitarian lines, unnaturally sharp and straight. It was strange that such a simple form could express so much, but you looked at a Francoist cross and you sensed all the harshness, rigidity and uninspired self-importance of his regime.

The crosses I had previously seen, however, were modest affairs, perhaps two or three metres high. Nothing had prepared me for the colossus that now appeared through the trees.

I knew immediately what it was, but was still taken aback by the scale of the place. The Valle de los Caídos was a vast mausoleum and basilica complex built by Franco after the war in the hills to the north of Madrid, intended as a memorial to the war dead and his eventual resting place. The structure was almost entirely carved out of the inside of a mountain, like a cave, while crowning the whole thing was a gigantic cross sticking out of the top of the rock.

'That,' Kiki said as I sat open-mouthed, 'is a hundred and fifty metres and two hundred thousand tonnes of religious devotion.'

The granite cross was so vast and imposing there was something quite obscene about it. For miles around, unspoilt countryside stretched in all directions; it was the kind of place you could imagine appealing to romantic, nineteenth-century sensibilities, all wild, untamed and emotive, with high cliffs, deep valleys and acres of virgin forest. And right in the middle of it all stood this strange, ugly structure, completely out of balance with both itself and its surroundings.

As we drove nearer on the winding mountain road an enormous plaza came into view at the foot of the carved-out rock – a semi-circular court framing the entrance to the basilica, and leading down a number of steps to an exposed and empty space that looked like a parade ground. I could make out a handful of figures walking around, some carrying what seemed to be flags.

'There won't be so many people there,' Kiki said. 'It can get quite busy, sometimes. Especially on the anniversary of Franco's death.'

The twentieth of November 1975 was still a day people remembered in Spain, even if only with a sigh of relief. I'd lost count of the number of people who'd told me they'd had a bottle of champagne sitting in the fridge at the time, waiting for the dictator finally to pass away.

'Young men from across the country congregate in Madrid and then walk out here as a kind of pilgrimage. Some of them even do it barefoot. I found out that a friend of mine was involved in it all a couple of years ago.'

'What did you do?'

'Nothing. Didn't bother me. But it was coming to an end anyway,' he said.

That was Kiki: try to pin him down in any way and he slipped effortlessly through your fingers. I'd found it slightly confusing that morning, not knowing whether to use masculine or feminine endings on adjectives relating to him. Normally it was all in the feminine. But the guise he'd chosen for this day was male, as though he'd changed his skin, and very quickly I'd found the matter took care of itself. Today he was a man, and despite being a rather boyish and slightly built man, something about the subtle energy surrounding him – just as it had been quite definitely that of a woman the day before – was now unquestionably masculine.

He parked his orange car under a tree at the edge of the complex and we began walking up to the basilica. A mixture of the mountain air and the gigantic absurdity of where we were was beginning to lift my spirits, and I suppressed a schoolboy urge to start goose-stepping around the place making Hitler salutes. Such a vast folly of a place tickled some surreal comic nerve within me.

'In the Middle Ages they spent centuries building some of the great cathedrals,' Kiki said. 'It took them twenty years to build this. Franco complained it was too slow.'

'Hardly comparable to a Gothic cathedral,' I said. A smile was playing on my lips. I felt light-headed. It was like a bizarre cross between the Eagle's Nest and the Vatican.

'You're very judgemental,' he said. 'But I can see you're glad I brought you.'

He took my hand and placed it on his shoulder for me to lean on as we walked across the great square, sunlight bouncing off every surface and glaring into our eyes. It would be a welcome relief from the heat to get inside this curious grotto of death.

Civil Guards eyed us with obligatory suspicion at the entrance, checking our bags and frisking us before letting us in. For a second it seemed I wouldn't be allowed to pass as I didn't have any ID on me, my passport having been taken along with everything else back in Saragossa. After explaining what had happened they relented. Later I almost wished they'd kept me out.

Rarely had a building produced such a sharp mood change in me as Franco's mausoleum when I stepped inside. The cheeriness I had felt outside and the sense of fun brought on by the sheer silliness of the place was transformed in an instant into dark, suffocating depression. The basilica consisted of a long tunnel-like nave with a cross at the far end, in classic Christian architectural style. But whereas Gothic cathedrals in particular were temples of light, this was little more than a dark, grim bunker, buried as it was inside a mountain. No natural light reached this far – kitsch electric fake torches hung from pillars instead, while striplights glowed up towards the vaulted ceiling. Beneath our feet the floor was black, while along the grey, damp-stained walls hung ghastly tapestries depicting apocalyptic scenes. A sense of claustrophobia gripped me at once, but I pushed on, caught between my curiosity and a desire to run back out into the square outside.

Kiki had edged away on his own and seemed to be counting the number of stones in each arch, his finger moving upwards as he mouthed numbers under his breath. They had needed twenty thousand workers to build the Valle de los Caídos and the vast majority of them had been Republican prisoners, forced to work in suicidal conditions on a hugely expensive project while the rest of the country went hungry in the harsh post-war years. Fourteen of the builders had died during the construction work, while there had been numerous mutilations. Construction had cost the equivalent of two hundred million pounds. Officially the monument was a memorial to all those who had died in the Civil War, but as so often with Franco, it was more a statement of victory and the crushing of his opponents and their vision of Spain. No mention of the other side was made at his inaugural address when the basilica was finally opened in 1959, while the small number of Republican dead buried there in the 1960s alongside Nationalists had in many cases been removed from graves around the country without even their relatives being informed. Only now were the children and grandchildren of some Republican soldiers beginning to discover that their relatives were buried alongside the very man they had been fighting against.

Franco had been obsessed by the building of the monument, and much of the architectural design was his own. It was said at the time that the Valle de los Caídos was the nearest thing he had to another woman.

Walking down the artless nave, I found Franco's headstone near the altar, with a simple inscription. It was deliberately placed so that he would appear as the 'head of the household', the main protagonist welcoming people into this space. Across from it was the grave of José Antonio. Franco exploited the legacy of the founder of the Falange to the full, setting him up as a fallen hero – he was far more useful to him dead than alive. The memory of the young, aristocratic *señorito* was turned into a cult Franco skilfully used for his own ends.

The guards on the door made sure no desecration took place here, but you almost felt they were unnecessary. You could hardly have hoped for a greyer, danker resting place for the Generalísimo.

Kiki found me outside, leaning against a pillar in the shade as I tried to shake off some of the melancholy the place seemed to have brought on in me. Out in the blazing heat of the open square a small group of men in dark army-style trousers were attempting to march in military fashion, carrying colourful flags and shouting slogans.

Kiki placed his arm on my shoulder. I watched as the young men turned first to the left and then to the right, performing some odd ritual only they seemed to understand.

'You've always insisted on being called a *transformista*,' I said. 'Never a *travesti*, a transvestite. Why?'

'*Travestis*,' he said, 'are caricatures. They only pretend to be women.'

He drew his arm away, placing his hands together as though in prayer.

'I don't condemn them. We're different, that's all.'

216

Below us, an older man to the side was barking orders like a sergeant-major. One of the boys had dropped his flag and was hurriedly picking it up and trying to carry on as though nothing had happened.

'I enjoy working at the club. It's a bit of a dive, but it's just nice to have a regular job.'

When he and Salud had been performing together, years before, they had shared the stage with a woman still having to bare her breasts at the age of sixty-five in order to pay the rent. Her tits might not have been what they once were, but the jokes and songs she performed as part of the act were so good no one really cared. There was something tragic and pathetic about her situation, nonetheless. Nobody wanted to end up like her.

'It's a show. I try to maintain as much dignity as I can. The *travestis* can give them the thrills.'

As far as Kiki himself was concerned, he was a being who could shift into either gender, with as little chance of being detected as possible. If anything, he was perhaps more convincing as a woman than as a man, when his small, slender body and cat-like walk made him stand out more. You sensed it was only as a woman that he could really slip by unnoticed.

'The audience is made up mostly of wealthy men in their fifties. With young mistresses wearing deaf-and-dumb trousers.' He paused. 'Pants so tight you can read their lips.' I laughed. From the grave faces down in the square came looks of scorn at such irreverence in this holy place. It was like a masked ball in reverse – everyone dressed the same and everyone with looks of utter seriousness. But a pantomime nonetheless.

'You think I play around with my identity?' he said, looking at the toy soldiers with their flags. 'I'm an amateur compared with this lot.'

We sat down on the grey flagstones. Vultures circled on whirling thermals rising from the overheated earth, while dusty sparrows flittered nervously around the litter bins. I looked towards the horizon, over the rising and falling contours of the land – plains, mountains and forests like different textures of skin – and remembered the things I admired about this country: the passion and the colour I had so fallen in love with when I'd first come, and which had carried me along over the years. With the things I had recently seen and experienced, my vision of Spain had become increasingly grey in the past weeks and months. As though lighting a spark in the gloom, Kiki was reminding me of the country I had always been drawn to. As he sat facing the performing fascists, I began to explain how I was feeling and how confusing I had found the last few weeks: discovering the pit – the *fosa* – near the farm, the right-wing wrestling match, getting arrested near Ceuta, and robbed just a few days before. How well did I really know Spain?

'You are like so many northern Europeans who have come here in the past,' he said. 'In Spain you find something that liberates you. I don't know what it is – perhaps the weather, the girls. But then you stop. You create a dream of what the place is, of what Spain is, and you refuse to go any further, to look outside this bubble you have created and get to know the country for what it really is.'

I closed my eyes. I thought I'd managed to break out of that trap and truly explore the country. Perhaps he was right.

'I used to dream about Paris, or New York – somewhere I could be more *me*. Where someone like me would be more accepted. But then I went to those places and you know what? I found the same prejudices as back here. OK, there are some differences, but I didn't discover the paradise I'd conjured up in my mind before I went.'

The soldiers had stopped their prancing about and were standing to attention to listen to an address being read out by a stern-looking middle-aged woman in a black dress.

'Your problem is that you came here and *did* find a kind of paradise. You *did* find something of what you were looking for. But that made you blind. Now you're discovering aspects of Spain you've always failed to notice, or hidden from, and you think you're falling out of love with the place.'

Perhaps it hadn't all been quite as he was saying, but essentially he was right. I remembered the phrase that had kept popping into my head when I'd found the farm – 'a piece of paradise', like a cliché from the property pages in a Sunday newspaper, as though paradise were something you could possess. It seemed I'd fallen into a trap, after all – of thinking my experience of the country was somehow complete, as though there was nothing left for me to learn or do here. There in the Valle de los Caídos, sitting next to Kiki, watching neo-fascists perform their rigid, colourful spectacle, it was as though I had been asleep.

'The only way you can love *de verdad*,' Kiki said, 'is to see everything there is to see of that which you love. Pick and choose and it will always come undone. You have to see whatever it is – a country, a person, an idea, even yourself – in all its complexity. Foreigners fall for a passionate image of Spain and that is all they see. But Spaniards themselves are blind. Everyone here talks about "the Two Spains" – throughout our history a long murderous struggle like Cain and Abel, or Goya's *Duelo a garrotazos* – those two giants in the middle of the countryside clubbing each other to death. On the one side a liberal, forward-looking Spain. On the other its traditional, authoritarian sibling. One Left, one Right. One dark, the other light. One male, one female. It goes on. And one always trying to impose itself on the other.'

He pulled his hair back tight over his scalp and redid the elastic holding his ponytail in place.

'Spain is both of these things and neither. The struggles

between the two sides will continue, it is part of the national make-up. You don't have to be limited by the visions of others, though. It's a question of looking, not just imagining.'

The intense afternoon heat was beginning to fade as we stepped back into his noisy orange car and started heading back to the city. In the square the young men were carrying out their final steps before the show came to an end. Under the verdant canopy above the mountain road, the darkness of the interior of the basilica seemed like a distant memory.

18

Orwell and the Civil War within the Civil War

*S*pain caught the attention of the world in the late 1930s because the most important political issue of the time – the struggle between Left and Right – was being played out in such sharp focus on its battlefields. The political divide born out of the creation of the Soviet Union found its first significant expression in the Civil War, in a foretaste of the later proxy battles fought around the globe once fascism had been defeated and the Cold War began. And just as Vietnam touched a nerve in a post-world-war generation, so Spain's war became one of the most pressing questions of its day, galvanizing thousands into action. The difference was that, whereas in the 1960s that energy was channelled into demonstrations against war, in the 1930s young people around the world were drawn to take part in the fighting themselves. A small number joined Franco's ranks. The majority caught the train south from Paris to help the Republic.

Some of those heading to Spain were artists and writers, a few already famous, others later to become so. Ernest Hemingway's

For Whom the Bell Tolls and André Malraux's *L'Espoir* are two books that emerged from their authors' experiences here. Laurie Lee waited longer before publishing an account of his time in the conflict in *A Moment of War*. Perhaps the most important literary impact the war was to have, however, was on George Orwell, not so much for his *Homage to Catalonia*, where he told of his time in Spain, but for the powerful experiences during the six months he was here that went on to inspire *Animal Farm* and *1984*, two of the most influential books of the twentieth century. If it hadn't been for what happened to him, and around him, in Spain, phrases such as 'double speak' and 'Big Brother' might never have entered the language.

Like many, Orwell was drawn to fight in Spain out of an urge to defeat fascism, his ambition being to shoot at least one fascist as a way of doing his bit for the cause. What he was unaware of, however, was how fractured the Republican side was. Most volunteers from abroad ended up in the communist-dominated International Brigades. Orwell failed to get in because of his suspect political views, and through contacts in the Independent Labour Party ended up instead in the militia of a small anti-Stalinist communist party known as the POUM – the Marxist Unification Workers' Party. The party was often labelled 'Trotskyite', as its leader, Andrés Nin, had been Trotsky's assistant some years earlier. The two men had now split, though, and the POUM was essentially an independent party on the left, with few arms at its disposal and its support largely limited to Catalonia.

Arriving in Barcelona with his wife at the end of December 1936, Orwell was immediately struck by the atmosphere in the city, which was still energized by the revolution that had taken place at the start of the war. A mass movement, mainly of anarchists, had defeated the military rising back in July and had subsequently brought about huge social changes. Most people wore workers' overalls, the formal form of address – *usted* – was no longer used, and there were no private cars on the roads. 'The working class was in the saddle,' as Orwell later wrote in *Homage to Catalonia*. Most of the main buildings in the city had been taken over by trade unions or workers' organizations, banners daubed the walls, and red and black anarchist flags flew above the roofs, revolutionary songs blaring from loudspeakers well into the night. It was all part of a stark cultural division that had developed between the Republican and Nationalist sections of the country. Whereas cities like Barcelona were all noise and promiscuity, areas under Franco's control were noted for their austerity and silence, with public notices calling on people not to talk about politics.

'There was much in it that I did not understand, in some ways I did not even like it,' Orwell wrote about what he saw, 'but I recognized it immediately as a state of affairs worth fighting for.' What he didn't realize, as he admitted, though, was that many members of the middle classes were either lying low for the time being or posing as members of the working class.

Orwell was assigned to the 'Lenin Barracks', where some one thousand men from the POUM underwent almost comical training for the front lines, being taught how to march after a fashion, but not how to take cover when under fire or how to shoot a gun – simply because there were barely any guns available. Only the sentries had rifles and Orwell was frustrated in his desire to be taught how to fire a machine-gun. Social equality was imposed on the ranks, with words like *señor*, 'sir', struck from the vocabulary. If a man disagreed with an order he could step out and argue the point with his officer. 'Discipline did not exist.' The 'uniform' was merely a half-hearted attempt by everyone to dress roughly the same, with corduroy breeches and jackets. Some wore party badges on their clothes.

Eventually Orwell was sent to the Aragon front, which was by this time fairly quiet after the rush of the first push from Barcelona towards Saragossa. The Aragonese capital remained in Nationalist hands, but the main theatre of operations was centred on Madrid. Orwell realized this and made further efforts to get transferred to the International Brigades and the heart of the action. Again he was thwarted, but this time by events on the ground.

A storm had been brewing among the various political factions within the forces lined up against Franco since the war had begun. It was merely a matter of time before it blew up. The different organizations divided roughly into two groups: those who thought the only way to defeat Franco was to have an orthodox regular army with a centralized and ordered society behind it; and those who felt revolution itself was a weapon against the fascist threat and favoured a decentralized army of loosely organized militiamen. Of the first persuasion were moderate Republicans and socialists, and the Communist Party, while on the other were most anarchists and the POUM. The communists were, at this point, strictly following Stalin's orders to make the party and the movement as a whole more acceptable to 'bourgeois' countries such as Britain and France, in an attempt to form an alliance against Hitler and Mussolini. As a result, communists were among the most well-organized and anti-revolutionary groups within the Republican ranks. Given that the Soviet Union was the only foreign power sending significant amounts of military assistance to the Republic, the Spanish Communist Party, which had been very small at the outbreak of the war, was wielding ever greater influence, backed by Soviet advisers sent over from Moscow to help the war effort. And as Stalin was busy 'purging' dissidents back home, so the cry for ideological uniformity and orthodoxy reached Spain. The POUM and the anarchists were in their sights.

The build-up to what would later be called 'a civil war within the civil war' occurred while Orwell was at the front, ignorant of the tension rising back in Barcelona. It was while he was on leave in the city, noticing that the distinctions between rich and poor seemed to have resurfaced all of a sudden, and trying to get some boots made for his size-twelve feet, that things came to a head and he found himself in the middle of the 'May Days'.

After months of tit-for-tat assassinations between communists and anarchists, the May Day processions for 1937 were cancelled in Barcelona for fear of trouble. Inflammatory articles had appeared in the anarchist and POUM newspapers, while the communist press preached 'unity' in the face of the common enemy while secretly plotting the downfall of the Republican prime minister, Francisco Largo Caballero. Orwell found it ironic that this most revolutionary of cities should be the only one where the twentieth anniversary of the Russian revolution was not being celebrated. Two days later, however, he discovered why. On 3 May a delegation from the local Catalan government tried to take over the telephone-exchange building in the centre of the city. Although it was theoretically controlled by both socialist and anarchist union members, the anarchists had the upper hand and it was feared they were listening in to official phone calls. Arriving with a group of armed policemen, the delegation was immediately forced back by anarchists firing from the upper floors. After several hours of negotiations it seemed the stand-off had been resolved, but the event triggered the resentment between the various parties that had been growing over the previous months.

By the next day armed men had taken over the streets and set up barricades, much as they had done at the start of the war. Barcelona was at war against itself. The anarchist union, the CNT, controlled most of the suburbs, but the centre was divided down the Ramblas, the main avenue at the heart of the city running from the Plaza de Cataluña to the sea. The communists and socialists were on the left-hand side, the anarchists on the right. Gunmen took to the rooftops and fired at any vehicle that moved. The situation was complicated by the fact that the anarchists themselves were now deeply divided. Some had taken the ideologically paradoxical step of joining the Republican government based in Valencia, while others, such as a group calling itself the 'Friends of Durruti', wanted a return to the glorious days of the previous July, when the military coup had been foiled in the city and a workers' revolution had spontaneously broken out. As far as they were concerned, the forces of the counter-revolution were on the march and had to be stopped.

Whereas in July the hard-line anarchists had been backed from all sides against the military rebels, this time their only potential allies were the POUM. Never great friends in the past, the two parties now found themselves pitched together against the local Catalan government and the communists, who were supported by crack teams from the Assault Guards.

Franco later liked to take the credit for what happened in Barcelona that May, saying he had a dozen agents working for him in the city at the time. It isn't clear how great a role they played in creating the conflict, but the various Republican factions were close to blows anyway. The communists saw this as their opportunity to eclipse once and for all the POUM, the anarchists and Prime Minister Largo Caballero – a man they had originally courted but now wanted removed.

As the fighting in Barcelona flared up, Orwell dashed up and down the Ramblas trying not to get shot as he moved between the Hotel Continental, where his wife was staying, and the Hotel Falcon down the road, which had become the POUM head-quarters. Once he had installed himself with his colleagues, he was placed on guard duty on the rooftop; periods of stalemate in the fighting were interspersed with sporadic shooting. Anarchist militiamen were said to be on their way from the front to storm the city, but eventually they were persuaded to hold back by the anarchist ministers in the Valencia government. The factions held their positions and the city remained divided. Tensions increased when a couple of days later the bodies of murdered anti-communists were discovered, including the brother of Francisco Ascaso, Durruti's best friend. Later the anarchists assassinated the socialist union leader Antonio Sesé, presumably in retaliation.

On the whole, however, as Orwell remarked, this 'mini civil war' was a static affair. 'So far as I could see, and from all I heard, the fighting was defensive on both sides. People simply remained in their buildings or behind their barricades and blazed away at the people opposite.' It was a time of 'violent inertia', and Orwell and others would take turns on guard duty before heading down to the Hotel Continental for meals. The place had become something of a refuge for people seeking respite from the troubles outside in the city, and was filled with foreign journalists, political activists and several communist agents, including a 'fat, sinister-looking Russian' who walked around with a revolver and a bomb attached to his waistband, whom they nicknamed Charlie Chan. As the days passed and still the stand-off continued, Orwell was fascinated to see how this man would corner all the foreign refugees in the hotel and explain how the conflict was all down to an anarchist plot. 'I watched him with some interest,' he wrote, 'for it was the first time I had seen a person whose profession was telling lies – unless one counts journalists.' Barcelona, and Republican Spain, was soon to be overrun by men like Charlie Chan.

As the conflict continued, Orwell began to get bored, having to spend hours on rooftop guard duty, reading Penguin paperbacks to while away the time. Very little actually seemed to be happening. A short-lived truce came and went, resulting in more gunfire. All the while he and his colleagues were in danger of being shot at by policemen on the roof of the next building. Eventually a peace agreement was reached between the various factions. The government in Valencia sent up more Assault Guards to take control of the city, and the fighting came to a halt.

According to official figures, a total of four hundred people had been killed in the fighting and a thousand wounded. Later claims would put the number killed as high as nine hundred. The red and black anarchist flag was taken down from the telephone-exchange building, where the conflict had begun, and replaced with the Catalan flag. 'That meant that the workers were definitely beaten.' Orwell – and most people in Barcelona, you imagine – was greatly relieved, if only because it was now safe to go out into the streets and buy something to eat – one of the greatest hardships of the previous days had been the shortage of food.

With the re-establishment of order came a handful of arrests – a wounded friend from the front had to spend eight days in a cell so crowded there was no room to lie down. And the atmosphere in the city underwent a sinister change. 'You had all the while the hateful feeling that someone hitherto your friend might be denouncing you to the secret police.' The campaign against the anarchists, and particularly against the POUM, had begun. The POUM newspaper was subjected to censorship so heavy it appeared with almost its entire front page blanked out. Meanwhile the communist press appeared as normal, denouncing the POUM in a cartoon as a party of 'fascists'. These independent, anti-Moscow Marxists, to whose militia Orwell was still attached, were being turned into the scapegoats for all that had happened. 'No one who was in Barcelona then, or for months later, will forget the horrible atmosphere produced by fear, suspicion, hatred, censored newspapers, crammed jails, enormous food queues and prowling gangs of armed men.'

Ironically, Orwell was approached at this time to see if he wanted to join the International Brigades. It would have meant being taken to the Madrid front, where he wanted to be, but this time he refused, claiming that after what had just happened he couldn't join any communist-controlled unit. 'Sooner or later it might mean being used against the Spanish working class.'

He left again for the positions of his POUM comrades on the Aragon front, but not before noticing how much better the Assault Guards were armed, with their new rifles sent from the Soviet Union, than the men actually fighting the enemy on the front lines. 'I suspect it is the same in all wars – always the same contrast between the sleek police in the rear and ragged soldiers in the line.' It was a sign of how much more importance was being placed on the political struggles back home than on fighting Franco. Not reading the signals, Orwell was still blind to how much danger he himself was in.

Not long after he arrived for his second stint at the front, he was shot in the neck, an experience which he described as being '*at the centre* of an explosion'. Realizing where he'd been hit, he assumed at first he was dying. Miraculously, though, the bullet missed the carotid artery and merely damaged his vocal cords. For some time he couldn't speak, and a doctor told him he would never recover his voice, although he eventually did. There now followed several weeks of recuperation, being carted around from the front to various hospitals, eventually ending up on the coast at Tarragona. Around him great political changes were taking place as a result of the 'May Days' in Barcelona, of which he was totally unaware. A couple of weeks after the fighting, the communists achieved their aim of bringing down Largo Caballero's government. They now moved in on the POUM.

Seriously wounded as he was, Orwell realized his fighting days were over and decided to return to England. He needed his discharge papers signing, however, a process which involved travelling back almost to the front line to get the right person's signature. This done, he returned to Barcelona.

The first sign that anything was wrong came when he walked back into the Hotel Continental and his wife immediately ran up, threw her arms around him and hissed into his ear, 'Get out!' Orwell didn't react straight away and she had to repeat what she'd said. A passing Frenchman and a POUM member of staff confirmed the situation: he was in danger. As she led him from the hotel, his wife explained that while he'd been away the POUM had been declared illegal and its buildings seized. Almost everyone associated with it had been arrested, and there was a rumour circulating that the party leader, Andrés Nin, had been shot. Even then it took Orwell time to realize the seriousness of the situation. 'It all seemed too meaningless.' But they had to get out of Spain as quickly as possible. It was only a matter of time before they came for him. The police had already raided their room at the hotel, and presumably the only reason his wife hadn't been taken in already was so that she could be used as a decoy. Although they didn't know it at the time, a warrant had been issued for the arrest of both of them by the newly created Tribunal for Espionage and High Treason, for being 'confirmed Trotskyites'.

Leaving the country was a complicated business, however, and required obtaining permission from three separate bodies, including the chief of police and the French Consulate. While their papers were being processed through the British Consulate, Orwell tore up his POUM militiaman's card and a photograph showing soldiers with the POUM flag in the background. He now had to pretend to be a well-to-do foreign tourist during the day, sleeping rough on the outskirts of the city at night for fear of being picked up. It took a couple of days to get their papers in order, a time during which Orwell could have been arrested at any instant. Nonetheless, he made an attempt to secure the release of his commanding officer, who had been detained along with other members of the POUM. Despite risking arrest himself by walking boldly into the War Department to demand a document he thought might save the man's life, the attempt failed.

Two days later, the Orwells and a couple of friends – John McNair and Stafford Cottmann – were escaping on a train. Luckily their names had not yet reached the border guards, and after a thorough search they were allowed over into France. As soon as they arrived they read a newspaper report announcing that McNair had been arrested for spying.

Had Orwell been caught – and Spanish inefficiency or sheer luck must have accounted for him getting away – he would almost certainly have been killed, or died while being tortured to make him 'confess' his treason. The POUM was accused of being in the pay of the fascists, a 'fifth column' organization. But if the communists had hoped for a rerun of the Moscow show trials, they were disappointed: Andrés Nin, the POUM leader, died refusing to incriminate himself. The communist education minister, Jesús Hernández, gave an account of his fate:

[Nin] was resisting until he fainted. His inquisitors were getting impatient. They decided to abandon the 'dry' method. Then the blood flowed, the skin peeled off, muscles torn, physical suffering pushed to the limits of human endurance. Nin resisted the cruel pain of the most refined tortures. In a few days his face was a shapeless mass of flesh.

Realizing they weren't getting anywhere, the communists devised an absurd scheme to get rid of him: Germans from the International Brigades were made to dress up as Gestapo commandos and kidnap Nin, being careful to leave 'clues' such as German banknotes at the scene. He was finally murdered and his body disposed of.

The repression of the POUM was merely an early step in the communists' brutal drive to power. Shortly afterwards they took over the workings of a newly created secret police, the SIM, which tortured and murdered suspected political heretics, including troops from the front, purely for not being supportive enough of the party. Early torture techniques involved beatings with rubber piping, mock executions and splinters placed under prisoners' nails. Visiting agents from the Soviet NKVD soon introduced them to more sophisticated methods, showing them how to build special cells with sharp bits of brick sticking up from the floor so that the naked suspect was unable to sit or lie down and was kept in constant pain. They also used powerful lights and strange noises to disorientate, when not resorting to the electric chair for quicker results.

Orwell managed to make it back to Britain after travelling up through France and crossing the Channel. It was a world away from the fighting south of the Pyrenees. 'The men in bowler hats, the pigeons in Trafalgar Square, the red buses, the blue policemen – all sleeping the deep, deep sleep of England . . .' In the words of his biographer, D. J. Taylor, Spain was 'the defining experience of Orwell's life'. Much of his later work was built on what had happened to him and what he had seen there. 'It was in Spain that, for the first time in his life, Orwell saw newspaper articles that bore no relation to the known facts, read accounts of battles where no fighting had taken place, saw troops who had fought valiantly denounced as cowards and traitors.' A world was coming into being where propaganda and 'double speak' – later it would be called 'spin' – played a dominant role, and the man who would open our eyes to its insidiousness and danger was there at its birth, and was very nearly its victim. Years before Snowball was banished from Animal Farm, or Winston Smith was persecuted at the hands of Big Brother in Oceania for 'thoughtcrime', Orwell himself had come close to suffering a similar fate in Barcelona.

19

Badajoz

*T*he air was so hot and dry it felt as though an electric charge had wrapped itself round my arms and legs like a creeping vine, slowing me and dragging me down as I trod the baking, broken pavements, past abandoned palaces and piles of rubble. A small, dark-eyed dog lay on its side in a shaded corner, its fur stiff and dusty, belly rising and falling in quick rhythm as it tried to cool itself. Like the dog, I tried to stay in the shaded parts of the street, hugging the sides of buildings as though seeking shelter from a rain storm, but the bricks and cement of the walls pushed their heat back in my face, almost forcing me into the deathly crossfire of the sun's rays. Common sense told me to fall into a bar or hotel and find sanctuary in an air-conditioned world, but there were things I wanted to see before my meeting with Manolo. Most other people, I felt, had already left town.

I heard Portuguese voices singing from a building site as I walked down from the citadel towards the bullring, their mournful cadences more suited to the sadness of the city, with its empty streets and scent of decay, than those of the Spanish to whom it belonged. Badajoz was pressed against the border, down in the southwest of the country, but it seemed a forgotten place, a ghost town in the making. The ancient Alcazaba, like the rest of the old quarter, was little more than an abandoned dump. It housed a museum and a library, but around these buildings all was neglect: weeds a metre high had taken root everywhere, broken bottles scattered the ground. The only sign of human care came from an old chapel set in the defensive walls that had been occupied by a gypsy family, their clothes hanging out to dry from rusting iron railings. It was a Spain that wouldn't have been unfamiliar to George Borrow or Richard Ford.

Outside the walls, nestling beneath them for protection, the city extended downwards, streets following the contours of the hill like river beds. Yet here every third or fourth house, usually a wreck, was for sale or abandoned. Blood-red paint which had once been daubed on the walls peeled in the sun, piles of broken brick and plaster had been shovelled into street corners, posters hung in faded shreds from billboards. I caught sight of a little baroque church squeezed in among all the decay, its walls scarred with black smears, and next to it an old men's bar with cracked wooden windows, through which I could see leathery sunburnt faces sipping scratched tumblers of red wine.

It could have been an attractive place, with its abandoned nineteenth-century colonial-style houses and *palacios*. These had once been proud buildings, yet now they had fallen into squalor. I continued walking through the streets. A man with his shirt open to the navel and thick grey chest hair stepped out from a nearby doorway with a whisky and ice in his hand, scratching his unshaven, glistening cheek as he crossed the road to a bar on the other side. Two drug addicts, all thin thighs and dirt-black clothes, feigned a swipe at me as they walked past. I ducked and they collapsed into hysterical laughter.

I went into the town hall to look for some information about the city, but I could find no one inside. Like the *Marie Celeste*, everyone appeared to have mysteriously jumped ship. I walked on, down towards the bullring. Something called the Athenaeum Club announced itself from the entrance of a semi-abandoned modern brick structure; large dry weeds poked out of the walls on the third floor.

Finally, my head spinning like a top, I reached the bottom of the hill and the site of the bullring. I had seen photographs of this notorious place and expected it, like the rest of the old town, to be a crumbling, weed-infested building, ignored and left to rot by a city that seemed to echo with the horror that had taken place within its walls years before. Yet here, at the epicentre of the city's woe, the structure which lay at the very heart of its dark secret, I found the first sign of change. The bullring was no longer there. In its place workmen were busy building a new, white, bullring-shaped structure which, according to a large announcement by the entrance gates, would eventually be a conference centre. Where once men had been slaughtered, now they would come to talk.

Badajoz had been at the centre of events in the Civil War in mid-August 1936, barely a month after the fighting had begun. After the bulk of Franco's Army of Africa had successfully crossed the Strait of Gibraltar to the Spanish mainland, a column began working its way quickly up the western side of the country, through the region of Extremadura, leaving a bloody trail in its wake. It advanced over 120 kilometres in just four days, killing any leftists and unionists in its path. Others with no involvement in politics, let alone with the Popular Front, were also murdered as the soldiers joked about carrying out 'agrarian reform'.

In the great push northwards towards Madrid, however, Badajoz, pressed against the Portuguese border in the south-west, got left behind. Stalling the advance, Franco's troops, headed by Colonel Yagüe of the Legión, swung westwards and pushed down on this pocket of resistance. At dawn on 14 August they launched their attack. The defenders were mostly badly armed militiamen, but with a handful of well-placed machine-guns on the town's ramparts they were able to inflict serious casualties on the legionaries. By midday one formation of Nationalists had entered the town and was fighting its way into the centre. Yagüe, however, was unaware of this and launched an attack on Republican positions at the Puerta Trinidad. Scores of his men fell, including Lieutenant Eduardo Artigas, who was 'gloriously blinded by a bullet through the eyes'.[24] By the time they broke through the defensive lines only a captain, a corporal and fourteen legionaries from the original assault force survived.

The city fell shortly afterwards, but the Legión had suffered its heaviest casualties of the conflict thus far – forty-four dead and several hundred wounded. Its revenge was cruel and bloody.

'No human force was able to contain the blind passion of the fighting legionary, his mind and reason all gone at the loss of his comrades,' wrote one witness.[25] The defenders were killed with anything to hand – grenades, bayonets, knives and guns. The last Republicans were shot on the altar of the cathedral. Piles of corpses were scattered around the city, while the streets ran red with blood.

Moroccan soldiers from the Regulares cut the testicles off their male victims for trophies and looted people's homes, often stealing from the houses of Nationalist sympathizers as well as Republicans. This was later explained away as a 'war tax' for their liberation. Booty taken in this manner was sent back to the soldiers' families in Morocco as a way of encouraging more men to enlist. The legionaries, on the other hand, didn't bother with the trinkets picked up by the Regulares, simply smashing out any gold teeth found in the mouths of their victims.

In the immediate aftermath of the battle, thousands of people were rounded up and herded into the bullring. Anyone with a bruise or a mark on his shoulder – a sign he had been firing a rifle – was taken in, as were all known Republican sympathizers and any unfortunates in the way. Teachers, lawyers, even a photographer, were all imprisoned. For the next few weeks they were systematically shot in batches. Afterwards their bodies were taken to the cemetery outside the city walls where they were doused in petrol, burned and buried in mass graves. Some were shot outside the cemetery itself.

Other massacres carried out by Franco's troops had occurred in relative obscurity. The killings at Badajoz, however, were read about all over the world, thanks to the arrival shortly after the city's fall of foreign journalists. 'SLAUGHTER AFTER CAPTURE OF BADAJOZ' ran the headline in the *Manchester Guardian* over a piece suggesting as many as two thousand had been killed – mostly by 'excited' Moroccan troops, or 'natives', as they then called them. A few days later, when interviewed by an American journalist, Colonel Yagüe seemed to suggest that double that number had been shot.

'Do you think I was going to take four thousand Red prisoners while my column carried on running against the clock?' he said when asked about the rumours and unconfirmed reports of mass bloodshed in the city. 'Of course we shot them.'

The news of the killings reached Madrid just as the first Nationalist aerial bombings of the city were beginning. There people reacted angrily, and scores of political prisoners held in the Modelo jail were taken out and shot by the militias in reprisal. The Republican government appeared helpless to prevent a massacre taking place under its very nose.

I was in Badajoz to meet a man who had been directly touched by the massacre in the city: Manolo's father and grandfather had both been murdered in one of the darkest chapters of the Civil War. Manolo represented much of where Spain was and where it wanted to go, but he was formed by events which took place almost seventy years earlier, when he was still growing in his mother's womb.

We met at a café on the top floor of a department store, a windowless cocoon of cool air and bland music which seemed like a buffer against the world and memories outside. Manolo was a bald, elderly man with large ears and drooping, sad eyes. I had come to hear his account of the massacre in the bullring at Badajoz, an event which still divided the country – according to some, it had never taken place at all.

I had spent a few more days in Madrid, recovering from the virus that had laid me low, gradually regaining my strength with the help of Kiki's cooking and good humour. With time, though, I had felt I should carry on – I had a growing sense that somehow, having reached Madrid, I had turned a corner. I was seeing dimensions of Spain I had previously closed my eyes to, and wanted to continue my exploration.

Kiki had told me about a new organization that was trying to revive Spain's memory of what had happened in the Civil War. The Asociación para la Recuperación de la Memoria Histórica was sponsoring digs around the country, at sites where Republicans had been shot and buried in unmarked graves. They said the bodies of over thirty thousand Spaniards were still lying in ditches around the country, places like the site Begoña had shown me. In a country like Spain, where the rites of death are so important, for decades thousands of families had been denied the chance to give their relatives a decent burial. Now at last it seemed that was beginning to change.

The organization was also playing an important role in raising awareness of what had gone on under the Franco regime. When the dictator had died, Spanish democracy was built on an agreement not to rake over the past, almost to pretend that nothing had happened – the so-called *pacto de olvido*, the 'pact of forgetting', that Miguel in Granada had mentioned. Now, though, as the last survivors of the Civil War were dying off, an effort was being made to remember events before it was too late. 'Recovering historical memory' was their watchword. Many of those involved were young people wanting to know what had happened, say, to a murdered grandfather the family had always talked of in hushed tones. Once Franco was in power, the Civil Guard police force acted with impunity in much of the country, a repressive law unto themselves. It didn't do to speak too loudly about the horrors of the past.

There were, however, a number involved in the organization who had been touched directly by the violence of the war. One of them was Manolo Martínez, the head of the local committee of the association in Badajoz.

Manolo spoke softly, his delicate pale hands lifting to touch his face as he told me his story. He was unusually mild-mannered and undogmatic. Spanish men often prefer to pontificate rather than communicate, handing down unquestionable gospel truth. But Manolo was different and the contrast was striking. He asked politely for a cup of coffee from the sulky teenage waitress and began to talk about his life.

'My father was twenty-six when he was shot,' he said. 'He was a socialist, linked to the town council. They picked him up and took him to the bullring, along with so many others.'

Behind him, up at the bar, the waitress was staring into space, twirling her hair around her finger while she bit the nail down on her thumb.

'They took my grandfather too,' he added. A neighbour, he explained, had told the Nationalist soldiers who had just conquered the city that he was 'living in sin'. His grandfather had been separated from his grandmother for some time by then, and had had children by another woman. The soldiers went round and arrested him.

Under the Republic, separation and divorce had been made legal. Many who had taken advantage of the new laws found themselves caught out when Franco took over, and soon discovered their new arrangements were not recognized by his authoritarian Catholic state. This was the first time I had heard of someone being shot for it, though.

'My mother was pregnant with me at the time,' Manolo continued. 'My father and I never knew each other.'

We fell silent for a moment. He sipped his coffee. In the background ambient music hummed above the low clatter of shop assistants on their afternoon shift. I was struck by the lack of self-pity in his voice. He was almost seventy, and had had an entire life to think about all this, but his simple, matter-of-fact delivery seemed at odds with the drama of what he was telling me. Something about the man both solicited and rejected sympathy.

'Our family had a house near the Puerta Trinidad, where much of the fighting to break into the city took place,' he continued. 'When the troops arrived my mother moved with the family to a relative's house near the train station. After breaching the defences, the Nationalist soldiers took over our house and turned it into a makeshift hospital. The Moors stole my mother's trousseau – all the sheets and curtains, that kind of thing – and then sold them to the neighbours for cash. When my mother finally got back home she had to buy it all back.'

There was another pause as he swallowed. Behind his glasses it was hard to read his expression. The sadness in his eyes seemed constant, as though fixed by the events he was describing; but, magnified by the distortion of his lenses, there seemed to flicker a whole range of responses and emotions within him: a steady, self-assured sparkle. I asked him if he knew where his father had been killed.

'I don't know,' he said. 'Either at the bullring or at the cemetery. They used to line them up against the wall by the main gates. My grandfather, though, was definitely shot at the bullring.'

His father's younger brother, he explained, was just a child at the time, but had been captured by the Nationalists and interned in the bullring with the thousands of other prisoners. One day he heard his father's name being called out from a list and then a few minutes later the stuttering of machine-gun fire as he was shot. Later the boy managed to escape from the bullring and survive.

'They were holding children there?' I asked incredulously.

'Oh yes,' he said. 'And women too.'

A woman in Badajoz had told him about her experiences: her father had been a socialist councillor and when the city fell he went to ground. As the Nationalists couldn't find him they arrested his wife and her son – the woman's mother and brother. She was just a girl at the time and went down to the bullring to see if her mother and brother were there. The guard opened the gate, saying, 'We've got loads here – have a look.' And she saw her mother and brother tied together. Later they were taken to the cemetery where they were shot embracing each other.

Manolo related these anecdotes with a certain flatness in his voice, as if it mattered little to him whether or not I was absorbing this information. It struck me that perhaps the only way he could describe these events was in this slightly dry, non-emotional way. To try to dramatize them or bring them alive might strike the wrong note.

The waitress came and brought more coffee, the stud in her exposed belly button glinting under the harsh department-store lights. I wondered how much she knew of what Manolo was telling me, if she cared about the bestial acts that had taken place only yards up the road from where we sat. A whole generation had been brought up not knowing anything about their recent past except the official textbook version about Franco's campaign to save the country from the Reds. This had been taught in schools for many years after the Generalísimo's death.

I asked Manolo about his childhood, about growing up without a father.

'I was always surrounded by mourning women,' he said. 'My mother, my grandmother, various aunts, all mourning like a wailing chorus in a Greek tragedy. All of them dressed in black.'

His eyes dropped for a moment.

'It was very hard adapting to the wider world when I was older,' he said without looking up. 'The world is male-dominated, *machista*, and I had no idea how to move in that environment. All my life I'd been with women. I had no male role models, no examples to follow. It took me a long time to adjust when I myself became a man.'

I asked if other children his age had gone through similar experiences.

He nodded. 'Some far worse. Plenty of women here were widowed and had to find a way of staying alive. They used to cross the border into Portugal to buy wheat and bread and other things that weren't available in the city after the war, then sell them to earn money. To get by the border guards they often had to sleep with the men on duty to pass with their goods.'

From the counter across the shop floor a woman wearing a yellow silk summer dress was complaining to a sales assistant about something she'd bought. She wanted her money back and was making sure everyone within a thirty-yard radius could hear her. Customers in the café fell silent as the woman's voice rose to a high-pitched whine. A long-suffering employee looked on passively, trying unsuccessfully not to betray with his face the thoughts that were passing through his mind.

Manolo went on talking, ignoring the scene that was catching everyone's attention. A lot of people his age, he was saying, didn't want to talk about any of this, still preferring the culture of silence that had prevailed since the 1970s. He had bumped into one man a few days previously – they had been at school together and his father, like Manolo's, had been shot in the bullring. 'Why are you digging all this up?' the man had said. 'Why not leave it alone?'

'He can't cope with it,' Manolo said. 'That's fine. I'm not asking him to talk. But for too long people have been afraid to say that all these things happened. Now it's time to speak out.'

It amazed me, after what Manolo had said, that there still seemed to be serious-minded people around – some historians, for example – who claimed that the massacre never took place. There was even a book about Badajoz during the Civil War that didn't so much as mention the bullring, claiming that in total only twenty people were killed when the city was captured. When I mentioned this, Manolo merely shrugged his shoulders. 'There'll always be people like that,' he said.

His expression was fatalistic, but not without confidence that the truth of what he was saying would eventually win through. Outside the country there were few doubts that the massacre had taken place. Only in Spain, where the Nationalists had won, did you hear denials.

Manolo's world had been destroyed before he was even born; he had been struggling with this all his life. And now finally he was able to say what had happened. But there was no shouting from the rooftops, no triumphalism or pretension in his words or his manner. He was, if anything, humbled by what life had given him, and treated his task now with a sense of responsibility.

As we finished our drinks, Manolo told me one last story. A man from Valencia had contacted him through the association, ringing him up out of the blue.

'Before the war, his father had been involved in some drama performance in support of a trade union,' Manolo said. Some time later he was involved in a freak accident at a petrol station and lost both his eyes and his hands. When the Francoists took over that area, anyone who'd been involved in the drama production was sentenced to death. But, because of his injuries, the man's father had his sentence commuted to life imprisonment. So severe were his disabilities that he was useless as a prisoner, so they commuted it again to house arrest. But now, under house arrest, in effect his entire family was subjected to a form of incarceration. 'If they lit a fire in winter,' Manolo said, 'the guards outside would come in, pull their cocks out in front of the women and piss on the flames to put them out.'

After fifteen years of this, the poor man asked for clemency, which was granted. But he still had to make some money. So father and son got involved in *estraperlo* – the black market. They'd go out on the train to the villages to sell stuff from the city, then bring goods back to sell from the country. Arriving back in Valencia in the afternoon, they couldn't get off at the station as they might be caught by the authorities. So they had to jump from the moving carriage a few hundred yards out. The son had to tell his blind, handless father exactly when to leap, otherwise he would fall to his death. For years this was how they lived.

Manolo leaned in towards me. 'You know what this man on the phone said to me? "They should have shot him in the beginning. It would have saved us so much pain."

'But, I said to him, at least you *had* a father there, a hero figure to look up to. That's what counts. I never had that. But the man just couldn't understand.'

As Manolo spoke, I began to see Spain differently, as a country that had suffered for centuries at the hands of tyrants, but which had emerged somehow intact, yet also subtly transformed, as if given greater strength. In his quiet, unassuming way Manolo was pulling away at the layers of fear which had wrapped around this country, by giving lectures, organizing conferences, simply by talking about what had happened. By breaking the silence that held the past in ice. For people outside the country, the Spanish Civil War was an episode in history; here it was part of people's own internal narrative. After decades of speaking in whispers, these stories could now be told out loud.

'I have always thought,' Manolo said as he got up to leave, 'that the most important thing is not what happens to you in life, but how you deal with what you are given. I have always tried to live by that.'

I sat sipping my coffee. Across the store the woman in the yellow silk dress was still arguing vociferously with the shop assistant.

20

The End

*T*he Civil War came to a rapid and sudden close in the spring of 1939, the final drama being played out on the docks of Alicante. Thousands of desperate people crammed on to the quay, scanning the horizon for any sign of ships that might rescue them from imprisonment and death at the hands of the advancing Nationalists. They had come from all over the country to this, one of the last ports held by the Republicans. British vessels, it was said, were on their way. One had recently passed by – Billmeir's the *Stanbrook* – and had taken over two thousand people away to safety. In the last days before final defeat, the refugees were praying that more like her would come and save them.

After the collapse on the front lines, the Nationalists were moving in fast as Republicans, hungry and weary after almost three years of war, spontaneously gave up the fight. There was only one thing to do: get out quickly before being caught up in the waves of reprisals that would inevitably come. Most members of the Republican government had already gone into exile. Those who had remained were on their way out, flying from danger in specially arranged aircraft or on foreign ships. They'd had their escape routes planned for weeks, not least those who had been urging the people to 'fight to the last man'. Republican Spain, a quickly shrinking piece of territory, had become a place of fear and chaos. But with no land borders left to them, there was only one direction in which people could run: towards the sea.

The hope in Alicante was that the British would finally come to their aid and help them fight against the fascists who were threatening the whole of Europe. The British, on whom everyone's hopes had rested through all these years of war. But the British didn't want trouble, and they didn't want war. Only days before they had recognized Franco as the legitimate ruler of Spain. They were determined not to upset him now.

Fifteen thousand people pressed against the sea, in fear of the Italian soldiers fighting for Franco who were moving quickly down to capture the city. Time was running out for the refugees. A glimmer of hope appeared in the form of two ships approaching the docks. But the captains took one look at the sheer quantity of expectant people on shore – many of them armed – and quickly turned back.

There was no means of escape: even the local fishing boats had been sabotaged in the days beforehand. And when an enterprising refugee managed to make the motor on one of them work, scores of people leaped on board and the boat quickly sank. Within minutes it lay at the bottom of the sea, unsalvageable.

As desperation grew and the Italians moved in closer, the suicides began. A man with a cigarette in his mouth slit his own throat and fell to the ground, bleeding to death. Two men shook each other by the left hand and shot themselves in the temple. Others threw themselves into the sea.[26] This was the last betrayal. Many believed they had been deliberately herded into this spot to make their capture and murder at the hands of the Nationalists that much easier. They preferred to take their own lives than hand themselves over to the enemy. Others hung on. They knew everything was lost, but decided to wait it out. Their duty was to escape and keep on fighting. As the suicides continued around them, a small group of men grabbed what they could and tried to make a run for it. They were soon caught outside the town by the Italians.

Then, from the castle on the hill overlooking the port, came the sound of machine-gun fire. The Nationalists had arrived. Panic set in, and some of the refugees threw suitcases full of saffron into the sea. They had been planning on taking the precious substance abroad to sell – something to get by on if they managed to leave the country. Seeping out, it stained the water below them yellow and red. And then, just at the last minute, a ship arrived in the port. Perhaps they were about to be saved after all. But as the vessel approached, it unfurled the Nationalist flag and played the Nationalist anthem to the thousands lining the port. The waiting had ended. There was nowhere left to go.

After the Nationalists' failed attempt to capture Madrid in the autumn and winter of 1936–7, the Spanish Civil War turned into a slow conflict of attrition, Franco gradually chiselling away at Republican territory while the Republicans in their turn launched offensives meant to divert Nationalist advances and deliver a decisive blow against the enemy. The mistakes of the First World War were often repeated. On the Republican side, tanks, when they were used, were usually spread out thinly along the front rather than formed into powerful columns. Land was won and lost at the cost of thousands of lives. Franco's German and Italian allies would often become exasperated at the Generalísimo's old-fashioned tactics: the Spanish war was costing them time and a lot of money. But Franco refused to change his methods. He wanted to keep the infrastructure intact while pursuing a war meant to 'cleanse' Spain of Marxism, Freemasonry and the world born out of the European Enlightenment, which in his mind was responsible for so many of the country's problems. A swift victory over the enemy would have created more difficulties in the rearguard and required repression on a scale even larger than was already being carried out.

After failing to break through at Madrid – but still trying to encircle the capital – Nationalist attentions had temporarily turned to the conquest of the southern city of Málaga, where Mussolini's Italian soldiers claimed an important victory. As well as sending significant military assistance, Hitler and Il Duce had both now officially recognized Franco's regime as the legitimate government in Spain, an event which Franco had described as 'the peak of life in the world'. Málaga became another notorious bloodbath, with perhaps as many as twenty thousand Republicans shot in the aftermath of its capture, much to the horror of the Italians. Arthur Koestler, who was in the city when it fell, described how exhausted militiamen would hang around on street corners, rolling cigarettes, waiting for the Nationalists to arrive and shoot them.

With this important port city in their hands, the Nationalists then turned their attentions to the strip of territory running along the northern coast which was cut off from the rest of the Republic. First the Basque Country, which had achieved virtual independence by this point, then Cantabria and finally Asturias all fell to Franco's armies. The Condor Legion played a significant role in this campaign, bombing Guernica into oblivion and then developing carpet-bombing techniques in Asturias. Republican offensives at Brunete, west of Madrid, and later on the Aragon front did little eventually to improve the situation, ending either in Nationalist counter-offensives which won back most of the territory lost, or a stalemate.

After the north fell, the Republic made two more large-scale attempts to turn the course of a war which was steadily going against them. Firstly a move was made to capture the town of Teruel, in southern Aragon, in the winter of 1937–8. It was a particularly harsh winter in a bleak part of the country. Temperatures dropped to twenty degrees below zero and guns and artillery froze. Heavy blizzards cut the Republican lines of supply from Valencia. Forty-six men from one brigade were shot for refusing to attack with empty rifles when their ammunition ran out. Eventually Republican forces captured the town, only to lose it again shortly afterwards in a Nationalist counter-offensive. Exhausted, they were unable to fight back as the Nationalists pushed on and took new ground. Within a few months they had reached the Mediterranean and cut Catalonia off from the rest of the Republic.

The last serious Republican attempt to turn the war came at the Battle of the Ebro, the river that gives the Iberian peninsula its name and which runs across the northeast of the country. A decisive blow there could have rejoined Catalonia with the remainder of Republican territory. It was the biggest battle of the war. By now the Republican army was a professional fighting unit rather than the previous collection of militias and a handful of officers who had refused to join the coup. But after rapid gains, the offensive stalled and was slowly pushed back. It was a disaster for the Republic, which essentially lost its army in the north as a result. When, shortly after in the late autumn of 1938, Hitler gave Franco yet more military supplies in exchange for iron-ore concessions, the balance tipped significantly in the Nationalists' favour. Taking advantage of the enemy's disarray, they launched an offensive against Catalonia at the end of December. Republican Spain was now hungry and desperate.

Within a month the Nationalists had reached the Pyrenees and the French border. The Republican government, its capital now in Barcelona, fled, the rump of the Spanish parliament, the Cortes, holding its last meeting at the border town of Figueres. Franco rejected all offers of a deal. There could only be unconditional surrender.

Barcelona, once the most revolutionary city in Spain, was now in Franco's hands. In a strange irony of history, the first Nationalist tank to enter the centre carried a celebrating German–Jewish woman on the front giving the fascist salute. She had just been released from a Republican jail where she was being held for 'Trotskyism'. Nationalist sympathizers came out on to the streets to welcome the conquerors, and masses were held in the open air by triumphant priests. Catalan was immediately banned as an official language.

Not everyone had stayed in the city, though. Hundreds of thousands of people were trudging slowly northward to the border in the hope of safety. Government cars carried officials along the packed roads at a snail's pace, while civilians with children and wounded soldiers had to walk to escape the advancing enemy. It was another cold winter, and the refugees had no shelter. Arriving at the border at the end of January 1939, at first the French refused to let them in. More and more arrived, though, many of them armed, and the French realized that if they didn't let them through they might fight their way over. At first civilians were allowed to cross the border, then a few days later the combatants, dumping their weapons in piles as they passed into France. They were herded like animals into makeshift concentration camps. Meanwhile they watched as lorries carrying the artworks from the Prado Museum in Madrid were driven through and on to Geneva for safe-keeping at the League of Nations. There had been fears for their security during the Nationalist assault on Madrid in 1936, so they had been taken first to Valencia and then on to Barcelona. Within a few months, once Franco's victory was complete, they would be back in Madrid. Not one piece from the famous collection was lost during these tortuous times.

Despite the loss of Catalonia, the Republic still possessed a third of Spanish territory – including Madrid and Valencia – and had half a million men at its disposal. Most of the government was in exile, though, and supplies of all kinds, particularly food, were pitifully low. The Army of the Centre had only 95,000 rifles and 1,400 machine-guns. The war could not be won as things stood, but there were two reasons to continue: the hope that a European war would soon start and that Britain and France would finally come to the Republic's aid; and the fear of reprisals if and when they were caught by Franco's men – better to die fighting than at the hands of a firing squad. Still, there were plenty who thought there was a chance of negotiating a better deal with Franco – if they could get rid of the communists.

The Republican prime minister at that point, Juan Negrín, despite his attempts to maintain a distance from the Communist Party, was a pragmatist who realized he had little choice but to work with Moscow and its agents in Spain. After the May Days the anarchists had lost power, and many army officers were attracted by the communists' discipline. Now, though, with the Republic falling apart around them, the thoughts of many turned to survival. And so in the last gasp before the end, the second 'civil war within a civil war' broke out. In early March 1939, a collection of anti-communist politicians and officers in Madrid overthrew the authorities, and when army units around the country declared in their favour, Negrín, who had returned from France with communist leaders and was holed up near Alicante, was forced back into exile. Soviet advisers realized which way things were going and got out as fast as they could. Many would later die back home in Stalin's purges.

This late coup got the Republic no further, though. Franco still insisted on unconditional surrender, communists or no communists. By late March there was nothing more they could do. Along the front lines Republican troops 'self-demobilized' en masse, dropping their weapons and heading for home rather than waiting for the order to surrender. With only pockets of resistance to deal with, the Nationalist armies again experienced the rapid conquest of territory they had enjoyed at the very start of the war. The last third of the country was taken in only three or four days. Refugees fled to the coast, hoping to find passage to safety. Valencia and Alicante fell on 30 March, Murcia and Cartagena the following day. From his headquarters, Franco, suffering from the flu – his first illness throughout the whole campaign – issued a statement: 'Today, with the Red Army captured and disarmed, Nationalist troops have achieved their final military objectives. The war has ended.' On 1 April the message was repeated throughout the day on Nationalist radio.

The European war that Republicans had so hoped for to save them from Franco didn't start until September of that year. Just days beforehand, Hitler and Stalin, until so recently at each other's throats on the fields of Spain, agreed the Nazi–Soviet Pact, promising not to fight each other while secretly dividing Poland between them. Franco, despite his debt to the Italians and Germans, managed to keep Spain out of the Second World War, although a few thousand hard-line fascist soldiers – the Blue Division – were sent as a token gesture to help on the Eastern Front. Spanish films were later made praising their 'heroism', using the blondest actors they could find.

Franco maintained an uneasy alliance with fascist Italy and Nazi Germany, meeting Hitler at the French border town of Hendaye in 1940. The Caudillo, with his Galician *retranca*, managed to sidestep further pressure from the Führer for Spain to enter the new European war, Hitler later remarking to Mussolini that he would rather have three or four teeth drawn than have to meet Franco again. Later, when he heard that Franco's government had declared the Virgin of the Fuencisla, the patron saint of Segovia, a full Field Marshal for her role in the defence of the town during the Civil War, Hitler announced he would never visit Spain under any circumstances. Franco was a canny player, though, and when by 1942 the tide against the Axis Powers was beginning to turn, he began to tone down overt support for the Nazis.

What for the rest of Europe became known as 'the war', for Spain was 'the post-war', *la posguerra*. It was a time of great hardship and famine: hundreds of thousands of men were held in concentration camps and jails, where many of them were shot or died of illness and neglect. Figures vary greatly, but at least fifty thousand people were executed during this time (there have been claims of up to three hundred thousand deaths), added to a possible two hundred thousand killed in the repression during the war itself. After the indiscriminate murders of the early months of the war, Franco had insisted on personally clearing all death sentences. He gave orders, though, that any appeal for clemency should only reach him once the sentence had been carried out, and often confirmed scores of executions while drinking his hot chocolate over breakfast, or while discussing matters of state with his ministers. Occasionally he would correct an order, specifying firing squad or garrotting as the means of execution depending on which political party the person was from. When the war ended, this process continued for several more years, well into the 1940s. Winning the war on the ground was only one stage of the process: defeated Republican Spain still had to 'redeem' itself for its original sin through blood. The Vatican took a similar view. Having supported the Nationalists throughout the Civil War, Pope Pius XII gave official thanks for

Franco's victory in 1942, at the very height of the Caudillo's repression of his countrymen.

Meanwhile droughts ruined the harvests and the people starved. Exiles who had fled Spain in the face of Franco's victory fared little better. Estimates put the number of Spaniards who left at around half a million, perhaps more. Some made it to Mexico and other parts of Latin America, others to the Soviet Union, but many countries closed their doors to the refugees. Britain allowed in just two hundred Republican leaders, including Prime Minister Negrín, who stayed there until moving to Paris after the end of the Second World War. With the fall of France to the Germans, some twelve thousand Spanish Republicans were sent to the Nazi death camp at Mauthausen. Only two thousand survived. Others managed to escape capture and joined the French Resistance, where their military experience proved invaluable. Others joined the Free French forces. Spanish troops were among the first soldiers to enter Paris with the Allies in August 1944. Several ended up in the Long Range Desert Group fighting the Germans in North Africa.

Despite the Allied victory in 1945, Franco stayed on in power for another thirty years. By the 1950s the Americans realized he was useful in their wider campaign against communism: US aid started to arrive and the country was brought back into the international fold. The Generalísimo eventually died in a hospital bed in Madrid on 20 November 1975, still ruthless and still very much in power, a nineteenth-century anomaly in the late twentieth century.

21

Perpignan

'My grandfather was imprisoned here once, just like me.'

Javier's hands moved in front of him in quick, confident motions, like a card shuffler's, giving shapeless form to the ideas and thoughts bubbling up in his neat round head while he spoke. He had barely stopped since he'd sat down, a torrent of words and gestures as he took full advantage of this unexpected visit and the limited time available to us. Few people came to see him at the prison – it was too far away, and meant a day's drive there and back at least. Not that the remainder of his family cared much for him anyway. Kiki had been coming the most: an old love affair that had ended years back had turned into a bond of loyal friendship. Kiki, Javier insisted, was the most real person he had ever met.

Perpignan prison was unrelentingly grey, as though autumn had come too soon to this derelict little place just over the Pyrenees: the sky, the blank concrete walls, even the windows of the waiting room all radiated a dull grimness, like a fog. It was strange to think that until the Treaty of the Pyrenees in 1659, this area had once been part of Spain – the mountains formed such an obvious frontier you felt nature herself had had a hand in deciding where one country ended and another began. But the previous owners had left an imprint of sorts in the local penitentiary, and while the prison guards were mostly blond and dressed in dark-blue uniforms spattered with the tricolour, the occupants of the prison and their relatives harked back to a previous age. Spanish inmates doing time in France were often transferred here to be as close to home as possible, while the imprisoned locals themselves looked as if they'd be more at home in the Triana district of Seville. Gypsies almost to a man, they crowded out the drabness of their surroundings with a collective colour and energy that almost made you want to commit some crime so you could join them on the inside.

I'd come across the women first, chatting and singing in the draughty waiting room while we waited for visiting hour to arrive. While their children climbed over scratched tables and chairs bolted to the floor, they'd sat down on the hard wooden benches, talking and bustling like a gaggle of geese. It was just another day – a chance to catch up with friends and have a natter. Those over forty came as they were, with house slippers and their hair tied back with bright elastic bands. The younger ones, though, had gone to town on their appearance, their faces freshly painted and navels exposed to the harsh wind, with skin-tight trousers and open-toed stiletto sandals. You sensed they were keen to show that looking good for their menfolk inside still mattered to them – a way of affirming fidelity by saying, 'I still want to be attractive for *you*.' They spoke in a curious patois that seemed to be a mixture of Castilian Spanish, Catalan, French and Caló. In their own minds, though, it was definitely Spanish.

'What's the matter?' I'd heard one of them say to a woman from Madrid who'd come to see her husband. Communication between them was proving difficult. 'Don't you speak Spanish?'

'They're crazy,' the woman had later said to me. 'God knows what they're speaking but it's not like anything I've ever heard before.'

It was one of the few times of the year when visitors were allowed to bring food parcels for the inmates. Kiki had warned me in advance – no chocolate liqueurs or alcohol of any sort. And nothing could be taken through in foil. I hurriedly helped the Madrid woman unwrap all her Ferrero Rochers one by one and place them in a plastic bag in the last few seconds before we were ushered in. A minute longer and she would have missed her chance to go through. It was her first time there and the guards had only just told her about the rules.

'They'll give him a few moments of pleasure, at least,' she said.

She handed the chocolates over to the guards with the other food she'd brought and rushed through as the doors were closing, smudging her make-up as she wiped away a tear welling up in the corner of her eye.

We'd filed through, eventually getting to the visitors' room after being made to stand for another ten minutes in an open courtyard that smelt of sewage. As a friend or relative of a criminal you were somehow made to feel guilty by association and suffer some degree of punishment in your turn. We passed a row of offices lined against one of the walls, knocked up from a collection of scrap windows and doors that someone must have picked up off a skip. Planks of oddly shaped wood held the complex together where it looked most in danger of falling down. A terrace of broken, grubby lockers stood along the adjacent walls, their doors hanging off or simply missing altogether. The gypsies, confident, assured, buffered by their weight of numbers, were untouched by it all. The Madrileña woman, chewing nervously on the inside of her mouth while she wrapped her white plastic coat tightly over her chest, looked close to breaking down. Sorry people in a sorry world. At least,

I thought, there were walls and a roof here: in the past Spaniards had been imprisoned in this part of France on nothing but a piece of bare frozen ground – and purely for being Spanish.

Javier had been in for almost a year after being caught with a right front tyre stuffed with cocaine as he was driving on a courier run to Italy. It was his second and supposedly last trip as he secretly tried to get some money together to pay for a risky new operation in the States that might just save his mother's life. The police had pulled him over and gone straight to where the drugs were stored, not even bothering to check the rest of the car. Pleading guilty from the start, he was tried and sentenced in less than a week, condemned to ten years and a half-million-euro fine for keeping quiet about whom he was working for. It was the state-appointed lawyer who explained how the supplier – an old friend of Javier back in Madrid – had probably been the one to tip the police off in the first place. In the pretend war on drugs, dealers often handed over little guys to the authorities, keeping the pressure off themselves while allowing politicians to show the public that 'something was being done'. In the meantime, a month afterwards, Javier's mother had died of her illness, condemning her son as a criminal on her deathbed, unaware of the sacrifice he was making. The rest of the family, equally ignorant, now blamed him for sending her to an early death. The only good thing that had happened in the past weeks was a reduction in his sentence and the fine. Those too, it seemed, were meant more for public consumption than anything else. With any luck he might be out and back in Spain in just over another year.

Kiki had told me little about Javier other than what had happened to him and that she went up to Perpignan to see him. She'd promised to go this time but the dates of her gigs at the club had been changed at the last minute, and so she was sending me instead, calling me in Badajoz where I was meeting

Manolo. I'd like Javier, she said, and he'd appreciate a visit, whoever it was from. And with that, and a brief physical description – twenty-five, very thin, dark hair, prominent nose – I'd set off, travelling across country to Barcelona and then on to Perpignan.

After everything that had happened to him, I'd expected to find a lonely young man, mourning his mother's death and his bad luck to have ended up in such an awful situation. No one benefited from him being locked up in here – stopping someone driving across Europe with seven kilos of party powder crammed inside his front tyre didn't seem like a particularly effective use of police time, especially when the authorities could have been after the person who had shopped him in the first place. Javier was a pawn in a game that seemed to move by itself – no one was actually in control.

He was, though, surprisingly cheery when I was shown to the table where he was waiting for me.

'Jason, my friend,' he said with a big smile. Forbidden by the world-weary guards from touching each other, it was the closest thing to an embrace he could give me. I noticed his big shiny white teeth framed by dark gums. Thin and dark-haired as Kiki had described, he also had a strong physical energy about him which seemed to radiate from his body like an electric field. He might not be well built, I thought in the fraction of a second when I first caught sight of him, but he was not the kind of person you'd ever want to get into a fight with.

We talked about Kiki at first, our common point of contact.

'Meeting Kiki was the best thing in my life,' he said simply. 'She – and now you – are the only people who have come to see me here.'

I warmed to him immediately, catching something of the incongruity of this spirited young man being in this loveless place. There was a light about him, immediately distinguishable from the rest of the prisoners in the room. The gypsies had street smarts, but there was a different kind of quickness in Javier's eye which you didn't often find, even outside prison.

I gave him bits of news from Madrid, as well as a private message from Kiki. He thanked me for bringing the food parcel.

'How are you getting on here?' I said. Expecting to hear about his mother's death and how he'd been unjustly put away, I put on my most sympathetic voice, shifting mentally into listening and comforting mode.

'Oh, it's a laugh!' he said. I gave a look of surprise.

'Don't get me wrong – wouldn't want to spend my holidays here *every* year, but there's plenty to be getting on with.'

'Fantastic,' I said, trying to adjust to this unexpected burst of enthusiasm.

'I'm learning to be a car mechanic. There's a workshop here and they let you do stuff. Just mucking about, really. Thing is, I've realized a lot of it is dead simple. You can fix all kinds of things in a car with a soldering iron and spanner. Most car mechanics are taking you for a ride.'

His hands moved restlessly in the space between us as he spoke.

'As soon as I get out I'm going to set up my own workshop and do it properly – you know, fixing people's cars for virtually nothing. None of this sending off for expensive parts from God-knows-where. *Sorry, my love, your new alternators still at the suppliers in Uzbekistan. The yaks are on strike.* If you do it cheap people will always come back. I'll be up and running in no time.'

There was no point going back to Madrid, he'd decided. Even though he'd told the police nothing about the operation, he was always going to be seen as a problem for the dealers back home: they'd assume he'd be asking them for money all the time to keep quiet, and would do all they could to run him out of town anyway. Now that his mother had died there were no family ties to take him back either. No, he was going to Seville, where his family had come from originally. He was picking up new skills and meeting new people: a new life was about to begin. It was almost as if coming to prison had been the best thing that had ever happened to him.

It was heartening to see him seemingly unbroken like this, even if I did wonder for a minute what kind of contacts he might be making behind bars. I quickly glanced around the room: the gypsies, with their mullet haircuts, were all talking seriously and manfully to their wives, who were giving them adoring looks. They could take this, you felt – it was part of life. The Madrid woman's husband, though, looked distraught and lost, his eyes like saucers in an expression of fear and shock. The woman had her back to us. From the hunching of her shoulders and position of her head, she seemed to be crying.

'Drug running,' Javier said, catching me watching them. 'Like me. Got caught off the coast in a boat with half a tonne of dope. He gets seven years, the kids buy their stuff from someone else, while the *kif* growers in Morocco who supplied him carry on as normal. Meanwhile suspicious quantities of his haul make it on to the market anyway, except that he's not getting any money for it.'

It was hard not to wonder what the point was of locking up people like him. Whom did it protect? And whom did it punish?

'The police here are corrupt,' said Javier. 'So are the guards. But at least they don't pretend not to be, so you know where you stand. One of the guards is having problems back home – thinks his wife's cheating on him. The word is, she probably is – with his own brother. But he's not been an angel himself either.'

'How do you know all this?' I asked.

'We find out about everything in here,' he said with a grin. 'Those walls are too thick for a man to get through. Believe me,

I've tried.' He winked. 'But gossip and information seeps through like a sieve. Especially about the guards. They all live next to the prison anyway. Sometimes I think they're the ones really in jail here. We'll get out eventually. They don't get released till they retire. And in the meantime they're all in and out of each other's wives like bunny rabbits.'

'Sounds like a soap opera,' I said.

'Oh, much better,' he said. 'We're allowed TVs here, but you have to pay to watch. I don't bother – what's going on around is much more interesting.'

'So what about this guard?' I asked.

'Well, I've given him a shoulder to cry on, so he's been helping me out a bit – extra cigarette rations, that kind of thing. Says he knows all about my case and will do everything he can to make sure I get out as soon as I can for good behaviour.

'Got to be careful, though,' he added. 'These guys have loyalty to no one. One minute they're your friend, the next . . .' He gave a thumbs-down sign.

'I'm so glad you came to see me,' he said, hardly pausing to take a breath. 'It's good to speak Spanish again.'

'I thought almost everyone in here spoke Spanish,' I said. And I explained about the people I'd seen in the waiting room.

'There are Spaniards here,' he said. 'But we're at the bottom of the pile. They treat the Arabs better than us – because they speak French.'

He told me how his cellmate was an Algerian. He was giving Javier French lessons in return for Spanish lessons and cigarettes – hence the usefulness of the guard.

'You'd think it would be one language for another, right? No. In here, Spanish on its own is not worth the same as French. That's why I have to give him cigarettes as well. I'm a second-class citizen.' He laughed. 'There's only one direction from here, though, and that's up.'

Everything, at every turn, was given a positive interpretation. If anyone was going to survive being in prison, it was Javier. He seemed to have the right balance of sensitivity and wit to hang on to who he truly was without falling into despair or hardening his outer shell. Prison often broke you or absorbed you. But Javier seemed to be successfully riding on the surface of it all. There was, though, something of an exotic and elegant wild animal about him, and it pained me to see him caged like this.

'Kiki told me you're interested in the Civil War,' he said.

I nodded, and without any prompting he started telling me the story of his grandfather.

Raimundo had been Javier's hero – a poet and a Republican, he had been exiled to Mexico after Franco's victory, but had returned to Spain in the early seventies, shortly before the dictator died, as the regime very slowly began to liberalize and pardon those it had fought against almost forty years before. He brought with him a son – Javier's father; his Mexican wife had died of emphysema.

'I'm a quarter Mexican. That's why there's an Aztec look about me,' Javier said with a smile. I hadn't noticed before, but now he mentioned it there was something about his cheekbones, and a glossiness about his very dark hair.

Raimundo had always been extremely close to his little grandson, and had been more of a father than a grandfather to him as Javier's own father passed restlessly through a series of jobs and relationships, never quite managing to settle in a country he had always been told was his real home. Eventually he had gone back to Mexico, leaving Javier in the hands of his Spanish mother and Raimundo. He hadn't been in touch for years. While his mother was out at work, the little Javier would sit with his grandfather, hearing stories about his time in the war, the ideals they had fought for, and his escape and journey to Mexico. Raimundo had been involved in schemes to expand the education system in

Spain during the early years of the Republic, bringing schools and teachers to rural areas where no one could read or write. But the war had come and he'd been shipped down to Valencia when the government debunked en masse from Madrid, and had then gone up to Barcelona for the last year of the conflict. He'd been one of the hundreds of thousands who'd walked through the snow over the Pyrenees into France in the final months as Franco's troops conquered Catalonia. And like so many others, once over the border he'd been imprisoned by the French authorities in a concentration camp not a great distance away from where Javier and I were now sitting.

Bullied by Britain and fearful of civil conflict within France's own borders, various French governments over the course of the war had failed to give the Spanish Republic the kind of assistance it would have needed to defeat Franco's army. Despite being of the same political bent as its Spanish equivalent – it was even called the Popular Front – the government in Paris preferred to maintain better relations with London, where the policy of first Baldwin and then Chamberlain was to prevent weapons from reaching Spain's elected government. Threats were even made at one point that Britain might tear up its historic accord with France and ally itself with fascist Italy and Nazi Germany if the French gave military assistance to the Republicans. And so France, ever the great hope to the north, failed to help its southern neighbour in any significant way and the Nationalists inched their way to victory. Worse, however, was yet to come.

By early 1939 a new government was in power in Paris under Edouard Daladier, a supporter of Chamberlain's appeasement policy towards Hitler. France now faced the reality of thousands of Spanish Republicans pouring over the border as they fled Franco and his bloody retribution. The refugees were seen as a threat – many of them were armed men who might bring their war with them. And so these tired, wounded, hungry, defeated people were rounded up as they crossed the border, stripped of their personal belongings in many cases, and placed in makeshift concentration camps in the area around Perpignan. Out of half a million Spaniards forced into exile at the end of the war, 275,000 passed through French hands. It was mid-winter and illness was rife, but no shelters or decent food were provided. Forced to survive on the bare ground, the refugees had to dig into the frozen earth with their hands to create some kind of shelter, washing themselves if they could in the icy salt water of the Mediterranean. Bread and a few other scraps to eat would be handed out, but there were virtually no medicines or treatment for the sick and wounded. Almost fifteen thousand died in the camps during the first six months. They were simply *les rouges espagnoles* – undesirables, facing death or destitution in their own country just a few miles away, or rejection in France from those they'd hoped would be their friends. The doors of Europe were closed to most Spanish refugees. There were few places to go.

Some, like Raimundo, were lucky and managed to make it to Mexico, one of the few countries that had supported the Spanish Republic throughout the war. Others were forcibly conscripted into the French Foreign Legion or joined the French in their fight against the Nazis only months later.

Javier told me all this in a hurried voice, aware that our time was short. A guard called out from the corner. They would soon be booting us out.

Stuck in the concentration camp, Raimundo might have ended up like so many others, but was recognized by a Republican government official with contacts, who made sure he was given passage to Mexico. But for that man, Javier said, he himself probably wouldn't be alive now.

Raimundo had started afresh in Mexico, marrying a local

woman and fathering a son. But like so many Spanish exiles, he dreamed of going home one day, and watched the Spanish news avidly for signs that the enemy who had defeated them years before might crumble and democracy be restored once more.

Eventually, after the death of his wife, he had decided to move back anyway while Franco was still alive, sensing that change was on its way and keen to catch it when it came. He was right: he lived to see the death of the dictator and the subsequent rapid collapse of the regime in the mid-1970s.

'In the end,' he used to tell Javier as a boy, 'Franco lost and *el abuelo* Raimundo won.' Franco might have had all the tanks and guns, but he didn't have time. 'Time,' he would say, 'was on *our* side.'

Javier's grandfather had died four years earlier at his home. Few things stayed the same for very long, he had said, but Spain was a democracy once more and he had seemed at peace. There was, however, one thing remaining he had always meant to do.

'Listen,' said Javier, 'could you do something for me?'

I picked up the flowers from a florist's in the centre of Perpignan and caught a train out to the coast. Argelès was a typical Mediterranean resort town, with views to the south of the rich green foothills of the Pyrenees lazily cascading into the water. Restaurants and beach apartments lined the sea front, with decorative palm trees and promenades for the holiday-makers, and playgrounds for the children. Now people paid money to come and lie on these sands, but fewer than seventy years earlier the beach had been a prison camp, a squalid and dirty open space with barbed-wire fences, where a hundred thousand Spaniards had been left to the elements while the world forgot about them and congratulated itself on having prevented another world war.

I walked along the shore, gusts of warm grey wind blowing in from the sea. The place was deserted, just a handful of bars still open at this tail end of the season. Already houses and villas were boarded up in preparation for the winter, adding to the nostalgic end-of-the-holidays feeling. Out at sea, tankers floated like miniature islands on the horizon, barely moving on the still, grey waters. A couple of seagulls cried mournfully overhead.

I tried to imagine the conditions that had existed here all those years ago, when Raimundo, then a young man, had been one of the many thousands held captive on this very shore. I'd seen photographs of the refugees with exhausted, defeated faces, men standing skinny and naked as they tried to wash their few scraps of clothes in sea water. There was nothing, though, like the image Raimundo had implanted in his grandson's mind. He had made a big impact on Javier. In some ways Javier seemed almost proud to be imprisoned here himself, as though he were following in his hero's footsteps. The future move to Seville was in the same vein: Raimundo had been born there before the family moved up to Madrid when he was a child. Perhaps in Andalusia Javier might feel at home.

A wounded militiaman had been in the camp, Raimundo had told him, just a few feet from where he and two other friends had tried to dig some kind of shelter. Shot through the lung, the man had developed tuberculosis, and with the cold and the hardship of the trek up to France in the snow, had had little strength left to take care of himself. He lay motionless on the hard, frozen sand, wrapping his greatcoat around him for warmth, his sickly breath hovering above his mouth like a fog. He was in his thirties, Raimundo thought, but his face was tired and grey, lines of defeat drawn along his increasingly pale skin. Gripped tight in his hands was a small framed photograph of a little girl. She was no more than three or four years old, with a centre parting and glossy brown hair falling down to her shoulders, a ribbon tied above one ear. Her face was bright, her large clear eyes filled with an expression of joy.

Raimundo and his friends tried to take care of the man, helping him walk the few paces to the sea to relieve himself during the first days, feeding him odd scraps to eat. But after a time he was unable to get up, even with their help, and he lay quietly on the beach, under a loveless sky, waiting for the illness to take its course. Still, though, he gripped the photograph in his fingers, pressing it to his chest with the little strength that remained to him, savouring the memory of the warmth of his lost little girl. She had used to dance *sardanas*, he had whispered to them.

There were no doctors or medicines to be had, and no way of getting hold of any from the French authorities. Raimundo and his friends did what they could, but the illness had taken him too far.

On the day the man died, the sun had come out briefly in the morning, tiny rays of light reaching the stiff, chilled bodies of the imprisoned refugees on the beach. For the first time in weeks half-smiles began to break out on people's faces.

At lunchtime he stopped breathing. The French officials were informed but did nothing for several hours. The face of the little girl stared up into the sky, pressed to her father's chest, smiling as she always had. Raimundo had never forgotten her.

By the following morning the man and the little girl had gone, her smile and expression of joy lost in the machine of French bureaucracy. By dusk that same day Raimundo himself was leaving the camp, taking his first steps towards a new life in exile in Mexico. He never found out the girl's name.

I stood by the shore and watched the grey little waves rolling and stroking the sand in their curious, rhythmic motion. With their wrapping crumpled in my hand, I scattered the flowers on the water's surface, where they were pulled out slowly by the current towards the south, down towards the Pyrenees and the border. Javier would have done it himself, he told me, but he knew when he got out he would be taken straight back to Spain. No time would be allowed for nostalgic visits to the nearby coast on behalf of his dead grandfather. I would be his representative, he'd said grandly, just as I was Kiki's now in coming to see him. His grandfather, wherever he was, would be watching and would bless us both. Many loose ends had finally been tied up for the old man by coming back to Spain, but this was one thing he had promised to do but never managed. The girl's face, and those days in the camp, had stayed with him for ever.

I walked back towards the town, past neat trimmed hedges of bougainvillea and carefully mown green lawns, catching sight of the 'beware of the dog' signs and security wires meant to keep the unwanted out.

'There is no such thing as history,' Raimundo had said to Javier. 'Only memories and interpretations. And they themselves are fluid. The past, your past, belongs to you: you can make of it what you want.' And the young man was methodically putting his words into practice. Kiki, in her way, was doing the same: it was what she had been trying to tell me all along, that day at Franco's grave. And it was what Manolo was doing back in Badajoz. There was no single version of events, either past or present – simply material with which we could choose to shape ourselves.

Over the previous months I had seen much of Spain that I had never wanted or meant to see: the worst of a place I had fallen in love with years earlier, listening to flamenco and with tales of the Alhambra ringing in my ears. Now the romantic image I'd built up had been broken and lay in pieces around me. And yet still, I found, I loved the country as deeply as before, perhaps even more so. I could not forget what I had discovered, nor apologize for it or ignore it: the haze of perfection had gone. Yet the love was there, fuller, and more rounded – neither despite nor because of what I had learned. I had been blind in my search for the essence of the country, imagining it to be something I could hold or possess, a truth that could be expressed in words, like a definition set in stone. But Spain changed, just as I did. Loving it meant exploring it and deepening my knowledge of it, a process that could have no end.

Epilogue

A cool sea breeze blows in from the south as I begin to walk up the steep-sided slope towards the farm. Pink- and red-flowering oleander bushes lining the edges of the dry river bed shake off a coating of dust in the circling air, their last colours of the summer blooming in the deep shade of the mountains. It hasn't rained for months and around me the landscape feels bare and hot.

Scrambling along the rocky dirt track, I turn up the road that leads to the *mas* – our little huddle of cottages. Along the verges the grass lies limp and yellow, the soil crumbling like sand. But amid this straw-coloured background come flashes of green, patches of life that have survived and seem almost to flourish despite the drought. Pine trees soar up into the sky.

As the path winds around the contours of the mountainside, the almond groves come into view. They too seem to have survived the summer well, with bright-green plump fruits hanging from their branches. Harvest time is only weeks away.

There are more butterflies now; with every step a score of

273

them scatter into the air. Like tiny fireworks, they shine a myriad of colours around my feet – shell blue, bright fox red, black, white, racing green and royal purple – enveloping me as I walk further up the hill.

I pass the freshwater spring as the path continues upwards; a frog leaps from stone to stone for safety as he senses the tread of my approaching feet. Around the edges of the little pool, rushes are beginning to sprout, absorbing the moisture seeping into the ground. Finches chatter in the Judas tree on the terrace below.

As I walk past a large holm oak, I hear a clicking sound coming from further up the slope. Turning, I see three ibexes staring down at me with dark, piercing eyes. Their horns stretch up from their heads, curved majestic arches a metre long. We stand for a moment gazing at each other, the ibexes as curious about me as I am about them. Sensing I pose no threat, they slowly start to move on, heads bobbing down to nibble on plants near the ground before glancing up again to see where I am. Eventually they skip up the mountainside with their powerful hind legs, their grey, black and tan fur blending seamlessly into the landscape. Long after they are out of sight, I can still catch the echo of their hooves pounding the rocks as they move to higher ground.

I approach the house under the shade of heavy, five-fingered leaves, and pick some of the last figs of the season, peeling back the skin and biting into the soft sweet flesh. Pink juices stick to my lips, my mouth tingling with flavour. Tomorrow I will pick the remainder and dry them. Salud has returned from her tour abroad at last: we'll be lighting the first fires of the autumn soon.

Begoña came up yesterday with the goats. I told her about my journey and about the things I've been discovering. She nodded silently as I mentioned where I'd been – places she has heard of but never seen. Her brown eyes glistened for a moment when I told her that people around the country were starting to open up unmarked war graves like the one she had shown me.

Perhaps, she wondered, one day they will come to look at our *fosa*.

Perhaps, I say.

Chronology of the Spanish Civil War

14 April 1931	Establishment of the Second Spanish Republic following the abdication of King Alfonso XIII
10 August 1932	General Sanjurjo leads unsuccessful *pronunciamiento* against the government
11–13 January 1933	Massacre at Casas Viejas
October 1934	Left-wing uprising. Franco uses Army of Africa to defeat rebels in Asturias
16 February 1936	Popular Front coalition of left-wing parties wins general election
12 July 1936	Police officer Lt José Castillo murdered
13 July 1936	Monarchist politician José Calvo Sotelo murdered
17 July 1936	Nationalist rebellion begins in Melilla and spreads to other parts of Spanish Moroccan territories
18 July 1936	Rebellion proper begins across Spain

19 July 1936	Rebellion crushed in Barcelona
20 July 1936	General Sanjurjo killed in air crash
End July 1936	German and Italian planes carry out airlift of Franco's troops from Morocco to the Spanish mainland
18/19 August 1936	Federico García Lorca murdered near Granada
September 1936	Nationalist troops relieve the Alcázar in Toledo; Franco named head of state by Nationalist generals
6 November 1936	Government flees to Valencia as Nationalists start assault on Madrid
20 November 1936	Anarchist commander Buenaventura Durruti dies after being shot during defence of Madrid; Falangist leader José-Antonio Primo de Rivera executed in Alicante prison
February 1937	Battle of Jarama starts as Nationalists try to encircle Madrid; Málaga falls to the Nationalists
8–23 March 1937	Battle of Guadalajara – Nationalist defeat
31 March 1937	Nationalists begin campaign in the north, starting in Basque Country
26 April 1937	Guernica bombed
3–9 May 1937	'May Days' in Barcelona
3 June 1937	General Mola killed in air crash
19 June 1937	Nationalists capture Bilbao
6 July 1937	Republicans launch offensive west of Madrid: Battle of Brunete begins
23 August 1937	Republican forces attack Belchite
26 August 1937	Nationalists capture Santander
21 October 1937	Nationalists capture Gijón and the war in the north ends

7 January 1938	Republicans capture Teruel
22 February 1938	Nationalists recapture Teruel
15 April 1938	Nationalists reach the Mediterranean at Vinaroz, splitting Republican territory in two
25 July 1938	Battle of the Ebro, biggest battle of the war, begins
15 November 1938	Nationalists win Battle of the Ebro
26 January 1939	Nationalists capture Barcelona
27 February 1939	Britain recognizes Nationalist government
28 March 1939	Nationalist troops enter Madrid
30 March 1939	Nationalists capture Valencia
1 April 1939	Franco declares the war over

Key Figures from the War

Republican

José-Antonio Aguirre, Basque regional president.

Manuel Azaña, war minister 1931; prime minister 1931–3, 1936; president of the Republic 1936–9.

Santiago Casares Quiroga, prime minister at the start of the Civil War.

Lieutenant José Castillo, police officer. Murdered July 1936.

Luis Companys, president of the Catalan regional government, the Generalitat, 1933–40.

Buenaventura Durruti, anarchist commander. Died November 1936.

Francisco Largo Caballero, socialist leader. Prime minister September 1936–May 1937.

General José Miaja, commander in defence of Madrid.

Dr Juan Negrín, finance minister 1936–7; prime minister May 1937–March 1939.

Andrés Nin, leader of the Marxist POUM party. Murdered 1937.

Indalecio Prieto, socialist leader. Defence minister May 1937–April 1938.

Major (later General) Vicente Rojo, negotiator at Toledo, chief of staff in Madrid.

Nationalist
José Calvo Sotelo, monarchist politician. Assassinated July 1936.

General Francisco Franco, leader of Nationalist movement from September 1936. Head of state until 1975.

José María Gil Robles, leader of the Catholic authoritarian CEDA coalition.

General Manuel Goded, leader of unsuccessful Nationalist rebellion in Barcelona. Executed July 1936.

General José Millán Astray, founder of the Spanish Foreign Legion. Friend and mentor to Franco.

General Emilio Mola, 'director' of the Nationalist rebellion. Died in plane crash 1937.

Colonel (later General) José Moscardó, defender of the Alcázar in Toledo.

José-Antonio Primo de Rivera, founder and leader of the Falange, Spanish fascist party. Executed November 1936.

General Gonzalo Queipo de Llano, 'radio general'. Captured Seville for the Nationalists July 1936.

General José Sanjurjo, anti-Republican conspirator, titular head of Nationalist rebellion until death in plane crash in July 1936.

General Hugo von Sperrle, head of the German Condor Legion.

General José Varela, monarchist military commander under Franco.

Colonel Juan de Yagüe, Falangist military commander under Franco.

Others

Niceto Alcalá Zamora, first president of the Second Republic, December 1931–May 1936.

Alfonso XIII, King of Spain 1902–31.

Federico García Lorca, poet and playwright. Murdered August 1936.

Miguel de Unamuno, philosopher, rector of Salamanca University.

Recommended Reading

There are many thousands of books on the Spanish Civil War. Here are a handful of English-language titles that might be helpful for anyone wanting to find out more about this fascinating period of history.

Anthony Beevor, *The Spanish Civil War* (Cassell, London, 2001). Good, general account of the war.

Franz Borkenau, *The Spanish Cockpit* (Weidenfeld & Nicholson, London, 2000). Eyewitness account of the war from behind Republican lines.

Raymond Carr, *The Spanish Tragedy: the Civil War in Perspective* (Weidenfeld & Nicholson, London, 2000). Excellent analysis of the social tensions behind the conflict.

Cecil Eby, *The Siege of the Alcázar* (Bodley Head, London, 1966). Gripping account of the events in Toledo.

Ronald Fraser, *Blood of Spain: an Oral History of the Spanish Civil War* (Pimlico, London, 1994). Oral testimonies from the period.

Ian Gibson, *Federico García Lorca: A Life* (Faber & Faber, London, 1989). Authoritative biography.

Gerald Howson, *Arms for Spain: the Untold Story of the Spanish Civil War* (John Murray, London, 1998). Extraordinary account of how the international arms embargo was a direct cause of the defeat of the Republic.

Paul Preston, *Franco: a Biography* (Harper Collins, London, 1993). Definitive biography of the dictator.

Nicholas Rankin, *Telegram from Guernica* (Faber & Faber, London, 2003). Biography of the journalist George Steer, with excellent section on the reporting of Guernica.

Hugh Thomas, *The Spanish Civil War* (Penguin, London 2003). Comprehensive and authoritative history of the period.

Gamel Woolsey, *Death's Other Kingdom* (Eland, London, 2004). Fascinating account of ordinary life in Andalusia during the first months of the war.

Notes

1   Montse Armengou and Ricard Belis, *Las Fosas del Silencio*, p. 27.

2   Michael Alpert, *BBC History Magazine*, April 2002.

3   Paul Preston, lecture at Gavilla Verde conference, Santa Cruz de Moya, October 2004.

4   Paul Preston, *Franco*, p. 142.

5   Hugh Thomas, *The Spanish Civil War*, p. 249.

6   Ian Gibson, *Vida, Pasión y Muerte de Federico García Lorca*, p. 567.

7   Enrique López Castellón, *Federico García Lorca: el poeta ante la muerte*, p. 65.

8   The following quotes from Queipo are from Manuel Barrios, *El Ultimo Virrey*.

9   Manuel Barrios, op. cit., p. 51.

10   Lawrence Dundas, *Behind the Spanish Mask*, p. 66.

11   Manuel Barrios, op. cit., p. 34.

12   Unnamed source quoted in Eladi Romero, *Itinerarios de la guerra civil española*, p. 100.

13 Cecil Eby, *The Siege of the Alcázar*, p. 128.

14 Cecil Eby, op. cit., p. 131.

15 Phil Ball, *Morbo: the Story of Spanish Football*, pp. 26–7.

16 'Death, Honor, and Loyalty: The Bushido Ideal', G. Cameron Hurst III, *Philosophy East & West*, V. 40 No. 4.

17 Joan Llarch, *La Muerte de Durruti*, p. 12.

18 Anonymous testimony quoted in Joan Llarch, op. cit., p. 71.

19 Juan Eslava Galán, *Una historia de la guerra civil que no va a gustar a nadie*, p. 150.

20 Hugh Thomas, op. cit., p. 470.

21 Diego Abad de Santillán, quoted in Hugh Thomas, op. cit, p. 484.

22 Testimony of Father Alberto Onaindía in Juan Eslava Galán, op. cit., p. 234.

23 Taken from Juan M. Riesgo, 'Guernica, la verdaderas causas', *La Aventura de la Historia*, April 2002.

24 Iniesta Cano, *Memorias*, quoted in Juan Eslava Galán, op. cit., p.100.

25 Juan José Calleja, quoted in Juan Eslava Galán, op. cit., p. 100.

26 Ronald Fraser, *Blood of Spain*, p. 502 ff.

Index